The Life of
Christ

The Life of Christ

Christ

365 daily readings

Rita & Neil McLaughlan
Trevor J. Partridge

Waverley Abbey House, Waverley Lane, Farnham, Surrey GU9 8EP

CWR, Waverley Abbey House, Waverley Lane, Farnham, Surrey, GU9 8EP, England.
Telephone: 01252 783761 Fax: 01252 783847 Registered Charity No. 294387

National Distributors
AUSTRALIA: CMC Australasia, PO Box 519, Belmont, Victoria 3216   Tel: (052) 413 288
CANADA: CMC Distribution Ltd., PO Box 7000, Niagara on the Lake, Ontario LOS 1JO
Tel: 1–800–325–1297
INDIA: Full Gospel Literature Stores, 254 Kilpauk Garden Road, Madras 600 010
Tel: (44) 644 1353
KENYA: Christian Products Ltd., PO Box 56495 Nairobi   Tel: (02) 567516
MALAYSIA: Salvation Book Centre (M), 23 Jalan SS2/64, Sea Park, 47300 Petaling Jaya, Selangor
Tel: (3) 7766411
NEW ZEALAND: CMC New Zealand Ltd., PO Box 949, 205 King Street South, Hastings
Tel: (6) 878 4408
NIGERIA: FBFM, (Every Day with Jesus), Prince's Court, 37 Ahmed Onibudo Street, PO Box 70952
Victoria Island   Tel: 01–2617721, 616832
REPUBLIC OF IRELAND: Scripture Union, 40 Talbot Street, Dublin 1   Tel: (01) 8363764
SINGAPORE: Campus Crusade Asia Ltd., 315 Outram Road, 06–08 Tan Boon Liat Building,
Singapore 169074   Tel: (65) 222 3640
SOUTH AFRICA: Struik Christian Books (Pty Ltd) PO Box 193, Maitland 7405 Cape Town
Tel: (021) 551 5900
USA: CMC Distribution, P.O. Box 644, Lewiston, New York 14092–0644   Tel: 1–800–325–1297

Design, typesetting and illustration by CWR Production
Photographs: Kagema Photo Library, Sonia Halliday Photographs
Cover photograph: Sonia Halliday Photographs
Course compiled by Rita & Neil McLaughlan.
Additional material by Trevor J. Partridge.
© CWR 1987, 1997

Printed & bound in Great Britain

ISBN 1–85345–009–X

First published 1986 as a bi-monthly six-part work and reprinted 1987

First single volume edition October 1987

Introduction

Christianity is Christ. What better way, then, to spend a year's Bible reading than in focusing on Him? Over a complete year this course will take you, day by day, chronologically through the life and ministry of Jesus.

To illuminate the setting, the events and the people of Jesus' life is one aim of the commentary, but it will also pinpoint sharply for us the adventure and challenge of living for Jesus today.

Additional verses from other parts of Scripture and further material for reflection, prayer, study and action are helps to this end, so that we might experience more deeply the fulness of life which Jesus gives and serve Him more effectively in our day.

The course is undated, so you can start at any time, and a ribbon marker is there for you to mark your path.

May this be a significant year for you of knowing and growing in the Saviour.

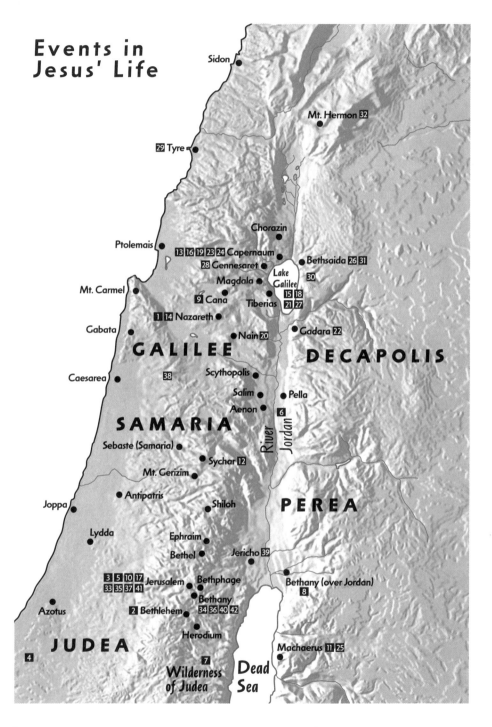

Events in Jesus' Life

Sidon

Mt. Hermon **32**

29 Tyre

Chorazin

Ptolemais

13 **16** **19** **23** **24** Capernaum

Bethsaida **26** **31**

28 Gennesaret

30

Magdala

Lake
Galilee

Mt. Carmel

9 Cana

Tiberias

15 **18**
21 **27**

1 **14** Nazareth

Gabata

Nain **20**

Gadara **22**

GALILEE

DECAPOLIS

Caesarea

38

Scythopolis

Salim

Pella

Aenon

6

SAMARIA

River Jordan

Sebaste (Samaria)

Sychar **12**

Mt. Gerizim

Antipatris

Joppa

Shiloh

PEREA

Lydda

Ephraim

Bethel

Jericho **39**

3 **5** **10** **17** Jerusalem
33 **35** **37** **41**

Bethphage

Bethany (over Jordan)
8

Bethany

Azotus

2 Bethlehem

34 **36** **40** **42**

Herodium

Machaerus **11** **25**

4

JUDEA

7
Wilderness
of Judea

Dead
Sea

Events in Jesus' Life

1 Birth announced
2 Birth
3 Presentation in Temple
4 Flight into Egypt
5 In Temple
6 Baptism by John
7 Temptation
8 First five disciples
9 Wedding at Cana
10 Clears Temple
11 John the Baptist imprisoned
12 Woman at the well
13 Healing of official's son
14 Rejected in Nazareth
15 Calls four fishermen
16 Teaches; heals man with evil spirit; Simon's mother-in-law; paralysed man; calls Matthew
17 Healing at pool
18 Heals man with withered hand; multitudes healed; chooses the Twelve; Sermon on the Mount; accused of being in league with Beelzebub
19 Heals centurion's servant
20 Raises widow's son
21 Calms storm
22 Casts out demons
23 Woman with haemorrhage; Jairus' daughter raised
24 Blind men see; dumb man speaks; Twelve sent out
25 Death of John the Baptist
26 Feeds the 5,000
27 Walks on the water
28 Heals sick
29 Syrophoenician woman
30 Heals many; feeds 4,000
31 Heals a blind man
32 Transfiguration
33 Woman caught in adultery; sends out the Seventy
34 Visits Mary and Martha
35 Heals blind man; at Feast of Dedication; heals sick man
36 Raises Lazarus
37 Plot against; withdraws to Ephraim
38 Ten lepers
39 Blesses children; two blind men healed; Bartimaeus healed; Zacchaeus converted
40 Mary anoints Jesus
41 Crucifixion; burial; resurrection
42 Ascension

List of features

He's always been there
John 1:1–14

Right at the beginning of his Gospel John establishes four facts about Jesus: 1, The Word is God. 2, He existed with God even before the cre-

"In the beginning was the Word ..."

ation of the world. 3, The world was created through Him. 4, The Word, Jesus, became flesh and as a man lived among men.

"In the beginning" reminds us of the first creation. John then leads us on to his subject, the new beginning, the new creation – Jesus, the Life and the Light of men.

Jesus didn't come to this world as an alien from outer space. He made the world. It belongs to Him. It's His home.

He came to His own people in the world, the Jews, to whom God had already revealed Himself in many ways, and with whom He had made an everlasting covenant. Jesus came home, to His family – and they didn't recognise Him. Think about the hurt, the rejection, He must have felt. Yet there were some then, as now, who received Him (v. 12). Have you received Him, *unreservedly*, into your life?

"For by him all things were created: things in heaven and on earth, visible and invisible, whether thrones or powers or rulers or authorities; all things were created by him and for him. He is before all things, and in him all things hold together" (Col. 1:16, 17).

■ QUESTION
What privilege is given to those who receive Him? (v. 12)

He gave them the right to be called children of God

Momentous event
Isaiah 9:6; Luke 2:11; Galatians 4:4

The Jews had had enough of kings who took unwise counsel, were defeated in battle, were anything but fathers to their people, and who had not achieved peace and prosperity. Isaiah wrote to them giving hope for the future.

"... God sent his son..."

"Everlasting Father" implies "One who is Himself eternal and able to give the gift of eternal life to others." "Saviour" has two meanings: "One who saves from" and "One who safeguards against". "Christ" means "the Anointed One" – the Messiah. Paul stressed that

the Son of God was "born of a woman" (Gal. 4:4) in contrast to the Greek gods who had goddess mothers.

Today's three verses agree perfectly – the prophecy written 700 years BC, details of His actual birth and the letter written 49 years later. Jesus completely fulfilled all the prophecies concerning Him. Think about the different facets of Jesus' character named in these verses.

"She will give birth to a son, and you are to give him the name Jesus, because he will save his people from their sins" (Matt. 1:21).

◤ KEY THOUGHT
God was born of human flesh so that humanity might be born to God.

▪▪▪▪▪▪▪▪▪▪ PROPHECIES ABOUT JESUS ▪▪▪ ▪▪▪▪▪▪

PROPHECY	FULFILMENT
Born of a Virgin	
Isa. 7:14 Therefore the Lord himself will give you a sign: The virgin will be with child and will give birth to a son, and will call him Immanuel.	Matt. 1:18 This is how the birth of Jesus Christ came about: His mother Mary was pledged to be married to Joseph, but before they came together, she was found to be with child through the Holy Spirit.
Slaughter of infants	
Jer. 31:15 This is what the Lord says: "A voice is heard in Ramah, mourning and great weeping, Rachel weeping for her children and refusing to be comforted, because her children are no more."	Matt. 2:16–17 When Herod realised that he had been outwitted by the Magi, he was furious, and he gave orders to kill all the boys in Bethlehem and its vicinity who were two years old and under, in accordance with the time he had learned from the Magi.
Escape into Egypt	
Hos. 11:1 When Israel was a child, I loved him, and out of Egypt I called my son.	Matt. 2:14 So he got up, took the child and his mother during the night and left for Egypt.

DAY 3

To destroy the devil's work

Genesis 3:15; Matthew 1:18

The first prophetic word about the coming of Jesus into the world was spoken to the serpent rather than to man. The primary purpose of Christ's coming to earth was to destroy the works of the devil (1 John 3:8).

"... with child through the Holy Spirit"

Because sin came into the world through a man, it had to be a Man who conquered sin. The word for the woman's seed, or offspring, in Gen. 3:15 is in the singular and can only refer to Christ. Our Lord, coming into the world as a Man born of a woman, would undo the damage caused by Adam's sin and conquer Satan completely through the Cross and His resurrection.

Note that the enmity is between the serpent's *offspring* and Christ, but Christ was to strike the *serpent* himself, crushing his head. Satan knows that he is a defeated foe. Do you know that? Are you living in the victory gained by Jesus on the cross?

"He who does what is sinful is of the devil, because the devil has been sinning from the beginning. The reason the Son of God appeared was to destroy the devil's work" (1 Jn. 3:8).

◆ REJOICE
Satan is a defeated foe – Christ is the victor!

DAY 4

Miraculous birth

Isaiah 7:14; Matthew 1:21–23

The miraculous birth of Jesus to a virgin is still a stumbling block to some who are known as Christians. Yet how else could God become man?

"... he will save his people from their sins" A child inherits characteristics from both parents. Jesus inherited His nature and character from His Father and His physical body from His mother. The Holy Spirit, the third Person of the Trinity, was instrumental in the conception of Jesus in a way which we don't understand – and don't need to understand. The miracle and the wonder of it is that God loved us so much that He wanted to come down and dwell with us.

All the other religions of the world demand that man must strive for acceptance by their gods. Our God, however, came down to us, right to our level, to live as a man, so that we might be lifted up to dwell with Him. The prophecy in Isaiah was a specific sign given to King Ahaz and, at the time, was probably not regarded as pointing to the Messiah. After Jesus came the meaning became clear and the prophecy took on a new and wonderful dimension.

"For to us a child is born, to us a son is given, and the government will be on his shoulders. And he will be called Wonderful Counsellor, Mighty God, Everlasting Father, Prince of Peace" (Isa. 9:6).

■ QUESTION
Look up Hebrews 1:1–2. In what other ways that you can think of did the coming of Jesus throw light on the Old Testament prophecies?

DAY 5

House of bread

Micah 5:2–4; Matthew 2:6; Luke 2:4–15

Bethlehem is a small town five miles south-west of Jerusalem, and also called Ephrathah to distinguish it from the other Bethlehem north of Nazareth. The name means "house of bread". Many years later Jesus was to say, as He broke the bread at the last super, "This is my body, broken for you ..."

"... the town of David ..." Bethlehem was the birthplace of David, who has a special place in Scripture as ancestor, forerunner and foreshadower of Jesus. David was a shepherd, and suffered rejection both from his own brothers and from

Saul, before he became a great king.

Micah's prophecy foretells that the One who was to come would be a shepherd and a ruler and that He would not be an ordinary man, but One whose origins are in eternity. The promise was literally fulfilled by Jesus' birth in Bethlehem, brought about by the requirements of the Roman census. It was fulfilled spiritually as Jesus declared Himself the Good Shepherd (Jn. 10:11) and King (Jn. 18:36, 37).

Jesus declared, "I am the bread of life. He who comes to me will never go hungry, and he who believes in me will never be thirsty" (John 6:35).

■ THANKS
Thank You, Lord, that the miracle of Your coming was not Your birth in Bethlehem, but that You've been born in my heart.

DAY 6

Everlasting kingdom

2 Samuel 7:12–13; Romans 1:3; Luke 1:31–33; Matthew 21:9

Although *covenant* is not a word mentioned in God's promise to David, it is very important in God's relationship with His people. His suc-

"Hosanna in the highest!"

cessive covenants with Noah, Abraham and Moses now culminate in the promise of an everlasting kingdom to be established through David's line.

The promise was partly fulfilled by Solomon when he built the temple in Jerusalem, but could only be completely fulfilled by Christ, the everlasting King of kings. The Jews looked forward to a coming King, their Messiah, born of David's line, who would free them from their oppressors and rule over them in peace and justice for ever. So the angel Gabriel's words to Mary would have immediately spoken to her of this promised Messiah. How amazed, how awestruck she must have been! Enter into the wonder and greatness of God's faithfulness. Use the words of Psalm 89:1-4 as a basis for worship, praise and adoration today.

"... to Jesus the mediator of a new covenant ..." (Heb. 12:24)

❚ QUESTION
What does the word *covenant* mean?

DAY 7

Wise men bow

Psalm 72:10; Isaiah 60:3, 6, 9; Matthew 2:11

Psalm 72 was written about King Solomon, who was also a type of Christ. Chapter 60 of Isaiah prophesies the coming glory of Zion when the light of God,

"... they bowed down and worshipped him"

the Messiah, will come to her. In both Scriptures the nations of the east are drawn to the glory and light of the kingdom of God, bringing their wealth as gifts for the King – gifts of gold, silver and frankincense.

The wise men who visited Jesus were representatives of the eastern nations, Gentiles coming to worship the Jewish King. They were astrologers, who recognised the birth of a great King because of a new bright star in the heavens. So they travelled a great distance to worship Him. Right at the beginning of Jesus' life on earth, it was clear that He had come not only to the Jews, but to all nations.

Do you pray for people of other nations, other religions? Many today live alongside people of other nations and cultures. Jesus came for them – reach out to them for Him.

"...the blessed and only Ruler, the King of kings and Lord of lords" (1 Tim. 6:15).

❚ KEY THOUGHT
The man who bows the lowest in the presence of God stands the straightest in the presence of sin.

Variety of forebears
Matthew 1:1–17; Luke 3:23–38

Genealogies may appear, at first glance, to be boring, but look again at some of the people mentioned here: Rahab, a prostitute; David, youngest son who became a great king; Ruth, an unknown girl from Moab; Zerubbabel, governor of Judah who rebuilt the temple; Amon, an evil king; Noah, the only righteous man in the world in his time.

"... Mary, of whom was born Jesus ..."

What a variety! Some famous, some infamous, some nonentities, yet all were chosen by God to be the earthly forebears of His Son, Jesus.

God still chooses a surprising variety of people to be His followers. Search your heart to see if you are guilty of judging fellow Christians by their present lifestyle, background, former sinfulness, way of speaking ... (Rom. 14:4).

Matthew, writing for Jews, establishes Jesus in the Messianic line from David, through His legal father, Joseph, and then back to Abraham, father of the Jewish people. Luke, a non-Jew, traces Jesus' line right back to Adam to show that He came to the whole human race.

"But God chose the foolish things of the world to shame the wise; God chose the weak things of the world to shame the strong" (1 Cor. 1:27)

■ STUDY
With the help of a good Bible commentary, study the theories for the differences between the two lists in Matthew and Luke.

THE LEGAL HEIR

Luke
Physical Descent

ADAM
Father of all mankind

Matthew
Legal Descent

ABRAHAM
Father of Israel

DAVID

EXILE

POST EXILE

JESUS CHRIST

Matthew's abridged genealogy shows Jesus as the legal heir to the Promises given to Abraham and David.

Jesus' descent is traced to the covenant heads, Abraham, promised a nation and the land of Canaan (Gen. 12:2,7) and David, promised a "son" whose kingdom would be everlasting (2 Sam. 7:12, 13, 16).

DAY 9

Angel's announcement
Luke 1:26–38

Imagine how Mary must have felt. A visit from an angel was astounding enough in itself, and his message even more so. Mary was probably in her early teens, her engagement to Joseph arranged by her parents.

"... you are to give him the name Jesus"

She was brought up to obey the Jewish law and to look forward to the promised Messiah but, as far as we know, nothing had prepared her for this astonishing announcement from Gabriel.

Luke tells us Mary was "greatly troubled". A very natural reaction! Yet, after Gabriel had reassured her and explained his message, Mary accepted it. She was in the world to serve God in any way that He chose. Think about her attitude and let God speak to *you* through the words of v.38.

The conception of God's own Son was unique, brought about by the power of the Holy Spirit alone without any human father. This is one of the fundamental truths of our faith in Jesus, Son of God. Ask the Holy Spirit to reveal to you the wonder, the truth of this amazing fact, that God became man and dwelt among us.

"But when the time had fully come, God sent his Son, born of a woman, born under law, to redeem those under law, that we might receive the full rights of sons" (Gal. 4:4)

▮ QUESTION
What names or titles are given to Jesus in this passage?

DAY 10

Joy in the womb
Luke 1:39–45

Elizabeth and Zechariah had been told by Gabriel that their son would be one who would prepare the way of the Lord, but Elizabeth was not aware that her young relative, Mary, was to be the mother of the long-awaited Messiah. The Holy Spirit revealed the presence of Jesus first to baby John in his mother's womb. He leaped for joy in the presence of His Lord. Then Elizabeth, filled with the same Holy Spirit, showed that God had also revealed the wonderful truth to her. Note Elizabeth's humility and complete

"... the baby in my womb leaped for joy"

lack of jealousy. Elizabeth had been chosen and greatly blessed by God, but Mary had been chosen for an even greater privilege and greater blessing. Elizabeth rejoiced with her and truly blessed her. Do you react with the same genuineness and sincerity when it seems that God blesses someone else more than you? Pray for the humility and generosity to rejoice with others.

Elizabeth blessed Mary for her *faith* (v.45). Mary's acceptance of the Lord's will was not passive. It was an active, faith-filled, embracing of His promise to her.

"Rejoice with those who rejoice" (Rom. 12:15).

▮ PRAYER
Lord, help me not to feel left out when You are blessing others, but to enter in to their blessings. Amen.

DAY 11

Unbounded rejoicing
Luke 1:46–56

Lyrical poetry is the "spontaneous over-flow of powerful emotion," declared Wordsworth. Mary spoke from a full heart and from her knowl-edge of the Old Testament, and the result is one of the most beauti-ful poems ever written.

"My soul glorifies the Lord ..."

It is a song of praise. Mary glorifies God for His goodness to her personally (vv. 46–49), and His mercy on all who fear Him (v.50). She speaks of God's concern for the oppressed and for His people, Israel (vv. 54 & 55). The Holy Spirit had given Mary great spiritual insight into the future ministry of her baby Son. Compare verses 51–53 with Luke 4:18–19.

Mary had progressed from her initial, troubled reaction to acceptance of God's will, and faith in His promise. Now that she had received confirmation of God's word from Elizabeth, Mary's spirit over-flowed in joyful realisation of what God had done – and would do. What can you praise God for in your life? Let your spir-it rise within you as you praise and thank Him right now.

"... yet I will rejoice in the Lord, I will be joyful in God my Saviour" (Hab. 3:18).

▌DECLARE THIS
I will praise You with all my heart today.

DAY 12

Mind put at rest
Matthew 1:18–24

It takes a very special person to be a suc-cessful foster parent or a step-parent – to love someone else's child as if it were your own. Joseph was such a person. Imagine the consternation, hurt and grief he must have felt when he discovered that his betrothed was preg-nant. Yet even in his mis-understanding he didn't want to hurt her by publicising her disgrace.

"... do not be afraid ..."

Betrothal was as legally binding as mar-riage in Jewish law, and could only be dissolved by a writ of divorce. However, God the Father was watching over His Son, Jesus. He also knew and understood Joseph's feelings. He sent an angel to reassure the young man and explain to him what was happening. Learn this about our heavenly Father: He doesn't leave us perplexed for long. Ask Him to explain things to you, and wait patiently and expectantly for His answer.

Joseph understood and obeyed the message from the angel because he knew the Scriptures and trusted God. He will-ingly laid down his own reputation to fulfil God's purposes.

"A man who lacks judgement derides his neighbour, but a man of under-standing holds his tongue" (Prov. 11:12).

▌EXAMINE
Examine your own heart today and ask God to create in it the attitude Joseph had.

Lowly birth

Luke 2:1–7; Matthew 1:25

In taking Mary as his wife, Joseph became the legal father of Jesus, fulfilling the prophecy that the Messiah would be of the line of David. So a family was prepared for the coming of God's Son into the world. Yet Mary and Joseph lived in Nazareth and the coming Messiah was to be born in Bethlehem.

"... there was no room for them in the inn"

For what reason would a considerate husband require his pregnant wife to travel 80 miles to another town? Nothing is impossible with God. He had it all in hand, and the census required Joseph and Mary to be in Bethlehem at exactly the right time, when Mary "gave birth to her firstborn, a son". Such simple and matter-of-fact words to describe the greatest event this world has ever known!

God became man and was born, not in a palace, but among the animals in a stable. Jesus, Saviour of the world, came to preach good news to the poor. Therefore He came as a poor Man. Are you prepared to relinquish your position in life for Him?

"He made himself of no reputation" (Phil. 2:7 AV).

✏ KEY THOUGHT

Christmas without Christ means a manger with no babe, a cross without a Saviour, a hope without heaven and a soul without salvation.

▪▪▪ ▪▪▪ ▪▪▪▪▪▪▪▪▪ A MANGER ▪▪▪ ▪▪▪▪ ▪▪▪▪▪▪▪

It was common at the time of Jesus' birth for a mother to lay her baby in a manger during the day. It was safe and warm in the clean straw. Every peasant house had a manger indoors, for the animals were brought in at night and tethered to it. It was made of small stones held together by mortar. It was also common in Palestine to use a cave as a stable and the manger would be cut out of the rock. After a baby was born, he or she was placed diagonally on a square cloth, which was folded round it. Then strips of linen were wrapped around it like bandages.

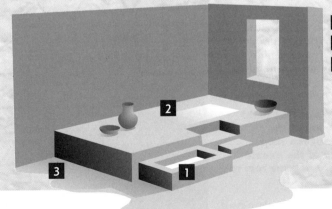

1 Manger
2 Raised living area
3 Livestock area

Welcomed by angels

Luke 2:8–20

The birth of Jesus was:

To the people of Bethlehem – an ordinary, everyday happening.

"... tidings of great joy ..." To Mary and Joseph – a very special, precious time.

To the angels in heaven – a stupendous, wonderful, unique event. A time of great rejoicing, and for giving all praise and glory to God.

In a very real sense Jesus is born into the world again every time a sinner repents and asks Jesus to live His life in him. When asked about a meeting he had just been to, a Christian said casually, "Oh, it was OK. Quite a few people got saved." The angels were rejoicing about *each one* (Lk. 15:10). How do you react?

The title "Christ the Lord", used by the angel, would have indicated to the shepherds that this was indeed the long awaited and expected Saviour of Israel. "Christ" (Greek) and "Messiah" (Hebrew) both mean "the Anointed One". The shepherds rejoiced with the angels and spread the good news. The people who heard it were amazed. Mary, however, "treasured" the happenings. Do you? Or is the story so familiar that it has lost its wonder for you?

"I tell you that ... there will be more rejoicing in heaven over one sinner who repents than over ninety-nine righteous persons who do not need to repent" (Luke 15:7).

MEDITATE

Meditate on the events of that night in Bethlehem. Let the joy of the angels, the eagerness of the shepherds, the amazement of the people and the peace of Mary become real to you as you praise God.

Right: a street in Bethlehem

DAY 15

Given His name

Luke 2:21–38

"Jesus, the Name high over all". "Jesus, Name above all names." How many hymns and spiritual songs can you think of which are about the Name of Jesus?

Jesus was given the name commanded by the angel although, traditionally, the eldest son would be named after his father. It is probably the best known name in history, whether loved or hated. It means, simply, Saviour – one who saves or safeguards. It is the Name at which every knee should bow (Phil. 2:9–11).

"... my eyes have seen your salvation ..."

Imagine Simeon's joy and delight at seeing the fulfilment of God's promise to him. The Holy Spirit had:

1. Revealed to him that he would see the Christ.

2. Caused him to be in the temple at exactly the right moment.

3. Given him instant recognition of the baby Jesus.

Anna, a very old lady, was also given the privilege of recognition and immediately gave thanks and spoke about the child. Why should these two elderly people be so aware of the presence of Jesus? Look again at verses 25 and 37b, and apply them to your own spiritual life. Is Jesus real to you? Are you aware of His presence in you, daily, wherever you are?

"Therefore God exalted him to the highest place and gave him the name that is above every name, that at the name of Jesus every knee should bow, in heaven and on earth and under the earth" (Phil. 2:9, 10).

■ **QUESTION**
What does Leviticus 12:8 tell us about Joseph and Mary?

DAY 16

Light to the Gentiles

Matthew 2:1–12

"The gospel ... is the power of God for the salvation of everyone who believes," wrote the apostle Paul, adding, "first for the Jew, then for the Gentile" (Rom. 1:16). Jesus was born into a Jewish family and was presented first to the Jews as their Saviour, and the promised Anointed One, the Christ. The coming of the wise men was the beginning of the fulfilment of prophecies that Jesus would also be a "light to the Gentiles" (Isa. 49:6; Lk. 2:32). The sign given to the wise

"When they saw the star, they were overjoyed"

men was one they would understand: a new bright star, heralding the birth of a King, and they brought Him costly gifts. The gold, frankincense and myrrh were later regarded as symbolic of Jesus' threefold office of King, Priest and Prophet. The fact that they came to a house, not a stable, indicates that their visit was some time after the birth of Jesus. Their arrival could, in fact, have been any time up to two years later.

The shepherds glorified and praised God; the wise men worshipped Him. Are these things a priority in your life?

"I have come into the world as a light, so that no-one who believes in me should stay in darkness" (John 12:46).

■ **KEY THOUGHT**
A wise man will not only bow at the manger, but also at the Cross.

GIFTS FOR JESUS

Gold, used as a precious metal in Palestine from very early times, was possessed by only a few. It was the symbol of a king.

Frankincense was a symbol of worship and holiness. A white, scented gum from the Boswellia tree, it was brought to Palestine by camel caravans from Arabia, the land of the Queen of Sheba.

Myrrh, symbol of suffering and death, came from the Commiflora, a thorny bush which grew in Arabia and East Africa. An oily, yellow gum with a very sweet scent, it was used for perfumes and cosmetics as well as for anointing the dead.

DAY 17

The right path
Matthew 2:13–18

I was once driving one of our children to a music lesson when, for some reason, I turned right from our driveway instead of left, resulting in a much longer journey. I was annoyed with myself for my mistake, until coming home by the usual route, I saw the aftermath of a very serious accident at a busy crossroads.

"Out of Egypt I called my son"

The Lord had protected us from being involved in that accident. God guides His people in many different ways, through Scripture, dreams, circumstances, prophecies, advice from other Christians – but more often, in my experience, by His still, small voice saying quietly, "Don't go that way – take this path."

Many of you will have had similar experiences. Perhaps it was an urge to look for a small child just as he was about to fall into a pond or wander into the road or an urge to phone a depressed friend just as she was thinking of taking an overdose. The word of the Lord is not always so specific as the dream that Joseph had but, like him, we need to listen and obey, for our own safety and that of others.

"Trust in the Lord with all your heart and lean not on your own understanding; in all your ways acknowledge him, and he will make your paths straight" (Prov. 3:5, 6).

■ THANKSGIVING
Lord, Your guiding eye is continually upon me. Thank You for Your protection.

DAY 18

Back to Nazareth

Matthew 2:19–23; Luke 2:39, 40

Joseph obeyed the message from the angel again, but when he arrived back in Judea he was shocked to find a potentially worse situation then when he had left. Archelaus, one of Herod's sons, was a notorious tyrant who was so cruel to the Jews and Samaritans that he was eventually exiled by the Romans for his brutality.

"... the grace of God was upon him"

Have you ever felt puzzled by God's leading? You've felt sure you were in His will, and yet the situation seemed all wrong? Perhaps God was saying to you, as He said to Joseph, "Keep going – trust me."

Joseph and Mary went back to Nazareth and at last settled down to a normal life in their home town. Jesus' life, from the time the family left Nazareth before He was born to the time they returned, had been hazardous and unsettled. Think about it. Yet all the time His heavenly Father had been watching over Him. It is not our circumstances that dictate our sense of security, but our relationship with God.

"'For my thoughts are not your thoughts, neither are your ways my ways,' declares the Lord. 'As the heavens are higher than the earth, so are my ways higher than your ways and my thoughts than your thoughts'" (Isa. 55:8, 9).

■ **MY CONFESSION**
In the midst of a confused world, I place my trust in you, Lord.

DAY 19

Teachers amazed

Luke 2:41–50

Jesus was suprised that His parents were anxious about Him. He was thrilled to be where He was. He knew He was safe and in His rightful place. There must be many young people who can identify with this attitude of, "I know I'm safe. Why should you worry about me?" But Jesus was without sin.

"Everyone who heard him was amazed ..."

There was no rebelliousness in Him, no intent to hurt His parents – simply a youthful lack of understanding of their natural fears. As soon as He understood, He was obedient. Young people, do you try to understand your parents' point of view?

Parents, do you see things from your children's viewpoint? Loving explanations achieve far more than angry accusations.

It was an exciting time for Jesus – the age at which every Jewish boy became a full member of the congregation. He would now be instructed in law, in fasting and in taking part in public worship, as well as starting to learn a trade. His understanding, under the tutorship of the Holy Spirit, however, was already far greater than that of His contemporaries.

"Don't let anyone look down on you because you are young, but set an example for the believers in speech, in life, in love, in faith and in purity" (1 Tim. 4:12).

◆ **FOR STUDY**
Read Proverbs 2:1–6 and write down what the Lord says to you through these Scriptures.

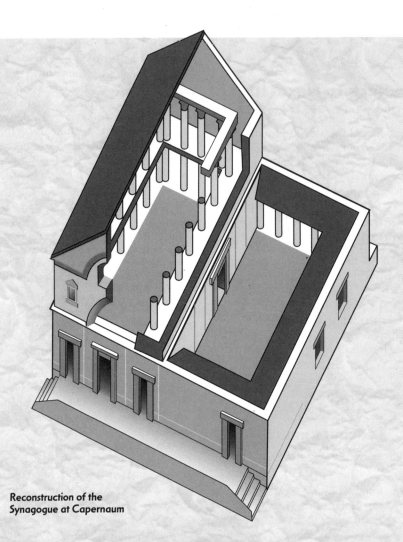

Reconstruction of the
Synagogue at Capernaum

THE SYNAGOGUE

According to Jewish law, ten or more adult men assembled together for the purpose of worship and to learn and fulfil God's will constituted a synagogue. The regular sabbath meetings began with the Shema, the first commandment, followed by prayers, the reading of Scripture and, if a competent person was present, exposition and teaching. The synagogue was a lay institution. No priest was necessary, but if one was present he was given a place of honour. The chief residing officer, the Ruler of the synagogue, was responsible for taking a scroll from the ark where they were kept and handing it to someone to read from.

Growing up
Luke 2:51–52

The word translated "grew" or "increased" in v.52 could also mean "kept advancing". Jesus was, humanly speaking, a normal boy at every stage of His life, but He kept advancing in wisdom as well as in physical stature.

"... Jesus grew in wisdom and stature ..."

The incident in the temple at Jerusalem showed us that by the age of 12 He already had a good grasp of the law of Moses and was eager to learn more. No doubt He diligently studied and understood the books of the prophets, particularly the prophecies relating to Himself.

At the same time Jesus would have been apprenticed to Joseph in the carpentry trade, learning practical skills and patience in working with the wood. He would also have learned public relations when dealing with customers. Our Lord was obedient to His parents, even though He was the Son of God. What tremendous humility and grace!

Do you keep advancing" in your spiritual life? Do you study the Scriptures diligently and seek understanding, using the gifts God has given you to His glory, and becoming more like Him day by day?

"... Christ, in whom are hidden all the treasures of wisdom and knowledge" (Col. 2:2, 3).

▌ MEDITATE
Meditate on Philippians 3:13, 14.

Preparing the way
Matthew 3:1–6; Mark 1:2–6;
Luke 3:1–6; John 1:6–18

What a tremendous privilege and responsibility John had in his ministry of preparing the ground for Jesus! Luke's historical background (3:1, 2) pinpoints the year as AD 26. Isaiah's prophecy shows the making of a road for a king to travel along.

"Repent, for the kingdom of heaven is near"

Compare it with the laying down of a red carpet for the Queen or, more accurately, the building of a new motorway. The bulldozers plough up the ground, rocks are dynamited away, houses and other buildings are pulled down, valleys filled in with tons of earth, bridges built and old roads diverted, the whole area levelled and smoothed.

This was John's commission: to prepare the minds of the people, to blast away the hardness of their hearts, pull down old traditions, fill in the emptiness of their religious lives, build bridges of repentance and change the direction of their lives so that when Jesus began His ministry there would be a people ready to listen.

What is your commission from God? Spend a few minutes asking and listening. What is God calling you to do today, and in the future?

"One sows and another reaps" (John 4:37).

▌ KEY THOUGHT
You do not do God a favour by serving Him. He honours you by allowing you to serve Him.

Jesus' Early Ministry

- **Nazareth** – Mary told she will bear God's Son
- **Bethlehem** – The Saviour born
- **Jerusalem**
  – Jesus debates in the Temple
- **Judean Wilderness (by the Jordan)**
  – John the Baptist preaches repentance.
  – Jesus baptised
- **Wilderness**
  – The temptation of Jesus
- **Aenon near Salim**
  – John continues baptising
- **Galilee (nr Capernaum)**
  –Disciples called
- **Cana** – Jesus' first miracle
- **Capernaum** – Jesus' home during Galilean ministry
- **Jerusalem** – Jesus cleanses the Temple
- **Sychar** – Jesus meets woman at the well
- **Nazareth** – Jesus rejected in His home town
- **Galilee (towns)** – Jesus teaches and heals
- **Lake Galilee** – Jesus walks on the water
- **Caesarea Philippi** – Peter's confession of Jesus

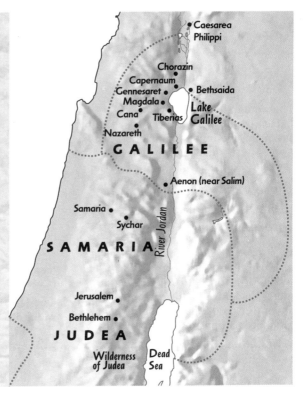

DAY 22

Call to repentance

Matthew 3:7–10; Luke 3:7–14

Strong words from John! He corrected the Jewish expectation that the coming Messiah would bring judgment to the Gentiles and free the Jewish nation from their oppressors.

"The axe is already at the root ..."

Judgment begins at the house of God (1 Pet.4:17). It was not their ancestry that would save the Jews, but their obedient heart attitude to God's laws worked out practically in their lives.

John's message was not the Christian message of grace, but the preparation for that message, bringing about conviction of sin and repentance. Matthew tells us that John's most scathing comments were directed at the Jewish leaders, the Pharisees and Sadducees, who had led the people astray with their false teaching.

"In the past God overlooked such ignorance, but now he commands all people everywhere to repent" (Acts 17:30).

◼ ASK YOURSELF
Am I ever guilty of thinking that others should be judged?
Do I rely on my Christian background for my salvation?
Am I willing continually to allow God to search my heart?
Am I quick to repent of sin?
Does my repentance show in practical ways in my life?

DAY 23

Introduced Christ

Matthew 3:11–12; Mark 1:7–8;
Luke 3:15–18

John's utter humility and acceptance of his role of forerunner is shown in these readings. He knew his commission from God and he fulfilled it. As the saying goes, "It takes more grace than tongue can tell to play the second fiddle well."

> **"He will baptise you with the Holy Spirit and with fire"**

John didn't try to go beyond his stated orders, and he made it quite clear to his hearers that there was One coming after him who was far greater than he.

This is what evangelism is all about – pointing the way to Jesus. Has someone ever tried to attach themselves to you as a Christian? It is flattering, but wrong. You must help them to put their roots down in Jesus and grow in Him.

John's introduction of Jesus is interesting. He announces Him not as Saviour, which would have the wrong connotation to his Jewish hearers, but a baptiser with the Holy Spirit and as Judge. Winnowing, separating the wheat from the chaff, is a picture of judgment and is a clear preparation for the effect that Jesus' teaching would have.

"... serve one another in love" (Gal. 5:13).

▌ QUESTION
How does John the Baptist fulfil Isaiah's prophecy? (Luke 3:4)

DAY 24

Lower than a slave

John 1:19–28

The task of removing sandals and washing hot and dusty feet was performed by the slaves of the household. When John described Jesus as "the one ... the thongs of whose sandals I am not worthy to untie," he was placing himself in a position lower than a slave in relation to our Lord. In preparing the way for Jesus, John taught, both by word and example, that the One who was to come after him was worthy of respect, honour and worship.

> **"... the voice of one calling in the desert ..."**

Consider your own attitude to Jesus: do you give Him the honour due to Him? Would younger Christians learn from your example how to walk humbly before God, to reverence Him and speak of Him in public?

There are many people nowadays who speak flippantly of Jesus, make fun of His Name, use it as a swear word, or blaspheme against Him. Do you stand up for Him like John the Baptist did, proclaiming humbly who He is and why He came?

"Be devoted to one another in brotherly love. Honour one another above yourselves" (Rom. 12:10).

▌ KEY THOUGHT
If we do not learn humility, we will learn humiliation.

BAPTISM IN ...

The Old Testament
Ritual "washing" or "cleansing" acts are a sign of purification from sin (Ex.30:17–21; Lev. 11:25; 15:8; 17:15; Num. 19:17, 18; 31:22,23).

John the Baptist's teaching
Baptism marked a deep repentance over sin (Matt. 3:5–11; Luke 3:3–17)
There was an urgency for God's Kingdom was near (Matt. 3:1–3)
It signified forgiveness for those who repented (Mark 1:4–5; Luke 3:3).

Jesus' teaching
Jesus spoke of His death as a baptism He had to undergo.
Baptism is to be understood in the light of Jesus' saving death and resurrection and is an identification with His redemptive work (Luke 12:50; Mark 10:38).
The Church is commissioned to make disciples and baptise them in (or into) the name of the Father, Son and Holy Spirit, so displaying whose they are (Matt. 28:19).

The apostles' teaching
Paul explains that baptism symbolizes the Christian's participation in the death and resurrection of Christ: he, too, has died (to his old life) and is raised to a new one (Rom. 6:3–4, 11).

With the Holy Spirit
Jesus baptises with the Holy Spirit, clothing us "with power from on high" (Luke 24:49).
Our Lord provides us with the means to be His witnesses on earth (Acts 4:27–33).

What a baptism!
Matthew 3:13–17; Mark 1:9–11; Luke 3:21,22

John's baptism was a baptism of repentance for the forgiveness of sins (Luke 3:3). Jesus had no sin. He needed no forgiveness, yet He insisted on being baptised to identify Himself with the people whom He came to save. It was an act of humility which also publicly signified His approval of John's ministry. It marked the beginning of Jesus' own ministry – and His heavenly Father put His seal of approval on it.

"This is my Son, whom I love"

It was a wonderful scene – all three Persons of the Trinity manifested at the same time. The Son was being baptised on earth, the Father speaking from heaven, publicly declaring Jesus to be His Son, and the Holy Spirit visibly descending from heaven to rest on Jesus, anointing Him for His earthly ministry.

Traditionally, baptism is a family, as well as a public, occasion. Jesus' heavenly family were present at His. Fathers, think about the words spoken by the heavenly Father in these Scriptures: Do you encourage your children with words like those? Do you give them confidence and security by showing your approval publicly?

"Humble yourselves before the Lord, and he will lift you up" (James 4:10).

◢ PRAYER
Lord, help me to live so that You may say to me, "This is my son, whom I love; with him I am well pleased" Amen.

Here He is!

John 1:29–34

It must have been a proud moment for John when he baptised Jesus, but even more so when he was able to publicly declare, "This is the One I've been telling you about!"

"Look, the Lamb of God, who takes away the sin of the world!"

John recognised Jesus as the Son of God because God had given him a sign (v.33). He recognised Him as the Lamb of God because he knew the Old Testament prophecies relating to the Messiah (cf Isa. 53:7).

Suddenly, it all tied together for John, and he must have felt that his hard years in the wilderness had all been worthwhile.

Can you imagine how thrilled and overjoyed John must have been to be actually in the presence of the One to whom he had dedicated his life?

When we tell someone about Jesus, perhaps for years with no result, it does seem hard at times. Yet when we see at last the Lamb of God taking away that person's sins and His new life planted in him or her, then it's worth it, isn't it?

"For you know that it was not with perishable things such as silver or gold that you were redeemed ... but with the precious blood of Christ, a lamb without blemish or defect" (1 Pet. 1:18,19).

▼ MY PROMISE
Lord, today I will seek to introduce someone to You.

Temptation resisted

Matthew 4:1–11; Mark 1:12–13; Luke 4:1–13

It was the Holy Spirit who led Jesus to the wilderness, *not* the devil. Christians often experience a spiritual low straight after reaching a spiritual mountain top.

"... It is written ..."

Everything then seems to go against us. If only we could see these times as testing times from God, chances to prove our strength in Him rather than to fall under an attack from the enemy!

Yes, the Father allowed the devil to tempt His Son, but only when He was ready to withstand him. Jesus, tempted when He was at His lowest ebb physically, proved that the Word of God is an effective weapon against the enemy. How well do you know the Bible? Are you ready to use Scripture as a sword to thrust at the devil?

Consider the difference between Adam's temptation and Jesus'. Adam was in a lush garden with plenty of food, a loving wife, tame animals – and he fell. Jesus was alone in a wilderness, starving, threatened by wild animals – and He stood firm. Think about this when you are tempted to blame your circumstances for sin.

"Do your best to present yourself to God as one approved, a workman who does not need to be ashamed and who correctly handles the word of truth" (2 Tim. 2:15).

▲ KEY THOUGHT
Ask how he resisted temptation, a little boy said, "I have a little talk with the devil and say, 'Get behind me Satan – and don't you dare push.'"

The first disciples
John 1:35-42

It seems that the writer, John, son of Zebedee, was the other disciple with Andrew in this passage, because of the precise time recorded. They had both been disciples of John the Baptist, who then pointed them to Jesus.

"We have found the Messiah ..."

It must have been a wonderful day for them in the company of the One they had been looking for. At the end of it Andrew is convinced that Jesus is indeed the Christ, the Messiah.

The incident of Andrew finding his brother and introducing him to Jesus always thrills me. You never know, when you "find" someone for Jesus, what their future potential will be. Simon Peter became the head of the Church in Jerusalem. That person you are praying for and witnessing to may be a future evangelist, missionary, minister ... so *don't* give up!

Jesus looked at Simon and saw in him what God was to make of him, not what he was. God always sees our potential rather than our weaknesses. Do you see people like that?

"The fruit of the righteous is a tree of life, and he who wins souls is wise" (Prov. 11:30).

■ **STUDY**
What does the word "disciple" mean? Look it up in a Bible dictionary.

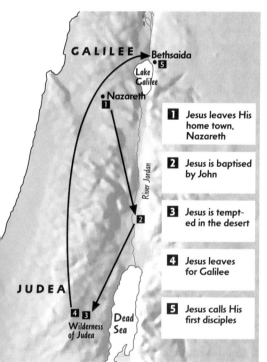

GALILEE ▶ Bethsaida
● **5**
Lake Galilee
● Nazareth
1

River Jordan

2

JUDEA

4 3
Wilderness of Judea
Dead Sea

1 Jesus leaves His home town, Nazareth

2 Jesus is baptised by John

3 Jesus is tempted in the desert

4 Jesus leaves for Galilee

5 Jesus calls His first disciples

Sharing the good news
John 1:43-51

It was time for Jesus to return from the Jordan valley to Galilee. He invited Philip to go with Him, along with Andrew, Peter and John. Like Andrew, Philip's first thought was to share the good news with someone else.

"... Follow me"

I wonder if Nathanael was asleep under that fig tree? The Jews often used fig trees as places of meditation, but Nathanael's grumpy attitude to the stupendous piece of news that Philip brought him suggests that he might have just woken up.

Or perhaps he was one of those pessimistic people who can't believe there is any good in anything. Whatever the reason for Nathanael's blunt remark, Jesus, by His word of encouragement and revelation, completely disarms him and wins him over. How do you react to criticism and sarcasm?

Nathanael gives three titles to Jesus: Rabbi (teacher), Son of God, King of Israel. Jesus responds with another title, Son of Man. Why do you think He did that?

"Whoever serves me must follow me; and where I am, my servant also will be. My Father will honour the one who serves me" (John 12:26).

⚑ PRAYER
Lord, I want to love and serve You with all my heart. Help me to follow You in obedience along the path You have set for me. Amen.

WEDDINGS

God's command to Adam, "Be fruitful and multiply" is taken by the Jews as binding, and that it is the duty of every man and woman to marry and produce children. Marriages were arranged by older relatives, but each man had to buy his wife.

Water into wine
John 2:1–11

The first miracle Jesus performed was a practical one. He answered a friend's need, supplying both quantity and quality. Do you pray about your practical needs as well as your spiritual ones?

"... the first of his miraculous signs ..."

Many Christians can testify of the Lord's miraculous supply line, but sometimes we forget to ask.

Once, when we were without money for a while, I cried out to the Lord for a bar of soap. There was a "plop" through the letter box – a full-size free sample of toilet soap! Ten minutes later, another "plop" – another bar of soap! The distributors had got muddled and covered our road twice. During the same period I asked the Lord for some fruit one day. I would have been content with a pound of apples, but the doorbell rang, and there stood a lady with a large basket of fruit of all kinds. "The Lord told me to bring you some fruit," she said. She had had a train journey and a walk each end to get to me, and I had only met her once before.

The Lord is good. He is generous and understanding. He really does supply *all* our needs.

"And my God will meet all your needs according to his glorious riches in Christ Jesus" (Phil. 4:19).

⚑ THANK YOU
Thank you, Lord, that there is no shortage in Your storehouse – Your supply never runs out.

Temple cleaned up

John 2:12–22

Jesus had visited the temple annually at Passover time, but this was the first visit after the start of His ministry. He was angered by the worldly intrusion into what should have been a sacred place.

"Zeal for your house will consume me"

The market in the Gentiles' court prevented people worshipping there. The noise and the smell pervaded the inner courts, too, hindering worship by the Jews. The exorbitant profits made by the money changers may have prompted Jesus to later say, "You cannot serve God and mammon."

Jesus took His authority as the Son in His Father's house, and drove them all out. The disciples remembered a prophecy from Psalm 69:9. John the Baptist's message (see reading and notes on Day 22) is also relevant.

The rebuilding of the temple had begun in 20 BC and was still not completed at this time, AD 26 or 27. So the Jews were completely mystified by Jesus' claim to be able to raise it in three days.

Think about your worship of the Lord. Is it pure, untainted by worldly attitudes and thoughts?

"Do you not know that your body is a temple of the Holy Spirit, who is in you, whom you have received from God? You are not your own" (1 Cor. 6:19).

▌ QUESTION
How should we worship God? See John 4:23; Psalm 96:8,9; Exodus 34:14.

Seeing into hearts

John 2:23–25

Jesus demands more of us than a faith based on supernatural signs. Many people were amazed, excited and drawn to Jesus by the wonderful things He was doing among them.

"... he knew what was in a man"

Their commitment, however, was only superficial and their motives were wrong.

Jesus saw into their hearts. He knew, and still knows, what human nature is like, because He was a Man. He knew that people do not like to be bored and will travel in search of new experiences, charismatic personalities or adventure. Many of the people who followed Jesus around Jerusalem were looking for just those things. When the going got tough they deserted Him.

What kind of commitment do you have to Jesus? Are you looking for thrills and excitement, the big meetings, camps, conferences? Or are you walking daily with Jesus, filled with His Spirit, ready to serve Him faithfully in the mundane things of everyday life?

"...The Lord does not look at the things man looks at. Man looks at the outward appearance, but the Lord looks at the heart" (1 Sam. 16:7).

▼ KEY THOUGHT
When the going gets tough, the tough get going.

DAY 33

Straight talking
John 3:1–12

Nicodemus was a member of the Sanhedrin and a very respected member of the community. Note that Jesus calls him "Israel's teacher", rather than "a" teacher. This may meant that he had some official position as teacher. He came by night probably because he was unwilling to be seen talking to Jesus in daylight. He acknowledged that Jesus was a teacher sent by God, as distinct from one who had qualified in a rabbinical school, but he didn't recognise Him as the Messiah.

"You must be born again"

Jesus came straight to the point. He had no time for discussion or theological arguments. Nicodemus would have relied on careful observance of the law and traditions of the elders for his salvation. Jesus explained that, in order to enter the kingdom of God, it was necessary to be born of the Spirit.

Nicodemus had to completely change his way of thinking and start again from the beginning. It was too much for him – he didn't understand. What do you base your salvation on? Have you really understood what it means to be born of the Spirit?

"He who has the Son has life; he who does not have the Son of God does not have life" (1 Jn. 5:12).

■ QUESTION
Read John 7:50,51 and 19:39. How do you think Nicodemus got on with his re-thinking?

DAY 34

So much love
John 3:13–21

Jesus went on to explain to Nicodemus that He is not just a "teacher sent from God" – He has come from heaven. He speaks of His death in the simile of Moses' serpent in the desert with its healing powers, and of His return to heaven.

Then, in the best-known and best-loved verse in the Bible (John 3:16), Jesus clearly spells out that He is God's Son.

"For God so loved ... that he gave ...."

It is good to look at this verse in context – as part of the continuity of Jesus' talk with Nicodemus. First, Jesus established the need of spiritual rebirth, rather than careful observance of the law as Nicodemus believed (v.3). Our Lord then elaborated on this principle (vv. 5–8). He rebuked Nicodemus for not understanding (vv. 10–12). Then He revealed Who He really was (vv. 13–17) and explained God's loving purpose in sending Him into the world.

Jesus finished with a challenge – giving Nicodemus a clear choice of beliefs (vv. 18–21). Have you ever led anyone into the Kingdom of God? How would you show a friend, in simple terms, how to become a Christian by using this passage?

"Therefore, if anyone is in Christ, he is a new creation; the old has gone, the new has come!" (2 Cor. 5:17).

■ MEDITATE
Meditate on the words, "God so loved ..." Receive His love for yourself.

DAY 35

Dealing with jealousy
John 3:22–26

All though Jesus' ministry we find that He divided His time between the crowds and His disciples.

We read today how He takes His disciples out into the country to spend time with them. But, as always, people followed, and many were baptised, not by Jesus, but by His disciples (4:2).

"... he spent some time with them"

Meanwhile, John the Baptist was still baptising elsewhere. His disciples got into an argument with a Jew, possibly a member of the Essene sect, about purification. It is interesting that, when his disciples went to complain to John, it was not about this Jew that they complained, but about Jesus. It seems that they were jealous that Jesus was attracting more converts than John.

It is a very common, humorous story, of human nature. Something or someone upsets you and you turn round and blame God, or perhaps your minister. Another church or fellowship appears to be doing better or growing faster than yours. Do you rejoice or complain? See the ridiculous as well as the spiritual side of it!

"... Christ loved the church and gave himself up for her to make her holy, cleansing her by the washing with water through the word" (Eph. 5:25, 26).

◆ PRAYER
Lord, give me grace to rejoice with those who rejoice and strength to make my complaints only to You. Amen.

- - -

DAY 36

Letting Jesus take over
John 3:27–36

What a wonderful reply to the disciples' complaint! John is completely humble. He rightly points out that he has always said that he is not the Christ and that, when Christ came, He would be greater than John.

"He must become greater; I must become less"

He is not jealous of Jesus' ministry, but rejoices in it. John was sent to prepare the way for Jesus and is now quite willing to step back and let Jesus take over.

Are you willing to take a back seat and step down if someone more able than you wants to take over your job? How do you feel if a younger Christian, perhaps one that you have led to the Lord, gets on faster or has a more prominent ministry than yourself? Rejoice, and give all the glory to God!

John the Baptist glorified God in all that he said. He constantly spoke of Jesus, prepared people to receive Him, introduced Him to the people. John testified as to who He is and finally, in this last record of his ministry, gives this glorious "Gospel-in-a-nutshell" in verses 35 and 36. It is worth learning these verses by heart.

"Do not think of yourself more highly than you ought, but rather think of yourself with sober judgment ..." (Rom. 12:3).

◆ KEY THOUGHT
The smaller we are the more room God has.

DAY 37

Wise departure

Matthew 4:12; John 4:1–3

These Scriptures mark the beginning of a new phase in Jesus' ministry: His return to Galilee. His decision to return to His home country was made because of the increasing hostility of the authorities.

"... he left Judea ..."

John the Baptist had been put in prison by King Herod because he condemned Herod's unlawful marriage. Anger against John must have been directed on to Jesus as well, because the two were closely associated. The Pharisees were concerned because Jesus was gaining so many followers. They regarded Him as a threat to their traditional teaching of the law. God the Father had work for His Son to do on earth. Therefore it was expedient that Jesus went to a safer place for the time being.

Jesus was wise – He didn't walk into, or remain in, danger unwittingly or unnecessarily. He took note of circumstances and acted accordingly. We can learn from His example. Occasionally we may have a definite leading of the Holy Spirit to go to a dangerous place, but we need to be very sure of His guidance. God takes care of His children. We are precious to Him.

"Be wise in the way you act towards outsiders; make the most of every opportunity" (Col. 4:5).

KEY THOUGHT
A wise man will make more opportunities than he readily finds.

DAY 38

Real refreshment

John 4:4–26

Jesus got tired and thirsty, just as you and I would on a hot and dusty journey, but He did not get fed-up and irritable as we might. He was ready to speak to this needy Samaritan woman.

"... whoever drinks the water I give him will never thirst ..."

She was surprised that a Jew should even speak to her – and she was amazed at what He said.

Notice how Jesus leads the conversation. Beginning with a simple request for a drink, He uses the water as a spiritual illustration. He doesn't directly answer her question (v. 12), but goes on explaining His illustration. She doesn't understand, so Jesus uses His gift of knowledge to awaken a sense of need in her, and a growing realisation of Who she is speaking to.

In v. 20 the woman brings up a controversial subject which could have led to argument, but Jesus parries it and leads into a deeper spiritual truth than she has ever heard before. Finally, He answers her question of v. 12 by declaring Himself to be the Messiah. Jesus' wisdom, knowledge and understanding surpass anything man can do.

"For the Son of Man came to seek and to save what was lost" (Luke 19:10).

QUESTION
Consider v. 24 carefully. How do we worship God in spirit and in truth?

A harvest reaped

John 4:27-42

The disciples could have thought the worst of Jesus when they found Him talking to an immoral woman alone, but such was His purity and uprightness that they didn't question His behaviour.

"... look at the fields! They are ripe for harvest"

They were surprised to find that Jesus' tiredness and hunger had been completely taken away by His obedience to the will of God. I wonder if you have ever experienced this?

It's true that one can be feeling weary, ill, depressed or spiritually low and be completely revived by ministering to someone else's need. Never let your own feelings hinder you from giving out to other people.

What a harvest for eternal life Jesus reaped by His conversation with that one woman! She told her neighbours and they came and heard for themselves. They urged Jesus to stay, and many more believed. Faith is not a second-hand experience, based on what others say. It must be born out of a personal encounter with Jesus and trust in the Lord Himself.

"On the last and greatest day of the Feast, Jesus stood and said in a loud voice, 'If anyone is thirsty, let him come to me and drink'" (John 7:37).

ASK YOURSELF
Are you telling your neighbours about Jesus so that they can meet Him, too?

An about-turn

John 4:43; Matthew 4:17; Mark 1:14-15; Luke 4:14-15

Having walked through Samaria and spent two days with the people of Sychar, Jesus arrived back in Galilee to find a welcome from people who knew Him.

"The kingdom of God is near"

News of all He had done in Jerusalem spread quickly, and the crowds were eager to hear His preaching in the synagogues.

Jesus continued with John the Baptist's call to "repent", and adds "believe" to it. Repentance means far more than being sorry for one's sins. It means, literally, "to have a change of mind," to turn back from going one way and to go the opposite way. The people were to turn from their sinfulness and live a completely new life.

"Believe" means "to put one's complete trust in". Jesus was calling the people to leave their old ways, to trust and follow Him, and to allow God to rule as King in their hearts. Does God rule in your life? Is there any part of you that has not come under His royal command?

"... if you confess with your mouth, 'Jesus is Lord,' and believe in your heart that God raised him from the dead, you will be saved" (Rom. 10:9).

QUESTION
What was expected after repentance and baptism in the Early Church? (Acts 2:38)

WATER – THE SOURCE OF LIFE

Water carries powerful spiritual symbolism in the Bible. It is, primarily, a cleansing agent. The Old Testament priests were instructed to wash themselves in the bronze basin which stood in the Tabernacle between the Tent of Meeting and the altar (Ex. 30:17–21). There they could see their own reflections in the basin and their need for cleansing. Hence the New Testament application is found in Eph. 5:26, which speaks of Christ having sacrificed Himself for the Church to make her holy "by the washing with water through the word". That purification is seen both as a once-and-for-all act in baptism and as a continuous process through meditating on, and obeying, the Word of God.

Water is a source of refreshment (Psa. 42:1; Isa. 55:1), a picture of God satisfying the heart which longs to know Him and do His will. Jesus told the Samaritan woman that He would give a continuous supply of living water to all who received Him (John 4:13, 14). Those who truly live for God are themselves like streams of water, giving life to those stranded in the world's deserts of sin and hopelessness (Isa. 32:2; 49:10; Jer. 17:8; Jn. 7:38). Water is a source of joy, the well of salvation from which we can continually draw (Isa. 12:3; Song of Songs 4:15). There, in Christ, the deepest needs are satisfied (Jn. 7:37).

Water is a picture of so much blessing from God, so it is not surprising that the opposite – drought – symbolizes devastating judgment (1 Kings 8:35, 36). And spiritual drought is upon our nation as a result of turning away from Him. This state should drive us to prayer for God, in His mercy, to send floods of revival.

DAY 41

Sincerity tested
John 4:46–54

The nobleman's son was dying and, in a last desperate attempt to save his son's life, the man travelled the 20 miles from Capernaum to Cana to find Jesus. What a sensible thing to do.

"Your son will live"

Often in a crisis Jesus is the only Person who can help. Do you turn to Jesus immediately when things go wrong, or do you rush about trying everything else first? We read in this passage that when the man heard, he went. He begged Jesus to save his son.

Jesus tested his sincerity. Was it just sensationalism he was after? No, it was a genuine concern for his son's life – there was an urgency in his plea for help. Isn't it amazing, then, that the nobleman accepted without question Jesus' simple words, "Your son will live"?

In the midst of his terrible anxiety, there was something about Jesus that stilled his fears and inspired perfect peace and trust. He came with worry and despair and went away with peace and hope. Jesus loves to answer desperate pleas.

"Jesus said to her, 'I am the resurrection and the life. He who believes in me will live, even though he dies'" (John 11:25).

▼ KEY THOUGHT
Peace rules the day when Christ rules the circumstance.

DAY 42

Rejected by the 'locals'
Luke 4:16–30

Galilee was a densely populated area in Jesus' time. News travelled fast and the whole countryside was buzzing with stories of Jesus' teaching and miracles.

"The Spirit of the Lord is on me ..." His family and acquaintances in Nazareth were eager to see and hear this local boy who had become famous. No doubt the synagogue was well attended on that particular Sabbath!

The people were listening. Jesus started teaching. He spoke of God's favour to the Gentiles in the face of Jewish unbelief. The people were furious. This wasn't what they had wanted – or expected to hear. They closed their minds to His teaching and drove Him out.

Are you prepared to listen to what God wants to say to you, even if it is not what you expect? Jesus knew the people's hearts, and He told them what they needed to hear. God knows your heart and He will teach you what you need to know – if you have open ears.

"And they took offence at him" (Matt. 13:57).

◤ EXAMINE
Examine Luke 8:8 and consider it in relation to yourself.

DAY 43

Entering into our suffering
Matthew 4:13–16

Jesus left Nazareth and went down to Capernaum on the north-west shore of Lake Galilee. Capernaum was an important town, the centre of the Roman government for Galilee and Jesus made it His base for His Galilean ministry.

"... the people living in darkness have seen a great light ..." It is referred to in Matt. 9:1 as "His own town," showing how clear was the break from Nazareth, where He had been brought up and spent most of His earthly life.

The districts of Zebulun and Naphtali had suffered terrible destruction and ravage in 734 BC. Isaiah's prophecy came as a ray of hope to the people of the time who had lost so much, and was fulfilled completely by Jesus: "The people living in darkness have seen a great light." The people who suffered the most were being blessed the most by having Jesus, the Light of the world, living among them.

God may allow us to go through times of suffering and desolation, but He doesn't forget us. If we are faithful, His reward is far greater than the loss.

"If we confess our sins, he is faithful and just and will forgive us our sins and purify us from all unrighteousness" (1 Jn. 1:9).

◤ FOR STUDY
Look on an Old Testament times map, find the districts of Zebulun and Naphtali, and relate Nazareth, Cana and Capernaum to them.

DAY 44

Fishers of men

Matthew 4:18–22; Mark 1:16–20;
Luke 5:1–11

"At once," "immediately," "without delay." Coming soon after Jesus' experience in His own home town, this response from the fishermen must have really gladdened His heart.

"... I will make you fishers of men"

What a contrast! Being a follower of Jesus may or may not require the giving up of a career and leaving one's home. It *does* require wholehearted, 24 hours a day commitment, complete loyalty and instant obedience.

Is there anything in your life that you need to leave behind in order to be a wholehearted follower of Jesus? Do you always obey instantly when Jesus calls?

Jesus said, "I will make you fishers of men." Not a command at this stage, but a promise. Jesus was to spend time with these men over three years, teaching them by word and example, re-shaping their lives and their thinking until He could confidently say, "Go into all the world ..." (Mark 16:15). He doesn't send us out unprepared. The miracle of the catch of fish was part of their teaching. Jesus could do what even the most experienced fisherman could not do.

"The Spirit and the bride say, 'Come!' And let him who hears say, 'Come!' Whoever is thirsty, let him come; and whoever wishes, let him take the free gift of the water of life" (Rev. 22:17).

MEDITATE
**Compare Luke 5:10b with Acts 1:8.
Compare Luke 5:5 with Gen. 1:21, 22.**

DAY 45

Lighting up the Scriptures

Mark 1:21–22; Luke 4:31–32

It was natural for Jesus to attend the local synagogue on the Sabbath. He had been used to this ever since childhood although, as He grew to adulthood, it must have irked Him to listen to the scribes misinterpreting and adding to the law given by His Father to Moses.

"... he taught them as one who had authority"

Now the time had come for Jesus to teach. He taught with authority, expounding and explaining the Scriptures as no one else had ever been able to. He did not, as the scribes did, just repeat the old traditional interpretations, but He threw new light on every subject. The people were amazed.

When you read and study the Bible, ask the Holy Spirit to shed His light on it for you, to help you understand and apply the truth to your life. The Bible is not for half-hearted reading and discussion – it is God's Word to *you*.

How illuminating Jesus' teaching must have been! Yet we who know more of His life than the people of Capernaum did can be even more amazed.

"But when he, the Spirit of truth, comes, he will guide you into all truth. He will not speak on his own; he will speak only what he hears, and he will tell you what is yet to come" (John 16:13).

KEY THOUGHT
The best time to read the Bible is as often as possible.

DAY 46
Absolute authority
Mark 1:23–28; Luke 4:33–37

The man with the evil spirit had probably attended the synagogue before – and possibly for years – without causing any trouble.

The presence of Jesus, however, caused the demon to cry out in fear. Just as the light shows up the darkness, so the holiness of the Son of God revealed the evil of the demon. The demon couldn't stand it. Note that the demon had *knowledge* – instantly recognising who Jesus was.

"... you are ... the Holy One of God!"

The demon had *power* over the man it possessed, but Jesus had absolute *authority* over the demon. Jesus' authority is now seen, not only in the quality of His teaching, but also in His command over evil spirits. His spoken word was sufficient to drive the demon out.

We need to remember that, no matter how much evil appears to surround us or attack us, the Name and authority of Jesus is effective against it. The Name of Jesus is high above every name. God is greater than any enemy. Whether the evil attacks from outside or from within, Jesus will deliver you – *if* you ask Him.

"... at the name of Jesus every knee should bow, in heaven and on earth and under the earth" (Phil. 2:10).

▉ I DECLARE
You can't touch me, Satan, because I am God's property. I take authority over you in Jesus' Name.

DAY 47
Healing the sick
Matthew 8:14–17; Mark 1:29–34; Luke 4:38–41

The three slightly different accounts of the healing of Simon's mother-in-law add authenticity to the Scriptures. No two witnesses see the same incident in exactly the same way. It is interesting that Luke, being a doctor himself, is the one who records that Jesus rebuked the fever before He took her hand and helped her up. She needed no convalescence. She started work right away preparing and serving the Sabbath meal, which would have followed the synagogue service.

"... Jesus healed many ..."

After sunset the people of the town could move their sick without breaking the Sabbath laws, and soon a huge crowd gathered outside Simon's house. Jesus healed each one. Notice the distinction between healing the sick and the driving out of demons. Jesus laid hands on the sick people, but demons were driven out with a word.

Whatever problem affects you, whether it is spiritual, emotional or physical, Jesus can set you free from it – *if* you ask Him.

"If you listen carefully to the voice of the Lord your God and do what is right in his eyes, if you pay attention to his commands and keep all his decrees, I will not bring on you any of the diseases I brought on the Egyptians, for I am the Lord, who heals you" (Ex. 15:26).

◆ PRAYER
Lord, look with pity on my pain
And soon my strength restore.
And grant me life and health again
To serve Thee ever more.

DAY 48

Every illness cured

Matthew 4:23–25; Mark 1:35–39; Luke 4:42–44

News about Jesus spread. People came flocking to hear this new, authoritative teaching, to bring their sick for healing and the demon-possessed to be set free. Matthew tells us that Jesus healed *every* disease and sickness. Luke says that demons came out of many.

> "... a solitary place, where he prayed"

If you have ever been in a large meeting where healing is taking place you will know the sense of excitement. People press forward to see what is happening, while from the back you can only hear, "I can walk." "Praise God, my hearing has come back." "Oh, the pain has gone!" The excitement mounts as someone gets out of a wheelchair ...

More important than all this to Jesus, however, was His relationship with His Father. So precious was their time together that Jesus rose while it was still dark to get away from the crowds and spend time alone with Him. Reflect on your own prayer times with your heavenly Father. Are they precious to you? Is there any way you can improve the quality, as well as the quantity, of time spent with Him?

"But Jesus often withdrew to lonely places and prayed" (Luke 5:16).

▼ QUESTION
What do you think Jesus spoke with His Father about?

DAY 49

Absolutely clean

Matthew 8:2–4; Mark 1:40–45; Luke 5:12–16

The leper came humbly to Jesus and said, "If you are willing ..." He was not questioning Jesus' power to heal the disease, but His compassion for an outcast.

> Be clean!"

The man had probably been rejected and unloved for so long that he doubted that anyone could love him enough to help him. Have you ever felt like that? There are many people who do.

God's love is boundless, immeasurable and available to anyone and everyone who comes humbly and asks. Is there something you would like to ask Jesus to do for you? Ask Him now.

Jesus touched the man. Usually this action would have resulted in ceremonial

LEPROSY

Leprosy in the Bible probably described a variety of different skin conditions, not only true leprosy, or Hansen's disease, as it is known today. Regulations for control of infectious skin diseases were given by the Lord to Moses (Lev. 13:1–45 and 14:1–32).

uncleanness to the toucher, but in this case it brought cleansing to the leper. Nothing could contaminate Jesus, who always showed special compassion to the poor and the sick and the unlovely. As Christians, we should follow His example. Is there anyone you know to whom you could show Jesus' love and compassion in a more positive way?

"Finally, all of you, live in harmony with one another; be sympathetic, love as brothers, be compassionate and humble" (1 Pet. 3:8).

▼ PRAYER
Lord, I believe. Please help my unbelief. Amen.

Above: the River Jordan

Nothing could stop him
Matthew 9:1–8; Mark 2:1–12; Luke 5:17–26

Jesus was facing a critical audience – at least in part. The scribes and Pharisees had come from far and wide to trap and find fault with Jesus' teaching. They crowded round Him, blocking the way for the man who was in real need.

"... your sins are forgiven"

Ask yourself if any critical attitude in you could be a hindrance to others finding Jesus.

Yet there was a way. The man's friends found a direct access to Jesus for him. Remember: other people can never completely block your way to Jesus. You have the right to direct access to Him through His blood shed on the Cross at Calvary.

Jesus then demonstrated another area of His authority – to forgive sins. His audience was not impressed. They had found the evidence they were looking for to accuse Him of blasphemy. But then, when the paralysed man got up and walked, they were all filled with awe and praised God. There are Christians today who look for signs and wonders, forgetting that the biggest miracle of all is the repentance of a sinner.

"Therefore, brothers, since we have confidence to enter the Most Holy Place by the blood of Jesus, by a new and living way opened for us through the curtain, that is, his body, and since we have a great high priest over the house of God, let us draw near to God ..." (Heb. 10:19–21).

▼ KEY THOUGHT
Repentance is being so sorry for sin that you stop sinning.

A clean break

Matthew 9:9–13; Mark 2:13–17; Luke 5:27–32

Before Matthew met Jesus he was:
• Employed by the Romans and therefore
• Despised by his fellow Jews as a collaborator and traitor.

"... Matthew got up and followed him"

• Ritually unclean because of his dealings with Gentiles.
• Probably greedy and dishonest.
• More interested in riches and influence than obedience to God's laws.

Why, then, did Jesus want him? Why did He single him out from all the tax collectors in Galilee? Let's look at him *after* he met Jesus. He:

• Followed his new Master immediately.
• Left a lucrative job to work for nothing.
• Made a complete break (the fishermen were able to take up fishing again, but Matthew couldn't go back to collecting taxes).
• Used his home to introduce Jesus to his colleagues, making a public declaration of his change of life.
• Became the writer of the first Gospel.

How has Jesus changed your life? Has the break with your old life been complete?

"He chose the lowly things of this world and the despised things – and the things that are not – to nullify the things that are, so that no-one may boast before him" (1 Cor. 1:28–29).

■ **QUESTION**
Read Luke 5:30–32 again. How did Jesus turn the complaints to good effect?

Giving up ritual

Matthew 9:14–17; Mark 2:18–22; Luke 5:33–39

Scribal tradition had added other fasts to the minimum required by Jewish law.

"No-one pours new wine into old wineskins"

The Pharisees fasted two days a week. John the Baptist's disciples evidently fasted voluntarily, whereas Jesus' disciples did not fast at all.

The time of Jesus' ministry on earth was to be a time of joy – a break between the ritual fasting of the Old Testament and the Spirit-led fasting of the Early Church. What does the Lord require of you regarding fasting?

Jesus' reference to the Bridegroom being taken away is His first indication that He would die before His disciples. He was to tell them this many times during His three-year ministry. He warned them and prepared them gently for His crucifixion – but they still didn't understand.

Jesus used the two everyday pictures of patches and wineskins to illustrate clearly that He had not come to patch up the old Judaic covenant, but to inaugurate a new one. The new teaching of Jesus required a new vessel, the Church.

"But this kind does not go out except by prayer and fasting" (Matt. 17:21 in footnote).

▶ **FOR STUDY**
Look up the New Testament references to the word "new" in a concordance. What new things did Jesus bring or give?

DAY 53

Living with us
Matthew 1:23; Isaiah 7:14; 9:6

"God with us. " Many Christians have their thoughts fixed on the idea that one day they will be "with God," in heaven, seeing Him face to face.

"... Wonder-ful Counsellor, Mighty God ..." That is gloriously true, but if that is our only hope of contact with God then we have missed a very important truth: God's desire is to dwell *here* with us.

Before the Fall, God walked with Adam and Eve in the garden (Gen. 3:8). His glory filled the tabernacle in the wilderness (Ex. 40:34), and the temple in Jerusalem (2 Chron. 7:1–2), but because His people were disobedient, our Holy God was unable to dwell with them on earth as He longed to. So Jesus came.

The Son of God came down to earth as a man to live among men so that we could understand the Father's heart. He died that we might be forgiven, cleansed and reconciled to God. He rose again that we might receive eternal life – have His life within us. He longs that you might understand and receive the truth of "Emmanuel," God with us, *today*.

"The Word became flesh and made his dwelling among us. We have seen his glory, the glory of the one and only, who came from the Father, full of grace and truth" (John 1:14)

◢ MEDITATE
Meditate on Ezekiel 37:26, 27; 2 Cor. 6:16; Eph. 3:17; 1 John 4:12; Rev. 21:3

DAY 54

The Lamb of God
Genesis 22:7–8; Exodus 12:3,7,13; Isaiah 53:1–12; John 1:29 & 36

A lamb, symbol of purity and meekness, would have presented two familiar pictures to Jewish hearers. First, there was the lamb of the sin offering sacrificed twice daily in Jerusalem.

"... like a lamb to the slaughter ..." There was also the Passover Lamb sacrificed once a year on the Day of Atonement. You may ask, "Which of these lambs did John have in mind when he called Jesus the Lamb of God?"

Jesus, in fact, fulfilled both types. On Calvary He took upon Himself the sin of the world, shed His blood and died in your place so that your sin might be permanently removed. As the Passover Lamb, Jesus set us free from death and from Satan's bondage. According to the timing in John's Gospel, Jesus' death took place at the same time as the Passover lambs were being sacrificed in the temple at Jerusalem.

Isaiah's prophecy reminds us of the meekness of the lamb which, unlike other animals, does not fight when attacked. Jesus went voluntarily to the Cross to do His Father's will.

"... I looked and there before me was a great multitude that no-one could count, from every nation, tribe, people and language, standing before the throne and in front of the Lamb" (Rev. 7:9).

▉ THANK YOU
Thank you, Lord, that You became my Passover Lamb, You became sin for me. I worship and adore You.

The Lord
Luke 1:67–80

The name *Yahweh* in Hebrew is often translated Lord, or Lord God in the Old Testament, but there was no equivalent word in Greek. The Greek word, *Kurios*, translated Lord in this passage, can also mean "sir" or "master", and is a term of great respect.

"... the rising sun will come to us from heaven"

Zechariah identifies the One who is coming, Jesus, with the Lord God of Israel – *He* has come and has redeemed His people (v. 68). God reveals to Zechariah through the Holy Spirit that his own son, John, was to prepare the way for the Lord Himself, the Messiah.

Today the title, Lord, has – for Christians – become identified with God in a more specific way than in the New Testament Greek. We use it with reverence, and our use of it implies that the whole of our lives have been given to Him. He is Lord and Master of every part of us and commands complete obedience. Can you call Him Lord?

"... the Lamb will overcome ... because he is Lord of lords and King of kings ..." (Rev. 17:14).

WORSHIP
My Lord and my God!

The Saviour
Luke 2:1–11; John 4:42

The Jews were looking for someone to come and save them from their Roman oppressors – a king or an army leader who would set their land free, enable them to live in peace and practise their religion as they had always done. Jesus was not that kind of Saviour.

"... a Saviour ... Christ the Lord"

God saw the people's deepest need: liberation from inward, not outward, oppression. Jesus (His name means "Saviour"), came to save people from the consequences of their sin (Rom. 6:23). Those who received Him were freed from slavery to sin and Satan, and came under His protection against all onslaughts of the enemy (Gal. 5:1).

What a wonderful Saviour we have! He sets us free to live our lives as God intends us to regardless of outward circumstances, past background or future worries. Do you know Jesus as your Saviour in that wonderfully complete way? Not only as initial Deliverer from your sin, but today, in every circumstance?

"Therefore he is able to save completely those who come to God through him, because he always lives to intercede for them" (Heb. 7:25).

KEY THOUGHT
The recognition of sin is the beginning of salvation. – Martin Luther

The Son of God

Matthew 14:22–33

The disciples had seen Jesus perform many miracles already. Why, then, should His command over the weather provoke their worship of Him as the "Son of God"?

"It is I. Don't be afraid"

They already knew that Jesus was God's Son because Jesus Himself had told them (Matt. 11:27). Demons had addressed Him as Son of God (Matt. 8:29). The disciples would have heard of the events at Jesus' baptism, though not all of them were present (Matt. 3:17). But it took a frightening experience to cause them to *worship* Him as the Son of God.

There is such a difference between knowing a fact in your mind and appreciating it in your whole being. The former does not change your life, but the latter does. The disciples had been afraid for their own lives in the storm on the lake – Jesus had saved them by miraculously stilling the storm. It was an intensely personal situation for them, and they worshipped.

That Jesus is the Son of God is a fact well documented in the New Testament. What does it mean to you personally? Does He command *your* worship?

"If anyone acknowledges that Jesus is the Son of God, God lives in him and he in God" (1 Jn. 4:15).

🔻 **MY DECLARATION**
I will fear no evil for you are with me.

JESUS WORSHIPPED ...

	At His birth	Matt. 2:2,11
	After walking on the water	Matt. 14:33
By a man born blind		John 9:38
After the Resurrection		Matt. 28:9, 17
At the Ascension		Luke 24:52
By the angels		Hebrews 1:6
In Heaven		Rev. 5:8, 12–14

That all worship is to be directed to the Lord God (Yahweh) is the clear teaching of the first two Commandments (Ex. 20:3–6) and of Jesus (Matt. 4:10). Yet the Son of God received and accepted such worship – a clear declaration of His divinity.

DAY 58

The Son of Man
Mark 2:1–12

"Son of Man" is the term that Jesus used most often to describe Himself in the Gospel narratives. Possibly it was because He wanted to emphasise that He was a human being, identifying Himself with the people He came to save.

"The para-lytic ... got up ... and walked"

The term is used in the Old Testament like that – to distinguish men from God. On the other hand, Jesus describes the Son of Man as coming on the clouds with power and glory (Matt. 24:30) and seated at God's right hand (Luke 22:69).

This corresponds to the vision in Daniel 7:13, 14.

Think about it. Jesus was born in the ordinary way to a young girl in Bethlehem. He grew up into a boy, then a man, with all the physical characteristics of a human being. He knows our weaknesses, understands our emotions and physical limitations.

This same Son of Man is seated at the right hand of God in heaven, interceding to His Father constantly on our behalf. Doesn't that give you a sense of security?

"For there is one God and one mediator between God and men, the man Christ Jesus" (1 Tim. 2:5).

✦ MEDITATE
Meditate on Hebrews 4:15, 16 – and act upon it.

DAY 59

The Christ
Matthew 16:13–20

"Messiah" (Hebrew) and "Christ" (Greek) both mean "The Anointed One". The Jews were looking for the Messiah, their coming King, expecting him to be a political leader.

"You are the Christ, the Son of the living God"

But Jesus was not what they expected Him to be. He was a humble Servant, obedient to His Father's will.

Jesus never openly declared Himself to be the Messiah, the Christ, because of the misconception about the purpose of the Messiah's coming. To have done so would have brought Him into conflict with the Romans. God the Father, however, revealed the truth to Peter, and Jesus was pleased that Peter grasped it. It was important, though, that the disciples should not spread the truth around then.

Can God trust you with secrets? Sometimes He will reveal truths to us that are not for sharing, but for prayer.

The name Christ was used as a second Name for Jesus in the Early Church, when the disciples fully appreciated who He was.

"We know that we are children of God, and that the whole world is under the control of the evil one" (1 Jn. 5:19).

✦ QUESTION
How did Peter use his revelation to good effect later? (Acts 2:36–41).

The helpless man
John 5:1–15

A pitiful scene. Chronically sick and disabled people waiting helplessly and hopelessly for the pool to become disturbed. It was there that Jesus singled out one man for healing. Maybe we shall never know why Jesus chose just that one.

"... See, you are well ..."

He has the sovereign right to heal whom He chooses when He chooses. The sick man didn't know who Jesus was and, even after Jesus had spoken to him, he was still looking to the water for his healing.

We must look in the right direction, and at the right Person, for healing. God can heal through doctors, surgeons, nurses and medicines, but I believe He loves His children to ask Him *first* to heal supernaturally – and He honours our faith.

The man in our story had no faith, but Jesus still healed him. One of the great principles in God's Word is that God is a helper of the helpless. God gives to those with nothing to give. Jesus teaches (John 9:3) that disease is not necessarily caused by sin, but 5:14 seems to imply that sometimes it can be. Think about it.

"And if the Spirit of him who raised Jesus from the dead is living in you, he who raised Christ from the dead will also give life to your mortal bodies through his Spirit, who lives in you" (Rom. 8:11).

QUESTION
Look at verses 14 and 15 again. For what purpose does Jesus give us health and strength?

The Jews' displeasure
John 5:15–23

A new phase had begun in Jesus' ministry. He was confronted with the open hostility of the Jewish leaders. ("Jews" in this context means the Pharisees and Sadducees.) They saw Jesus as a threat to their authority. He was violating their laws and claiming a special relationship with God.

"... the Father loves the Son ..."

Jesus, Son of God, was perfectly obedient to His Father's will at all times and He kept the law given by God to Moses. He had no time, however, for the additional, petty laws created by the Pharisees. His words, "My Father", were blasphemy to the Pharisees, and punishable by death. In spite of the hostility of His hearers, Jesus used the opportunity to teach them further amazing truths about Himself.

Jesus was never deterred by rejection, criticism or threats. He began in utter humility (v. 19), and went on in complete confidence and security in His Father (v. 20). From those two platforms He could proclaim the truth about Himself. You, too, can have that same confidence in your Father's love for you. In that perfect place of security you can be completely free to do His will.

"For you did not receive a spirit that makes you a slave again to fear, but you received the Spirit of sonship. And by him we cry, 'Abba, Father'" (Rom. 8:15).

THANKSGIVING
How thankful I am that, through the Son, I have come to know You, Father.

POOL OF BETHESDA

Located in the N.E. part of Jerusalem, the Pool of Bethesda consists of twin pools cut out of rock and fed by a spring. The pools were surrounded by five porches which gave shelter to cripples. The arrangement of these porches is similar to that demonstrated by Dr F. Bliss as having existed in Roman times at the Pool of Siloam. Steep winding steps led down to the pools. Excavations have uncovered on the wall of one of the porches a fresco depicting an angel in the act of "troubling the waters". It was believed that when the waters were disturbed (probably by the intermittent flow of the spring), the first person to enter the pool would be healed of whatever disease he had. The story implies that the incident occurred outside the city walls, as to carry a bed on the Sabbath would have been forbidden by Jewish traditional law. The name "Bethesda" means "House of Mercy".

the river, death – on the other, life.

That is how clear-cut Jesus' message of life is to us. Conversion is a radical change, not a gradual moral improvement. Read verse 24 again and make sure you understand it well enough to explain to someone else.

Having established the difference between death and eternal life, Jesus went on to explain the authority given to Him by His Father. Jesus will judge us. But because He has been a Man on this earth and knows our temptations, weaknesses, human emotions, and because He is also God, holy and righteous, He will judge us justly and rightly. Doesn't it give you confidence and hope to know that? We have a righteous Judge who has been in our shoes and understands us.

"For he has set a day when he will judge the world with justice by the man he has appointed. He has given proof of this to all men by raising him from the dead" (Acts 17:31).

▓ EXAMINE
Look up 1 Cor. 11:31, consider its meaning and implications and then take any appropriate action.

He speaks of His authority
John 5:24–30

Imagine a great forest fire burning everything in its path. It comes to a wide river

"... I seek not to please myself but him who sent me"

and stops. All living creatures on the side of the fire will die. Nothing can save them unless they cross the river to peace and safety on the other side. On the one side of

His witnesses
John 5:31–47

Jesus was concerned that His critics should have every opportunity to understand who He was and to respond to Him. He didn't reject them because of their hostility, but gave a reasoned discourse using words and arguments that they would understand. He quoted four witnesses: John, His Father God; His works; the Scriptures. All testify that Jesus is the Son of God, the Messiah.

The Jews of that time had ample opportunity to talk to Jesus, listen to Him, see His miracles and study the Scriptures concerning Him. Some followed Him and understood. Some became bitter and angry and rejected Him.

"...the Scriptures that testify about me ..."

What do you think the difference was between those who accepted and those who rejected?

Jesus commended the Jews for their diligence in studying the Scriptures (v. 39), but what was He unhappy about (v. 40)? When we read the Bible, we should become conscious of the reality of Jesus as we allow Him to feed us spiritually through His Word.

"Do your best to present yourself to God as one approved, a workman who does not need to be ashamed and who correctly handles the word of truth" (2 Tim. 2:15).

THOUGHT
The Christian who is careless in Bible reading is careless in Christian living.

DAY 64

What about the Sabbath?
Matthew 12:1–8; Mark 2:23–28; Luke 6:1–5

In the Pharisees' eyes, the disciples were harvesting and threshing the corn. That was work and was unlawful on the Sabbath. But in Jesus' and His disciples' eyes they were eating because they were hungry.

" ... the Son of Man is Lord of the Sabbath"

God is concerned with our heart attitudes and our motives far more than detached observance of rules and regulations. He gave us one day a week to rest, to worship Him, to enjoy His presence and to be refreshed for the six work days to follow.

It is one of His love gifts to us for our benefit. Let us guard it jealously, and resist all attempts by governments and society to take it away from us.

The Jewish Sabbath began on Friday evening with a special family meal. On the Saturday all the men, and some of the women, would attend the synagogue. Jesus regularly observed this custom. The early Christians began by observing the Sabbath, but it soon became the custom to worship on the first day of the week – the day Jesus rose from the dead.

"For six days work is to be done, but the seventh day is a Sabbath of rest, holy to the Lord ..." (Ex. 31:15).

ASK YOURSELF
How do I spend Sundays? Am I pleasing the Lord in my attitude and actions on His special day?

SEVEN HEALINGS ON THE SABBATH

1. The invalid at the Pool of Bethesda (John 5:1–9)
2. The man born blind (John 9:1–14)
3. The demoniac in Capernaum (Mark 1:21–27)
4. Peter's mother-in-law (Matt 8:14–15)
5. The man with a shrivelled hand (Mark 3:1–6)
6. The crippled woman (Luke 13:10–17)
7. The man with dropsy (Luke 14:1–6)

Your Journey with Jesus...

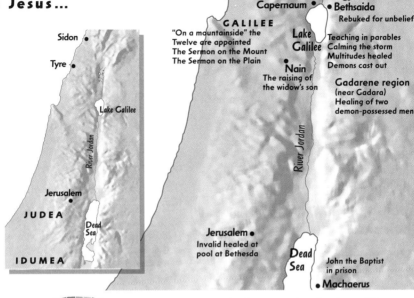

The centurion asks for healing of his servant
Capernaum •
• Chorazin & • Bethsaida
Rebuked for unbelief

GALILEE
"On a mountainside" the Twelve are appointed
The Sermon on the Mount
The Sermon on the Plain

Sidon •
Tyre •

Lake Galilee

Lake Galilee

Nain
The raising of the widow's son

Teaching in parables
Calming the storm
Multitudes healed
Demons cast out

Gadarene region
(near Gadara)
Healing of two demon-possessed men

River Jordan

Jerusalem •
JUDEA
Dead Sea
IDUMEA

Jerusalem •
Invalid healed at pool at Bethesda

Dead Sea

John the Baptist in prison
• Machaerus

DAY 65

The man with the withered hand

Matthew 12:9–14; Mark 3:1–6; Luke 6:6–11

What a contrast of attitudes and emotions we see in this short story! The Pharisees and Sadducees were coldly oblivious to the man's needs, fearful for their own reputation and furious to the point of having murderous thoughts about Jesus.

"Stretch out your hand"

Jesus, on the other hand, was full of compassion for the disabled man. Our Lord was also angry and distressed on his behalf and completely fearless in the face of opposition.

Put yourself in the disabled man's place. Jesus is the same today, and that is the way He feels about any problem that may bother you. On the Cross He overcame the opposition once and for all. Realise the depth of His love and compassion for you and the extent of His power to help you.

Notice two things about the healing: Jesus did it openly in front of the congregation, despite the presence of the Pharisees. He healed by a spoken word alone, which in no way could have broken the Sabbath laws. It was permitted to comfort a mourner or to visit a sick man and pray for him on the Sabbath. The Pharisees were fearful of Jesus' power, not just annoyed at His disregard for their laws.

"But he was pierced for our transgressions, he was crushed for our iniquities; the punishment that brought us peace was upon him, and by his wounds we are healed" (Isa. 53:5).

◢ MY DECLARATION
Lord, You are not only Saviour, but healer. I trust You today for healing.

DAY 66

Multitudes healed
Matthew 12:14–21; Mark 3:7–12

Jesus never advertised Himself. There were no publicity campaigns for Him. He ordered the evil spirits *not* to proclaim who He was. Yet multitudes flocked to Him for healing. Look at the map on the previous page to see how widely His fame had spread (Mark 3:8).

Jesus had what the people needed – the power to heal the most distressing bodily diseases, and He gave freely to all who came to Him.

"... he healed all their sick"

The demands on Him were tremendous in terms of spiritual power, stamina, emotional giving, continual compassion and the sacrifice of personal privacy. But Jesus, anointed by the Holy Spirit, was equal to it all. Jesus has called you to be His follower, to do the works that He did, and He will anoint you for whatever particular work He is calling you to. You must be prepared, like Him, to give *your* all.

One of the reasons why Jesus silenced the demons was that they knew Him to be the Messiah. Jesus did not want to be looked on as the expected earthly king and deliverer. He came as Himself – a humble servant.

"... I am the Lord, who heals you" (Ex. 15:26).

■ EXAMINE
Is there any way in which your attitudes should change in the light of today's reading? Ask Jesus to change you.

DAY 67

The twelve apostles chosen
Mark 3:13–19; Luke 6:12–16

"One of those days Jesus went out to a mountainside to pray, and spent the night praying to God" (Luke 6:12). There

"... Jesus went out to a mountainside to pray ..."

is no reason to believe that Jesus did this after a quiet day, or that He expected to be able to rest the following day. Yet so important was the choice He had to make that He took time to talk to His Father about it.

Examine how much time you spend in prayer, and whether you worry over important decisions or pray about them. Also ask yourself whether you make your own choices or leave the choice to the One who already knows the ultimate result.

Jesus chose the 12 apostles just as He was about to be overwhelmed by the multitudes. He needed loyal, reliable followers to help Him. But more than that, He wanted to spend time with these men, to teach, train, help them to understand who He was and what was to happen to Him. They were men to whom He would entrust the leadership of the future Church. They were all imperfect, had their weaknesses and failed Him in one way or another. Jesus, however, chose them for what they could become – not what they were.

"He chose the lowly things of this world and the despised things – and the things that are not – to nullify the things that are, so that no-one may boast before him" (1 Cor. 1:28, 29).

▲ MEDITATE
Read 1 Corinthians 1:26–30 and meditate on the fact that God has chosen you for a purpose. Have you discovered that purpose and are you seeking the fulfilment of it in your life?

DAY 68

Dealing with demonic powers
Luke 6:17–19

Jesus used His authority in casting out demons. We have already seen that these evil, or unclean spirits recognised Jesus for who He was. They were afraid of Him and often cried out in His presence.

"Those troubled by evil spirits ere cured ..."

Jesus had absolute authority over them – they *had* to obey His command and leave.

There is a clear distinction in the Scriptures between those who were sick and those troubled by evil spirits, although sometimes a spirit could cause symptoms of sickness or disability (see Luke 9:39). Whatever the cause of the problem, each sick person who was touched by Jesus was healed.

JESUS DEALS WITH DEMONS

They knew Him (Mark 3:11; Luke 4:34; Acts 19:15)
They feared Him (Luke 8:28)
They obeyed Him (Mark 5:13)
They were cast out of human beings by Him:
1. A Capernaum demoniac (Mark 1:25; Luke 4:35)
2. A Gadarene demoniac (Matt. 8:32; Mark 5:8; Luke 8:33)
3. A dumb demoniac (Matt 9:33)
4. A demoniac girl (Matt. 15:28; Mark 7:29)
5. A demoniac boy (Matt. 17:18; Mark 9:25; Luke 9:42)
6. A blind and dumb demoniac (Matt. 12:22; Luke 11:14)
7. A woman with an 18-year infirmity (Luke 13:10–17)
8. Mary Magdalene (Mark 16:9; Luke 8:2)

Jesus is the same today as He was all those years ago – His power is available to heal and set men and women free from demonic powers. If you are constantly troubled by evil thoughts or have some deep-rooted inner problem or fear, seek Jesus. He may release you immediately or He may lead you to a minister or counsellor who will pray with you and speak that word of authority which will set you free.

"... That power is like the working of his mighty strength, which he exerted in Christ when he raised him from the dead and seated him at his right hand in the heavenly realms, far above all rule and authority, power and dominion, and every title that can be given, not only in the present age but also in the one to come" (Eph. 1:19–21).

MY DECLARATION
On the Cross of Calvary, you were defeated Satan. I resist you in Jesus' name. Jesus is Lord.

DAY 69

The Beatitudes
Matthew 5:1–12

Jesus was always in demand! He found it hard to get away from the crowds, who marvelled at His teaching and wanted Him to perform more healing miracles. Yet Jesus knew His priority was to teach the disciples, to prepare them for the task of going out into all the world to preach the Gospel after His death and resurrection.

Our Lord had much to teach them when they came and sat with Him on the mountainside. The Beatitudes, or what Billy Graham calls "beautiful attitudes", showed them – and they show us

– what Christian character should be like, what qualities need to be demonstrated:

•Poor in spirit: Humility, conscious of a constant need for God's strength. •Those who mourn: Grief over sin, for mankind ignoring God, love for the lost. •Meek: Submissive to God's will. •Hungry and thirsty for righteousness: Seekers of God in prayer for Him to revive decadent society. •Merciful: Readily forgiving those who wrong us. •Pure in heart: Consciences constantly cleansed by His blood.

"Blessed are the ..."

•Peacemakers: Restorers of right relationships. •Persecuted: For standing for Jesus.

Jesus doesn't promise us an easy time (vv. 10 & 11), but He *does* promise us His strength and tremendous reward.

"But the pot he was shaping from the clay was marred in his hands; so the potter formed it into another pot, shaping it as seemed best to him" (Jer. 18:4).

◗ PRAYER

Lord, I place myself afresh into Your hands and ask that You, the Potter, will mould these qualities in me.

CHRISTLIKE QUALITIES

Tick the boxes which apply to you:

"Blessed are the poor in spirit..."
Matt 5:3 – humility. An honest appraisal of oneself: the heart of a servant (Matt. 23:11, TLB)

"Blessed are those who mourn ..."
Matt 5:4 – deep sensitivity. A strong awareness and keen interest in what is happening to others (Rom. 12:15).

"Blessed are the meek ..."
Matt. 5:5 – joyful submission. A willingness to yield to a higher authority (Mark. 14:16).

"Blessed are those who hunger and thirst for righteousness ..."
Matt. 5:6 – spiritual appetite. A healthy desire to know more of God (Phil. 3:10).

"Blessed are the merciful ..."
Matt. 5:7 – ready forgiveness. Being prepared to forgive others as readily as God has forgiven us (Col. 3:13, TLB).

"Blessed are the pure at heart ..."
Matt. 5:8 – righteousness. Living uprightly through the grace and strength God provides (Phil 4:13, TLB).

"Blessed are the peacemakers ..."
Matt. 5:9 – right relationships. Developing right attitudes between ourselves and others (1 John 1:7, TLB).

"Blessed are those who are persecuted because of righteousness ..."
Matt. 5:10 – total commitment. Putting God first in all of life's situations (1 Pet. 3:16–17, TLB).

SELF-CENTRED CHARACTERISTICS

☐ **Pride and egocentricity** ☐

☐ **Insensitivity and lack of compassion** ☐

☐ **Anger and impatience** ☐

☐ **Apathy and indifference** ☐

☐ **Bitterness and resentment** ☐

☐ **Impurity and uncleanness** ☐

☐ **Condemnation and criticism** ☐

☐ **Compromise and fear** ☐

DAY 70

Salt and light

Matthew 5:13–20;
Luke 14:34, 35

The illustrations of salt and light counteract the false image of a downtrodden, persecuted Church that could be taken

"... let your
ght shine ..."

from verses 11 and 12. Salt gives flavour when it is sprinkled lightly over food and it preserves when used liberally.

Light dispels darkness – it is meant to be seen. Light lifts the spirits and shows the way. It also shows up darkness in contrast.

Think about these illustrations in the light of Jesus' prayer in John 17:15 and 18. Look at how much contact you have with "the world" and whether you are the salt and light to your non-Christian neighbours, workmates, colleagues. You must not allow your light to be hidden from the world by your busyness with home and church affairs.

In verses 17–20 Jesus reiterates His respect for the law of Moses and for the prophets. Although He was at odds with the Pharisees for their additions to the law, Jesus agreed with, and exactly fulfilled, the Old Testament Scriptures. Verse 20 must have puzzled His hearers. See if you can explain how your righteousness can exceed that of the Pharisees.

"For God, who said, 'Let light shine out of darkness,' made his light shine in our hearts to give us the light of the knowledge of the glory of God in the face of Christ" (2 Cor. 4:6).

ACTION
Make a list of your non-Christian friends, or your spheres of influence in the world. How is your light affecting them? Be determined to share Jesus with someone today.

DAY 71

Anger, adultery and divorce

Matthew 5:21–32

Thoughts and relationships are more important to God than an outward appearance of goodness. Most of us have

"... be recon-
ciled to your
brother ..."

a cloak of respectability which we wear when the occasion demands it.

We learn quite early in life to cover up our feelings of anger, dislike and (later) wrong sexual desires (i.e. lust), in case people see what we are really like and reject us. God, however, knows our hearts and our thoughts – we can't hide anything from Him.

Be honest with your thoughts about the people you worship with every Sunday. See if there is any ill-feeling, contempt, unforgiveness, immoral desire, anger or any wrong thought in you, towards any brother or sister in the Lord. Also see if you are aware that someone is holding something against you.

Allow God to search your heart. Ask His forgiveness and cleansing for any sin that He shows you. Put it right with the other person if necessary and then – forget it! Jesus' death set us free from sin – sinful thoughts and attitudes as well as actions.

"... Peter ... asked, 'Lord, how many times shall I forgive my brother ...?' Jesus answered, 'I tell you, not seven times, but seventy-seven times'" (Matt. 18:21, 22).

PRAYER
Use Psalm 139:23,24 as a basis for a time of prayer with God today.

DAY 72

Vows and revenge
Matthew 5:33-42

The law of Moses allowed oaths as a protection against dishonesty (vv. 33-37). But Jesus came to implant truth in our hearts so that we no longer need to swear to the truthfulness of what we are saying. Faith in Jesus brings us back to the simplicity of complete honesty and openness. We do not need to argue vehemently or to back our opinions with strong words. Truth stands up for itself – it needs no defending.

"But I tell you ..."

Jesus went on to turn human attitudes upside down (vv. 38–42). A cloak was a blanket used for warmth during the day and as a cover by night. It could not lawfully be sued for, yet Jesus tells his hearers to give even this essential piece of equipment away.

A Roman soldier could lawfully compel a civilian to carry his luggage for one mile, often at great inconvenience to the civilian. Carrying it for two would be tiring, time-wasting, annoying – and called for truly loving your enemy. Examine whether you are willing to put yourself out for people.

"Do not repay evil with evil or insult with insult, but with blessing, because to this you were called so that you may inherit a blessing" (1 Pet. 3:9).

▪ QUESTION
How far are you willing to go for other people? Read Philippians 2:4–8.

DAY 73

Love for enemies
Matthew 5:43-48

It can be difficult loving people who are unkind to you. Elisabeth Elliott took her two-year-old daughter and went to work among the Aucas in South America – back to the people who had murdered her husband, Jim. Richard Wurmbrand, who suffered for years in Communist prisons, could write, "I denounce Communism but I love the Communists ... there is a better weapon against Communism than the nuclear bomb: it is the love of Christ."

"Be perfect ..."

An African Christian who was cruelly beaten and nearly blinded during the troubles in Rwanda in 1961, wrote, "All the time they were beating me, I couldn't help singing and saying, over and over again, 'Jesus be praised!' I kept praying for them very much all the time."

Testimonies like these are numerous. Christians through the ages have been persecuted and have loved those who tortured them, imprisoned them, killed their families, stole their goods. Jesus prayed for forgiveness for those who nailed Him on to the cross. Think about that when you are angry or hurt.

"If your enemy is hungry, give him food to eat; if he is thirsty, give him water to drink" (Prov. 25:21).

▪ THOUGHT
It is hard to express love with a clenched fist.

THE LAW OF GOD

"You have heard it was said ..."

Do not murder, and anyone who murders will be subject to judgment. (Matt. 5:21)

Do not commit adultery. (Matt. 5:27)

Anyone who divorces his wife must give her a certificate of divorce. (Matt. 5:31)

Do not break your oath, but keep the oaths you have made to the Lord. (Matt. 5:33)

Eye for eye, and tooth for tooth. (Matt. 5:38)

Love your neighbour and hate your enemy. (Matt. 5:43)

THE SON OF GOD

"But I tell you ..."

Anyone who is angry with his brother will be subject to judgment ... (Matt. 5:22)

Anyone who looks at a woman lustfully has already committed adultery with her in his heart. (Matt. 5:28)

Anyone who divorces his wife, except for marital unfaithfulness, causes her to become an adulteress, and anyone who marries the divorced woman commits adultery. (Matt. 5:32)

Do not swear at all ... Simply let your 'Yes' be 'Yes', and your 'No', 'No'. (Matt. 5:34 & 37)

Do not resist an evil person. If someone strikes you on the right cheek, turn to him the other also. (Matt. 5:39)

Love your enemies and pray for those who persecute you. (Matt. 5:44)

"Do not think that I have come to abolish the Law or the Prophets; I have not come to abolish them but to fulfil them. I tell you the truth, until heaven and earth disappear, not the smallest letter, not the least stroke of a pen, will by any means disappear from the Law until everything is accomplished." (Matt. 5:17–18)

DAY 74

Giving
Matthew 6:1–4

It is very tempting, when we give a gift, to let someone else know about it. It is gratifying when we see a child enjoying a toy to be able to say, "I gave him that for his birthday."

"Be careful ..."

Think about this passage before you dismiss it.

No, we don't blow trumpets when we make our offering at church – we don't announce to the congregation the amount we give. But there are other more subtle ways of disobeying Jesus' instruction here: "We gave our old car to Mary." "I'm just going round to Mrs Harris to take her this pie." "This dress will just fit Sally, I'll give it to her."

The illustration of the left hand and right hand was used by the Arabs as a symbol of closest fellowship. Jesus is saying that we shouldn't even tell our closest friends about our giving. Think about why this is so important. Two things can spoil our giving – pride and unwillingness. If you let your giving be known, you are in danger of pride.

"Each man should give what he has decided in his heart to give, not reluctantly or under compulsion, for God loves a cheerful giver" (2 Cor. 9:7).

MY PROMISE
Lord, You've given so much to me. According to the measure of the abundance You have bestowed on me, I will continue to give to You.

Prayer and fasting

Matthew 6:5–18

The Greek word *hypocrite* means literally "actor". We've all probably heard people praying long and complicated prayers in a prayer meeting, enjoying the sound of their own voices. They are not praying to God, but playing to the gallery.

The way Jesus taught His disciples to pray was very simple. I believe He gave this prayer as a pattern or example, rather than as a set prayer to be learned and repeated.

"This, then, is how you should pray ..." It is worth really studying. Think about it sentence by sentence, write down your thoughts on it and use your notes to guide your own private prayers. It is interesting that Jesus picked out only one sentence to elaborate on – dealing with forgiveness. Verse 15 is categorical – there is no way round it. God longs to forgive you for all your sin. See if there is any unforgiveness in your heart that is grieving Him and hindering Him from forgiving you.

Jesus said *when* you fast, not *if*. Although Jesus' disciples did not fast while Jesus was with them, fasting was practised in the Early Church – and still is today.

"And pray in the Spirit on all occasions with all kinds of prayers and requests. With this in mind, be alert and always keep on praying for all the saints" (Eph. 6:18).

▪ FOR STUDY
Look up, with the aid of a Bible concordance, all the occasions when Jesus prayed and then make a list of the characteristics of His prayer life.

Riches in heaven

Matthew 6:19–24

From time to time we ought to examine how important earthly possessions are to us. Here Jesus is talking about *attitudes* rather than actualities.

"... store up for yourselves treasures in heaven ..." It is not wrong to buy a microwave oven if the time saved by using it is spent profitably for the Lord, or to have a large car if you use it to give lifts to those without one. But what about your neighbour? There may be something he needs that you have the power to give.

Before you buy, ask yourself if there is someone with a greater need – that's laying up treasure in heaven. Verses 22 and 23 are figurative. The eye stands for vision, insight, ambitions and interests. If your vision for your life is wrong, your whole life will be disastrous. But if your vision for your life is for Christ, for wholehearted service to Him, your whole life will be full of His light.

We cannot be double-minded in our commitment to Christ – He calls for our complete surrender, 24 hours a day, seven days a week. "All that I am, all that I have is His."

"The blessing of the Lord brings wealth, and he adds no trouble to it" (Prov. 10:22).

▪ ACTION
Make a list of your goals in life. What things are important to you? Prayerfully put them in the right order.

DAY 77

God and possessions
Matthew 6:25-34

There is plenty to worry about in this world apart from personal matters – the nuclear bomb, unemployment, strikes, disasters. These things are real and anything might happen tomorrow. Satan would try to divert our attention from God by putting anxious thoughts in our minds about real and necessary needs.

"... seek first his kingdom ..."

Note that the things Jesus mentioned – food, drink and clothes – were necessities, not luxuries. We are not even to worry about such vital things.

Our loving, caring heavenly Father knows exactly what you need and He will supply it. What a freedom that gives us! Freedom to put Him first, to spend time in His Word, in prayer, in worshipping and serving Him. It is amazing how time stretches when you do this – you still have time for the practicalities of daily life as well.

If, when you receive your pay cheque, you give to the Lord first, the rest of your money will cover your needs. Receive your Father's love. Realise that He cares for you, understands and is able and willing to supply *all* your needs.

"And my God will meet all your needs according to his glorious riches in Christ Jesus" (Phil. 4:19).

■ MEDITATE
**Ponder on these Scriptures:
2 Corinthians 10:5; 1 Peter 5:7;
Phil. 4:6**

DAY 78

Judging others
Matthew 7:1-6

God once showed me very dramatically in a dream how absurd it is for me to judge someone else. In the dream I saw a corpse lying on our compost heap at the bottom of the garden – a horrible, stinking, rotting corpse.

"Do not judge ..."

As I looked in horror, it lifted a bony finger and pointed it in criticism at someone else.

I realised that the corpse was me. "All our righteous acts are like filthy rags" (Isa. 64:6). There is nothing good in me – nothing that could possibly have the temerity to point out a fault in someone else.

Yet, in my new life in Jesus, washed and cleansed by His blood, having taken all my faults and failings to Him to deal with, I can in humility offer to help a brother or sister remove a sin from their own life. We can only help another from a position of purity and humility.

"You, therefore, have no excuse, you who pass judgment on someone else, for at whatever point you judge the other, you are condemning yourself, because you who pass judgment do the same things" (Rom. 2:1).

◆ EXAMINE
Search your heart for any judgmental attitudes or criticism of your fellow Christians, and confess them to God.

Our heavenly Father
Matthew 7:7–12

Jesus emphasised again the care that our heavenly Father has for us. Jesus knew His Father. He was one with Him. He longed for His disciples to understand the overwhelming love and generosity of the Father.

"Ask ... seek ... knock..."

Understand how much the Father wants to give to you.

Bring all your needs to Him, ask Him about things you don't understand, cry out to Him for deliverance from a sin, knock at His door for opportunities of witness and service. Your Father wants you to talk to Him about all your problems and difficulties – just as earthly fathers want to hear about the day to day doings of their children.

Earthly fathers love to give presents to their children, but they can't always give as they would like to. We parents sometimes make mistakes, but our heavenly Father knows the best for us. He answers our prayers according to His perfect knowledge of us, unreservedly and abundantly. Snug and secure in this assurance, we can obey the command in verse 12 to love others in the way that we would like them to love us.

"A father to the fatherless, a defender of widows, is God in his holy dwelling" (Psa. 68:5).

■ **REJOICE**
"All good gifts around us are sent from heaven above. Then thank the Lord, then thank the Lord for all His love."

Further teaching
Matthew 7:13–23

The way into the Christian life is like passing through a turnstile. Only one person at a time can go through with a ticket – without any luggage or other encumbrances. Commitment to Christ is an individual matter.

"By their fruit you will recognise them ..."

Jesus is the door and also the ticket (as it were). We must leave behind all our worldly cares and ambitions. There's something else about the turnstile: it is one way only. Once in, there is no going back.

For the first time (v. 15) Jesus warned His disciples about false prophets. He was to warn them again several times. We can recognise true followers of Christ by the lives they lead – not just by their words. Today there are many sects and cults which preach part of the truth of the Word of God, but not all of it. They sound good to start with, and entrap many people. Test them by the whole Word of God and by their lifestyles.

Don't be fearful of verses 21–23. If you are in Christ, seeking to do your Father's will, and have His love in your heart, then you are secure in His kingdom. The warning is for those seeking their own glory.

"But the fruit of the Spirit is love, joy, peace, patience, kindness, goodness, faithfulness, gentleness and self-control ..." (Gal. 5:22, 23).

■ **LEARN MORE**
There are excellent Christian books and leaflets about sects and cults. Ask at the local Christian bookshops or your National Distributor.

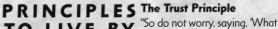

PRINCIPLES TO LIVE BY

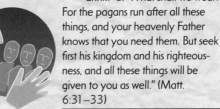

Matthew 5–7

The Investment Principle

"Do not store up for yourselves treasures on earth, where moth and rust destroy, and where thieves break in and steal. But store up for yourselves treasures in heaven, whether moth and rust do not destroy, and where thieves do not break in and steal." (Matt. 6:19–20)

The Love Principle

"So in everything, do to others what you would have them do to you, for this sums up the Law and the Prophets." (Matt. 7:12)

The Judgement Principle

"Do not judge, or you too will be judged." (Matt. 7:1)

The Trust Principle

"So do not worry, saying, 'What shall we eat?' or 'What shall we drink?' or 'What shall we wear?' For the pagans run after all these things, and your heavenly Father knows that you need them. But seek first his kingdom and his righteousness, and all these things will be given to you as well." (Matt. 6:31–33)

The Prayer Principle

"Ask and it will be given to you; seek and you will find; knock and the door will be opened to you. For everyone who asks receives; he who seeks finds; and to him who knocks, the door will be opened." (Matt. 7:7–8)

DAY 81

The wise and the foolish man

Matthew 7:24–27; Luke 6:46–49

The emphasis in this parable is again on the importance of *doing* the will of God, not just hearing about it. There were evidently a lot of "hangers on" in Jesus' time – people who flocked round Him, enjoyed His teaching, were excited by the miracles He did, but who were not prepared to change.

Over the past fortnight we have been studying Jesus' teaching together. We must be careful to put into practice what we learn, so see if His words have changed your attitudes or actions in any respect. Jesus Himself is the Rock (1 Cor. 10:4) and our new life depends on our faith in Him. We need to dig through the sands of vague beliefs, traditions, hearsay and secondhand knowledge and base our

"... it had its undation on the rock"

Christian faith, beliefs and doctrines firmly on the Word of God. We conscientiously examine the Scriptures ourselves and allow the Holy Spirit to teach us.

We need, too, to dig through the mud of self-righteousness, goodness, respectability, old habits and apathy, and base our whole lifestyle on Jesus' example and teaching. With faith and actions firmly based on the Rock, we have no fear.

"Do not merely listen to the word, and so deceive yourselves. Do what it says. Anyone who listens to the word but does not do what it says is like a man who looks at his face in a mirror and, after looking at himself, goes away and immediately forgets what he looks like. But the man who looks intently into the perfect law that gives freedom, and continues to do this, not forgetting what he has heard, but doing it – he will be blessed in what he does" (James 1:22–25).

▮ **GOD'S WORD**
Read it through; Pray it in; Note it down; Work it out; Pass it on.

DAY 82

Jesus' authority
Matthew 7:28–29

There are five great discourses of Jesus in Matthew's Gospel (the Sermon on the Mount is the first), and each ends in the same way, "When Jesus had finished ..."

"... he taught as one who had authority ..." (see 11:1; 13:53; 19:1; 26:1). Jesus was an excellent teacher. He used many different teaching methods – illustrations, parables, rhetoric, logical progressions, repetition and Hebrew poetic forms.

Our Lord adapted His teaching easily to suit His audience, whether it was one person or a huge crowd. And He knew when to stop. But it was His authority which really amazed His hearers. Some definitions of authority are: right to enforce obedience; personal influence over opinion; weight of testimony. Jesus had authority because He is the Son of God and the Word of God. He was teaching on subjects that He knew because He was the Author.

Jesus spoke with assurance because He knew His teaching would give life to His hearers. Although people respected Him for His authority, it is only those who obey Him who receive the full blessings.

"The Spirit gives life; the flesh counts for nothing. The words I have spoken to you are spirit and they are life" (John 6:63).

QUESTION
Where did Jesus derive His authority from? Think about John 17:2 and Hebrews 12:2.

DAY 83

Poverty and riches
Matthew 8:1; Luke 6:20–26

Some commentators believe that Jesus' discourse given in Matt. 5–8 is the same occasion that Luke describes in 6:17–49.

"Woe to you ..." But Matthew sets the scene on a mountain (Matt. 5:1) and Luke "on a level place" (Luke 6:17).

Jesus repeated His teaching often in different words to different people in different places. Some of the lessons here are the same, but others are new.

Jesus does not commend poverty, hunger and grief for their own sake, but if they are endured gladly for His sake there will be great reward in heaven. We must be willing to endure hardship for Him.

Jesus does not condemn wealth outright. Money used wisely and given gladly will further the kingdom of heaven. But when riches are kept selfishly they become a curse. A young man who spent time in Africa with a Youth With A Mission team suffered a culture shock on coming home to Britain. After months of living a simple life it was really shattering to see the many shops here full of the food and luxuries which we take so much for granted. Think carefully about this.

"For we brought nothing into the world, and we can take nothing out of it" (1 Tim. 6:7).

THOUGHT
Money is a good servant, but a poor master.

DAY 84

Bless your enemies

Luke 6:27–36

The punchline in this passage is the last verse: "Just as your Father ..." We who know the end of Jesus' life on earth can understand His teaching much more easily than could the people of that day.

"... Love your enemies ..."

"God so loved ... that He gave His only Son ..." God is so merciful, so willing to forgive the wickedness of the world, so loving towards *His* enemies, that He sent His Son to die at the hands of some those enemies.

Jesus loved the enemies who were crucifying Him so that He could say,

"Father, forgive them." The only way we can fulfil the command to love our enemies is by letting God's love flow through us to them.

I have to be willing right at that moment of pain or hurt to allow His forgiveness and love to flow through me to the person who is, for the moment, my enemy. It helps at that moment to look at Jesus suffering for me on the Cross.

"If your enemy is hungry, give him food to eat; if he is thirsty, give him water to drink. In doing this, you will heap burning coals on his head, and the Lord will reward you" (Prov. 25:21)

▌ **PRAISE**
Lord, Your grace is more than sufficient to enable me to respond to my enemies with Christlikeness.

DAY 85

Do not judge

Luke 6:37–42

Jesus here expands the teaching given in Matthew to explain more fully the principle of reciprocal attitudes. If you are a critical person, others are likely to criticise you. If you forgive, you will be forgiven. If you are stingy, you will receive little. Generosity, however, will be rewarded with abundance. This principle applies to your relationship with God as well as relationships with other people. So if you feel you are missing out in any way, search your own heart and actions.

"Can a blind man lead a blind man?"

God is not speaking to me:
"How much time have I spent with Him?"

So-and-so is criticising me:
"Have I ever thought or spoken evil of them?"

I was given short change in the supermarket:
"Have I short-changed God in my giving?"

There's a wall between me and God:
"Is there someone I haven't forgiven?"

People don't come to me with their problems:
"Is there a glaring fault in me so that people don't trust me?"

God wants to use you in His service, according to the gifts and talents He has given you. Don't let wrong attitudes get in the way.

"A generous man will prosper; he who refreshes others will himself be refreshed" (Prov. 11:25).

▌ **FACT**
Justice is truth in action.

A tree and its fruit

Luke 6:43-45

Jesus sums up His teaching on actions and attitudes by talking about the heart. None of us can produce good deeds and right attitudes by striving after them if our hearts are not right.

"... out of the overflow of his heart his mouth speaks"

But if our hearts are right with God, cleansed and renewed by the blood of Jesus, filled with His love, then our outward lives will show it.

A tree does not strive to produce fruit – if the conditions are right, fruit occurs naturally, the natural fruit for each type of tree. Examine what kind of fruit is produced in your life. The whole of Jesus' teaching in the Sermon on the Mount, and in Luke 6, is given to us as a guideline, so that we can test our lives against it and see where we are failing. We cannot live successfully in our own strength – we must allow His life to flow through us, as the sap flows through a tree, renewing, strengthening, beautifying and producing growth and fruit. If the Holy Spirit shows you a fault or failing in your life, confess it and ask Jesus to correct it. Open up your heart in that particular area for His abundant, perfect life to flow in.

"Out of the same mouth come praise and cursing. My brothers, this should not be" (James 3:10).

■ ACTION

Take some time today to examine the words you say to others in the light of Jesus' teaching.

The centurion's servant

Matthew 8:5-13; Luke 7:1-10

Luke, in giving a fuller account of this incident than Matthew, makes it clear that the centurion himself did not meet Jesus, but sent first a Jewish deputation and then some friends.

"... I have not found any-one in Israel with such great faith"

A Roman centurion was roughly equivalent to a British Sergeant-Major, and was in charge of 100 men. Each time centurions are mentioned in the New Testament they are spoken of favourably (Matt. 27:54; Acts 10:1, 22:26; 27:43).

Jesus was amazed! He had not met faith like that among His own people. It must have been an encouragement to Him after the hostility of the Jewish leaders, and He recognised the faith of this Gentile as the beginning of the fulfilment of prophecy (Psa. 107:3; Isa. 49:12; Luke 2:32).

The centurion describes himself as a man *under* authority. His commands are only obeyed because he had the authority of Rome behind him. He recognised in Jesus that same position – Jesus had His Father's authority behind Him and, therefore, His commands were obeyed. If you obey your Father's will, then your words will carry that same authority.

"Now faith is being sure of what we hope for and certain of what we do not see" (Heb. 11:1).

■ STUDY

Read Hebrews chapter 11 and then turn to the Old Testament to read about the exploits of faith those characters were commended for.

DAY 88

The widow's son
Luke 7:11–17

Nain is about 25 miles from Capernaum in southern Galilee. In our last story Jesus was asked for help – here it was His own compassion that prompted Him to go to the desolate, bereaved lady.

If you have ever tried to comfort a **"... I say to** friend whose loved one has died, you will know **you,** that tremendous love and **get up!"** tenderness that welled up in Jesus as He looked upon that funeral procession.

"When the Lord saw her, His heart went out to her and He said, 'Don't cry.'" Those simple words tell us so much about Jesus. Think about His love –

don't hesitate to tell people who are hurting that Jesus loves them and longs to reach out to them with comfort and help. Know His love and compassion for yourself when trouble hits you.

The difference between us and Jesus is that we often feel so helpless when confronted with another's grief. But Jesus, Son of God, raised up the dead man and gave him back to his mother. This, the first time Jesus restored a dead person to life, resulted in news of Him spreading even further afield.

"Brothers, we do not want you to be ignorant about those who fall asleep, or to grieve like the rest of men, who have no hope" (1 Thess. 4:13).

■MEMORISE
It is useful to commit verses to memory for use in helping people through difficult times, e.g.: 1 Peter 5:7; Deut. 33:27; John 14:27.

DAY 89

A forerunner
Isaiah 40:3; Matthew 3:1–3; Mark 1:2–4

During the next few days we will be looking at some of the Old Testament prophecies about Jesus' life. It is thrilling to discover how exactly the life of Jesus fulfilled these prophecies, given at different **" ' Prepare** ent times by different people hundreds of years **the way for** before His birth. **the Lord ...'"** In the East it was customary to send messengers ahead of a king to ensure that the road was fit to travel on and that adequate preparation was made for the visit. The same thing happens today before royal visits. John was just such a messenger. Both at the scene of his work, "the

wilderness," and the work itself of calling people to repentance, he fulfilled Isaiah's prophecy. John knew that he was a forerunner and took care to proclaim that the One coming after him was far greater than himself.

John's ministry was acknowledged by all four Gospel writers, confirming that Jesus was, in fact, the expected Messiah. The work of preparation of people's hears to receive Jesus is still important. Each one of us has a part to play in preparing the way for Him.

"Repent, then, and turn to God, so that your sins may be wiped out, that times of refreshing may come from the Lord" (Acts 3:19).

▲ MEDITATE
Jesus Himself confirmed that John fulfilled Isaiah's prophecy –
Luke 7:26–28. See also John 3:31.
Meditate on the relationship between these two men.

DAY 90

Anointed by the Spirit

Isaiah 11:1–5; Luke 3:22; John 3:34

> **"The Spirit of the Lord will rest on him ..."**

Isaiah predicted that the Messiah would be no ordinary man – He would have supernatural qualities. The aspects of the Holy Spirit given here are all to do with government – wisdom, understanding, counsel, power, knowledge, the fear of the Lord, judgment and decision.

Jesus was to be anointed as King – a wise ruler and judge.

Jesus was always One with the Holy Spirit, from eternity to eternity, just as He was One with the Father. The three Persons of the Trinity are inseparable. At Jesus' baptism God gave a sign of the Holy Spirit's anointing on His ministry for all the people to see. This was a confirmation of prophecy as well as seal of approval by the Father on His Son's work.

The Holy Spirit came upon Jesus in a special way, empowering Him for the start of His full-time ministry. The words of John the Baptist in John 3:34 sum up the scope of the Holy Spirit's power. God will anoint you, too, for every work that He has called you to – *if you ask Him.*

"... the Holy Spirit descended on him in bodily form like a dove. And a voice came from heaven: 'You are my Son, whom I love; with you I am well pleased" (Luke 3:22).

MY CONFESSION

Lord, so often I attempt to do things in my own strength. I confess my weakness and acknowledge again that it's " 'Not by might nor by power, but by my Spirit,' says the Lord Almighty."

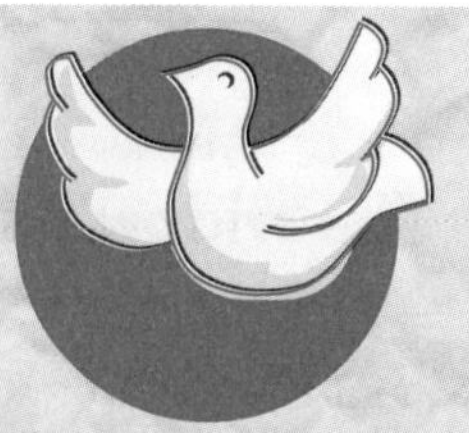

JESUS AND THE HOLY SPIRIT

Born of the Spirit
"The Holy Spirit will come upon you [Mary], and the power of the Most High will overshadow you. So the holy one to be born will be called the Son of God." (Luke 1:35)

Anointed by the Spirit
"The Holy Spirit descended on him in bodily form like a dove" (Luke 3:22); "How God anointed Jesus ... with the Holy Spirit and power." (Acts 10:38)

Led by the Spirit
"Jesus, full of the Holy Spirit, returned from the Jordan and was led by the Spirit in the desert." (Luke 4:1)

Empowered by the Spirit
"Jesus returned to Galilee in the power of the Spirit." (Luke 4:14)

Full of the Spirit
"For the one whom God has sent speaks the words of God; for God gives the Spirit without limit." (John 3:34)

Quickened by the Spirit
"And if the Spirit of him who raised Jesus from the dead is living in you." (Rom. 8:11)

DAY 91

Bringing salvation
Isaiah 61:1, 2a; Luke 4:16–21

Without Jesus the earth is in darkness. Without Him people are enslaved to sin and death, from which there is no escape. The poor have no hope of escaping from their spiritual poverty unless Someone rescues them.

"... the Lord ... has anointed me to preach ..."

When Adam sinned all mankind became subject to sin, sickness and toil (Genesis chapter 3). God gave Moses the law to help His people to live to please Him, plus sacrifices to cover their sin. But the people failed to keep the law. Only God Himself could bring salvation. The people were completely helpless to save themselves – so are we.

It is significant that Jesus stopped reading halfway through verse 2 of Isaiah 61.

He came on earth to proclaim the year of the Lord's favour. The day of vengeance, or judgment, is yet to come. Jesus came to preach and teach. He healed the sick and cast out demons. He preached mainly to the poor, common people, because the leaders wouldn't listen. But it was on Calvary that our salvation became complete, when Jesus defeated Satan, sin and death once and for all.

"She will give birth to a son, and you are the give him the name Jesus, because he will save his people from their sins" (Matt. 1:21).

WORSHIP
I worship and adore you, Lord, my redeemer, Saviour, provider, healer and King.

DAY 92

Worker of miracles
Isaiah 35:5–6; Matthew 11:4–5

Old Testament prophets such as Elijah and Elisha had performed miracles. They had even raised people from the dead. But never had anyone performed miracles on such a scale as Jesus.

"The blind receive sight..."

Hundreds were healed of incurable diseases; the demon-possessed were set free and thousands listened to His preaching. It seems strange that John the Baptist should have to ask "Are You the One?" Jesus reassures him with this reference to Isaiah's prophecy, with which John would have been familiar.

I wonder if you can imagine the scale of Jesus' miracles? We have large evangelistic campaigns and healing services, during which marvellous things happen and many people are healed, but I don't think we have yet seen anything on the scale of Jesus' ministry.

Read what Jesus said in John 14:12. What a wonderful statement! We *will* see greater miracles, greater works and greater crowds of people following Jesus. If we believe Jesus at all, then we believe *all* He said.

"This, the first of his miraculous signs, Jesus performed in Cana of Galilee. He thus revealed his glory, and his disciples put their faith in him" (John 2:11).

MEDITATE
On John 14:12–14 and pray it into being.

DAY 93

Light to the Gentiles
Isaiah 42:1–6; Luke 2:32; Acts
13:45–48

The Jewish leaders of Jesus' time did not understand that their promised Messiah would also bring light and salvation to the Gentiles. They had closed their eyes to the Old Testament prophecies about the Gentiles and were looking for a Jewish king who would overthrow and bring judgment on the foreigners.

"... a light for revelation to the Gentiles"

How easy it is to see only what we want to see in God's Word! Pray as you read the Bible for an open heart to receive *whatever* God wants to speak to you about. Simeon probably did not realise the full meaning of his prophecy when he spoke under the power of the Holy Spirit. It wasn't until some years after the Resurrection that first Peter (Acts 10:45) and then Paul realised the full implication of Jesus' work on the Cross.

Jesus is the Light of the world, the Light for all people, all nations. The salvation He offers is for Jews and Gentiles alike – *"whosoever* will may come."

This was a stumbling block at first in the Early Church. Had they read and understood the Old Testament prophecies it may not, and need not, have been.

"Is God the God of Jews only? Is he not the God of Gentiles too? Yes, of Gentiles too, since there is only one God, who will justify ... by faith ..." (Rom. 3:29, 30).

◢ EXAMINE
Read Revelation 5:9–10. Are you conscious of any prejudice in your heart against any nation, race, or type of person?

JESUS –

A STUPENDOUS MIRACLE

Christ was born of a woman; yet He made woman. He ate and hungered, drank and thirsted; yet He made corn to grow on the mountains, and poured the rivers from His crystal chalice. He needed sleep; yet He slumbers not, and needs not to repair His wasted energy. He wept; yet He created the tear duct; He died; yet He is the ever-living Jehovah, and made the tree of His cross. He inherited all things by death; yet they were His before by inherent right. What else can we do but bow in reverence before such a stupendous miracle!
F. B. Meyer

DAY 94

Blessing to the Gentiles
Isaiah 11:10; Romans 15:8–13

Paul was convinced that we are "all one in Christ Jesus".

In this letter to the Christians at Rome he gives practical teaching on our unity. In our passage he reminds the Jewish members of the Church of the Old Testament prophecies about the Gentiles.

God had told His chosen people over and over again that His mercy and blessings would be extended to the Gentiles. Although God chose Israel to play a very special part in His plan for this world, (don't forget, Jesus was a Jew), yet He never forgot the rest of us. All that Jesus achieved on the Cross is available for all mankind. His resurrection power, the outpouring of His Holy Spirit, and every other gift is for you. The command is to "Rejoice" and "Praise the Lord." Stop and think for a few moments of all that God has made available to you. Use these verses to help, and write down what you find: 1 Thessalonians 5:9; Romans 5:17; 1 Corinthians 1:5; Galatians 3:26; 5:1; Ephesians 1:7. Rejoice! Thank Him! Praise Him!

"... Praise the Lord, all you Gentiles ..."

"In his name the nations will put their hope" (Matt. 12:21).

QUESTION
Can you think of individual Gentiles in the Old Testament who were blessed by God?

Above: view of the Jordan valley from Mt. Nebo

DAY 95

Rejected by men

Psalm 69:7, 8; Isaiah 53:3; John 1:10–11; John 7:5

We have been reading of the huge crowds that followed Jesus in Galilee. Yet our Lord was also despised and rejected. The Father and the Son both knew that Jesus' earthly ministry would end on the Cross. That makes it all the more wonderful that the Father gave and Jesus came!

Jesus' own brothers did not believe in Him. That must have hurt, but it's not unusual that one's close family are the strongest critics of any gift or calling. We should,

"He was despised and rejected by men ..."

instead, encourage members of our own family in their gifts and talents.

Jesus was rejected in Nazareth, His home town, and despised and feared by the Jewish leaders, the Pharisees and Sadducees. The common people flocked to hear Him, drawn by His power to heal, His teaching and the miracles He performed. But when He was arrested everyone deserted Him, even His 12 disciples. No-one was prepared to suffer with Him. Remember, it was His own special people who gave Him up to be crucified, because they didn't recognise who He was.

"He came to that which was his own, but his own did not receive him" (John 1:11).

ASK YOURSELF
Are you willing to suffer rejection and persecution for Jesus' sake?

DAY 96

Jesus commends
John the Baptist

Matthew 11:2–15; Luke 7:18–20

John the Baptist was in prison. He may have been feeling depressed, discouraged and perplexed, wondering why he, herald of the Messiah, should be imprisoned while our Lord was in the world.

"'I will send my messenger ...'"

Jesus offered no comfort, but sent the messengers back with words that would remind John of the Old Testament prophecies concerning the Messiah (Isaiah 61:1; 35:5, 6).

John was expecting the Messiah to bring judgment – Jesus came to save, heal, deliver and rescue. Things were not turning out the way John expected, but Jesus encouraged Him to hold on (Matt. 11:6). We, too, can draw encouragement from Him to keep our faith when things seem to be going wrong.

Jesus regarded John very highly, as He emphasised to the crowds: "I tell you the truth: Among those born of women there has not risen anyone greater than John the Baptist ...". John prepared the way for people to enter the kingdom of heaven. We who have the privilege of being born of the Spirit through faith in Christ, have a place in that kingdom.

"And he will go on before the Lord, in the spirit and power of Elijah, to turn the hearts of the fathers to their children and the disobedient to the wisdom of the righteous – to make ready a people prepared for the Lord" (Luke 1:17).

⚑ FOR STUDY
Compare Matt. 11:14 with Malachi 4: 5,6. How did John's ministry fulfil v.6?

DAY 97

Unresponsive people

Matthew 11:16–19; Luke 7:31–35

Jesus showed how ridiculous were the people's opposite reasons for rejecting both Himself and John the Baptist. John was too stern, Jesus too relaxed. Jesus compared the people to children who would neither play at weddings or participate at funerals.

"... wisdom is proved right by her actions"

Those who do not want to listen to God's voice will find any excuse not to.

It is possible to be so critical of a preacher or evangelist that we don't hear his message. We need to be responsive to what God wants to say to us regardless of preaching methods or mannerisms.

Jesus' grief and yearning for the Jewish people comes over in this passage. He so longs for them to understand and to respond to Him. He has patiently taught, by example as well as words; He has healed them, and shown them miracles, even raising one from the dead, and still they won't listen. He wants us to enter into His grief and yearning for this present generation. We must pray, and take every opportunity to present Jesus to our friends and neighbours.

"Woe to you, teachers of the law and Pharisees, you hypocrites! You are like whitewashed tombs, which look beautiful on the outside but on the inside are full of dead men's bones and everything unclean" (Matt. 23:27).

⚑ ACTION
List five of your non-Christian friends and relatives, then pray for them specifically today and at least once a week.

Unbelieving towns
Matthew 11:20-24

Chorazin, about three miles north of Capernaum, is not mentioned elsewhere in the Bible but, clearly, Jesus had performed miracles there (see John 21:25).

"... the day of judgment ..." There were two Bethsaidas – one on the west of Lake Galilee where Andrew, Peter and Philip lived, the other on the north east of the Lake where the 5,000 were fed. Tyre and Sidon, on the Mediterranean coast, were heathen cities.

Think about what Jesus is saying in verses 21 and 22: those who have not had the opportunity to believe will be judged more leniently than those who have. God has given His Word to you and me. He has revealed His Son to us and given us every opportunity to know Him, to love and serve Him. We will be judged accordingly.

Let us be tolerant and zealous for those who haven't yet had those opportunities. The word to Capernaum is even stronger. It refers to a prophecy about Satan (Isa. 14:12-15). Those who aspire to great heights will fall to great depths. Jesus' anger was directed against the pride and complacency of those who didn't recognise their sin.

"See to it, brothers, that none of you have a sinful, unbelieving heart that turns away from the living God" (Heb. 3:12).

▌THOUGHT
There are a thousand ways of pleasing God, but not one without faith.

Invitation to rest
Matthew 11:25-30

The response of Jesus' heart to the anger and grief that He felt for the unbelieving towns was to turn to His Father in praise.

What a lesson we can learn from this! We should look at our response when we get upset. The wrong reaction is to mull over the situation in our mind, become more angry, bitter, anxious and worried. The right response is to turn the situation over to our Father and praise Him for His goodness and care.

Jesus thanked His Father for the good in the situation and acknowledged His wisdom in revealing the truth to simple people. He reminded Himself of the special relationship between Father and

THE YOKE OF JESUS

An obvious meaning of the word "yoke" in the Bible is that of bondage or slavery (see Jeremiah chs. 27 and 28). In Lamentations 3:27, the word means "disciplining sorrow", while in Jeremiah 5:5, it is used to symbolise "the law of God." This last use became popular with the Jews at a later period, and the phrase is employed by Christ in this sense in Matthew 11:29-30. Here "my yoke" means "the service of God as I teach it", rather than the common interpretation, "the sorrows that I bear", and the emphasis is on "my". The contrast is not between "yoke" and "no yoke", but between "my teaching" (light yoke) and "the current religious teaching" (heavy yoke).

Above: teams of oxen yoked together ploughing in an olive grove

Son, and then He turned His attention to those people who did want to listen to Him.

"Come to me ..."

What a loving, gentle Saviour we have! Jesus as a carpenter would often have made yokes for the animals. Each one was fitted to the shape of the animal, smoothed and polished to prevent chafing. That is the kind of yoke He has for you if you are willing to wear it: smooth, easy, light – because He is taking the strain.

"There remains, then, a Sabbath-rest for the people of God" (Heb. 4:9).

▼ THANKSGIVING

Thank you, Lord, that your yoke is easy and your burden is light. I rest in you today.

At Simon's home
Luke 7:36–50

Simon the Pharisees had shown an interest in Jesus, going as far as inviting Him to dinner. From his words,

"Your sins are forgiven"

"If this man were a prophet ..." we can guess that he wanted a closer look at Jesus to draw his own conclusions about His claims. But Simon showed Him none of the usual courtesies offered to a guest.

The "sinner" or harlot, in contrast, showed Jesus her love, her care and practical help. To wash the feet of a guest was a usual custom, and it was not uncommon to rub them with perfumed ointment to prevent chapping in the hot, dry country. This woman, however, went much further – she was extravagant in her service to Jesus.

Simon, coldly respectable, would have been horrified that the prostitute had even entered his house. Jesus, pure, loving and compassionate, saw her heart and accepted her ministrations gratefully. We, too, must see beyond the outward appearance of repentant sinners and welcome them like Jesus did. Notice that it wasn't her love that saved the woman – it was her faith.

"In him we have redemption through his blood, the forgiveness of sins, in accordance with the riches of God's grace" (Eph. 1:7).

◤ PRAYER

Lord, help me to see others as you see them and to love them as you do. Amen.

Women who accompanied Jesus

Luke 8:1-3

Jesus embarked on a major travelling campaign to Galilee with His 12 disciples and a small band of women. We don't read very much about these women, but there is no doubt that they played an important part in the spread of the Gospel. From their own resources they provided food for the team, found them places to sleep at night and did their washing.

"... who ministered to him ..."

Mary Magdalene is often identified with the prostitute in the previous chapter, but there is no evidence for this. She and Joanna were among the women who went to the tomb after Jesus' death (Luke 24:10). Jesus had a great respect for women. They were faithful followers, giving their money and their services willingly and lovingly.

We, too, must willingly do the more menial tasks, such as make the tea or clean the church after a function there, working "as unto the Lord". Even the every-day tasks you do around your own house are a practical evidence of your love for Jesus – if your attitude is right.

"She opens her arms to the poor and extends her hands to the needy." (Prov. 31:20).

▼ **FOR FURTHER THOUGHT**
Proverbs 31:10, 11 & 20; Romans 12:13.

WOMEN IN JESUS' LIFE ▪▪▪ ▪▪▪ ▪▪▪ ▪▪▪▪▪▪▪

Women played an important part in Jesus' life. His mother, Mary, was a quiet, deeply spiritual woman, wholly submissive to God's will. She was probably widowed before Jesus started His public ministry. Not fully understanding her Son during His lifetime, she was nevertheless present at the Cross and was with the other disciples at Pentecost.

Mary and Martha of Bethany were friends of Jesus, who offered Him hospitality and ministered to Him. It was Jesus they turned to when their brother Lazarus died.

The small band of women who ministered to Jesus and His disciples in Galilee included Mary Magdalene, Mary the mother of James and Joses, Joanna, Susanna, Salome and others. They were present at Calvary and took spices to anoint Jesus' body after His death.

It was to a Samaritan woman that Jesus first revealed His Messiahship (see John 4:25–26), and His first appearance after His resurrection was to another woman, Mary Magdalene (see Mark 16:9). Both were formerly women of questionable moral backgrounds.

Life of Christ   69

DAY 102

Accused of madness
Mark 3:20–21

Jesus' family were, naturally, concerned about the direction His life had taken. They didn't understand – how could it be right that He didn't have time to eat, sleep or lead a normal life? It seemed to them that He had carried things too far. This often happens today, particularly with young Christians whose parents are not Christians.

"... his family heard about this ..."

It is right for parents to be concerned, and it is right for people, young and old, who feel they have a special calling from God, to listen to advice. Often an older Christian will say, "Wait, you are not ready yet." God is never in a hurry – a call will be followed by a period of preparation and spiritual training. Be very sure of what God is saying to you before you move out in a new direction for Him.

Jesus *was* sure of His call and His work. He was sure of the timing of the start of His ministry. He was in constant touch with His Father. He knew just what He was doing – and He was doing it with a sound mind.

"Amazed and perplexed, they asked one another, 'What does this mean?' Some, however, made fun of them and said, 'They have had too much wine' " (Acts 2:12, 13).

QUESTION
Who else was accused of being insane? (Acts 26:24). What does God promise us? (Isa. 26:3).

DAY 103

Beelzebub
Matthew 12:22–30; Mark 3:22–27

The Jewish teachers had an even more serious accusation against Jesus, born out of jealousy and hatred. Beelzebub, meaning "lord of the fly," referred to none other than Satan himself, the prince among demons.

"He who is not with me is against me ..."

Jesus, who knew what the Jews were saying and thinking, called them and confronted them. Notice the difference between darkness and light: the Jews talked about Jesus behind His back, but Jesus faced them openly and spoke directly to them.

Jesus started from their own premise and showed how absurd it was. The progression is important – a kingdom, a household, Satan. The smaller the entity, the more disastrous the division is. Jesus "tied up the strong man", Satan, by defeating him during the temptation in the wilderness, and finally by His death and resurrection.

Satan is a defeated foe. Jesus had absolute authority over every demon that He came across. Because of Jesus we need have no fear of evil. We, too, have authority, in Jesus' Name, over Satan and his demons.

"He who does what is sinful is of the devil, because the devil has been sinning from the beginning. The reason the Son of God appeared was to destroy the devil's work" (1 John 3:8).

MEDITATE
Look at Psalm 23:4; 1 John 3:8; Ephesians 1:20–21; James 4:7–8. Is there any fear of evil in your heart, or any compromise with it?

DAY 104

The unpardonable sin

Matthew 12:31–37; Mark 3:28–30

Many people have been worried and confused by these verses – unnecessarily so, because they have taken them out of context. Jesus had been accused of being possessed by Beelzebub and of casting out demons by his evil power. Jesus drove out demons by the power of the Holy Spirit (Matt. 12:28).

"... by your words you will be acquitted ..."

The Jewish teachers were, therefore, attributing the work of the Holy Spirit to the devil. Their whole attitude and thinking were wrong. They called light darkness and white black. This is the sin against the Holy Spirit – an unrepentant, wilful, defiant rejection of His work of shedding light on our darkness and convincing us of sin and of evil.

God gives men many opportunities to repent, but continued vehement, hurtful opposition to the Holy Spirit cannot be forgiven. Notice that Jesus did not say that the teachers had committed that sin, but gave them a very strong warning.

"If we confess our sins, he is faithful and just and will forgive us our sins and purify us from all unrighteousness" (1 John 1:9).

▇ QUESTION

How would you counsel someone who felt that they had committed the unpardonable sin?

DAY 105

Folly of seeking a sign

Matthew 12:38–45

"Adulterous" in this context means "unfaithful to God". The generation into which Jesus came were people who had forsaken idolatry during their Bablylonian exile, but whose present hardness of heart and unbelief had led them into a worse condition.

"... one greater than Jonah is here"

Jesus contrasts the willingness of the Queen of Sheba to listen to Solomon's wisdom and the repentance of Nineveh when Jonah preached with the rebelliousness and hardness of heart of Jesus' generation.

It was foolish of them to ask for a miraculous sign. God had already spoken to them in many ways, and they were in the presence of the Son of God Himself. What more could God do to convince them?

Be careful to respond to the revelation of God which He gives you through Scripture, preaching and the presence of the Holy Spirit. Jesus teaches (vv. 43–45) that the truth applies both to a generation and to an individual. The casting out of evil must be followed by the positive indwelling reign of the Lord Jesus Christ.

"Jews demand miraculous signs and Greeks look for wisdom, but we preach Christ crucified: a stumbling-block to Jews and foolishness to Gentiles" (1 Cor. 1:22, 23).

▌ MY DECLARATION

Lord, I am convinced you are my Saviour. I need no sign: I simply gaze at the Cross.

His mother and brothers

Matthew 12:46–50; Mark 3:31–35; Luke 8:19–21

Jesus' family arrived, as we read four days ago, because they were concerned and wanted to rescue Him from His "way-out" lifestyle.

"... the will of my Father ..."

They may have heard rumours of the Jewish leaders' jealousy and hatred of Jesus and feared for His safety.

Any parent will understand the frustration that Mary must have felt when she couldn't even get through the crowd to talk to her Son, to reason with Him. But Mary and her other sons were wrong. Jesus had to show them that His spiritual relationship with His Father in heaven, and with those who also did His will, was more important than that with His earthly family.

Family relationships are important to God. We know Jesus loved and cared for His mother (John 19:26–27). If members of our family, however, seek to come between us and God's will we need to remember that our *primary* allegiance is to God. Jesus places His emphasis again on *doing* God's will. We are to hear and to do God's will in our lives.

"Still another said, 'I will follow you, Lord; but first let me go back and say good-bye to my family.' Jesus replied, 'No-one who puts his hand to the plough and looks back is fit for service in the kingdom of God" (Luke 9:61, 62).

■ QUESTION
Are you encouraging members of your own family in God's will? See Ephesians 5:25–27 & 6:4; Proverbs 31:10–12,23.

The parable of the sower

Matthew 13:1–9; Mark 4:1–9; Luke 8:4–8

These passages mark the beginning of two new elements in Jesus' ministry: 1, He begins to teach in parables. 2, His teaching is directed more towards His disciples.

"... he told them many things in parables ..."

The crowds are still there, but Jesus begins to train the Twelve more directly. A parable is a story which illustrates one spiritual truth. Jesus used simple, every-day illustrations with which His hearers would all be familiar.

There are parables around us, too. An Anglican minister once told me that in his first curacy his vicar set him the task of writing two parables a week from things that he heard or saw around him during his work. It really opened his eyes to see and understand what God wanted to say to him.

We can relate spiritual truths to our modern world just as Jesus did in His time. Try it. Jesus' closing words indicate that He intended His parables to be thought over seriously – to be meditated upon until the full spiritual meaning became clear.

"The one who sows to please his sinful nature, from that nature will reap destruction; the one who sows to please the Spirit, from the Spirit will reap eternal life" (Gal. 6:8).

▲ ACTION
Keep your eyes and ears open during the day, and write a modern parable about something you see or hear.

Purpose of the parables

Matthew 13:10–17; Mark 4:10–12; Luke 8:9–10

The secrets or mysteries of the Kingdom of God are those things which can't be understood by our human minds. God sheds His light on the "secrets" for those who are truly seeking and committed to Him.

"Why do you speak ... in parables?"

The Holy Spirit reveals truths to us that we could never grasp with our own intelligence.

Jesus went on to quote from Isaiah 6:9–10 – a judgment of spiritual blindness on a nation that had hardened its heart towards God. Many of the people who crowded round Jesus came only for the excitement of the healings and miracles. They were not prepared to acknowledge Who He was and follow Him in the true sense of the word.

It was for that reason that Jesus began to speak in parables, so that those who truly wanted to would understand His teaching and those who were there for the "kicks" would drop away. How whole-hearted is your commitment to Jesus? He longs to reveal the mysteries of the kingdom of God to you. He will if you open your heart fully to Him.

"The man without the Spirit does not accept the things that come from the Spirit of God, for they are foolishness to him, and he cannot understand them, because they are spiritually discerned" (1 Cor. 2:14).

■ COMPARE
Matthew 13:12 in the light of Matthew 7:7.

Jesus explains

Matthew 13:18–23; Mark 4:13–20; Luke 8:11–15

This is one of the few parables that Jesus explains. As a good teacher, He gives the disciples a pattern to follow so that they may understand His parables in the future.

"Don't you understand this parable?"

You may have been tempted to skip through this parable quickly because it is so familiar.

But read it again from Matthew, imagining yourself as the soil. Let's be careful how we receive the Word of God day by day. Ask God to search your heart and reveal to you any faults or hindrances to the growth of the seed in your life. Do not be content with less than a hundredfold growth.

Read the story again in Luke, putting yourself in the place of an evangelist sowing the seed. The seed is the Word of God, a living organism which will produce life in those who hear and receive. Examine the kind of seed you are planting in people's hearts. It must never be clever arguments, half-hearted beliefs, vague theories, church traditions, but *the living Word of God*. Then we shall see fruit in the lives of others as a result of our sowing.

"Do not merely listen to the word, and so deceive yourselves. Do what it says" (James 1:22).

◀ MEDITATE
Colossians 3:16 The Word dwelling in me.
Heb. 4:12 The Word working in me.
2 Tim. 4:2 The Word going forth from me.

A lamp under a bowl
Mark 4:21–25; Luke 8:16–18

Coming straight after the explanation of the parable of the sower, this illustration relates directly to Jesus' previous words in Mark 4:11 and Luke 8:10: "The

"If anyone has ears to hear, let him hear" secret of the kingdom of God have been given to you." Jesus is the Light of the world – it was not His purpose to conceal His light from the disciples by speaking in parables that they could not understand. He uses a ridiculous illustration to emphasise the comfort that He was giving them.

The disciples had heard and partially understood. They had seen and partially believed. Therefore they were told to pay particular attention to their Master's teaching because He longed to show them more and give them clearer understanding.

Jesus is the Light who shows up our darkness. We can only approach the Light as we are prepared for Him to eradicate our darkness. Any hidden things in our lives need to be exposed and dealt with.

"My dear brothers, take note of this: Everyone should be quick to listen, slow to speak and slow to become angry" (James 1:19).

■COMPARE
Contrast these passages with Matt. 5:14–16. There Jesus is urging His disciples themselves to shine as lights in the dark world.

HOLINESS

It breathes in the prophecy,
Thunders in the Law,
Murmurs in the narrative,
Whispers in the promises,
Supplicates in the prayers,
Sparkles in the poetry,
Resounds in the songs,
Speaks in the types,
Glows in the imagery,
Voices in the language,
Burns in the Spirit,
Challenges in the parables.

F.B. Drysdale

The growing seed
Mark 4:26–29

Even today, with all our modern technology and scientific research, we have not managed to come up with an alternative to planting and harvesting for producing food. Chemicals, colouring and flavouring *are* added, but the bulk of our diet still depends on the soil, the germination of seeds and the weather.

These are God-given conditions. The harvest depends on Him. So it is with the spiritual harvest. We fulfil our responsibility of sowing

"This is what the kingdom of God is like ..." the seed of God's Word in men's hearts, but He waters and warms until the seed germinates, grows and comes to full harvest. We cannot do God's work for Him. We cannot change people's lives or produce the right fruit – only sow the seed.

This is true both of the harvest in individual lives and the final harvest when we will all be gathered in for the final judgment and the marriage feast of the Lamb. I find that comforting. It takes all the striving and stress out of my own personal spiritual growth, my witnessing to non-Christians and counselling of other Christians. The harvest is God's responsibility.

"He who goes out weeping, carrying seed to sow, will return with songs of joy, carrying sheaves with him" (Psa. 126:6).

FOR FURTHER THOUGHT
Study Isaiah 55:10, 11; 1 Cor. 3:5–9.

Parable of the weeds
Matthew 13:24–30

Matthew writes of the "Kingdom of heaven," Mark and Luke of the "Kingdom of God." It is the same kingdom, established under the rule of Christ the King.

"The kingdom of heaven is like ..." The Jews regarded God as King and were looking for a Ruler to free them from the Roman oppression. Jesus came, setting people free from sin, sickness and oppression of demons. When He died and rose again He established the new life of His kingdom for ever.

Jesus conquered Satan and is the absolute Ruler, yet He told these parables to explain that on earth His kingdom will grow slowly, as men and women turn to Him and allow Him to rule in their lives. In the age to come, when there will be a new heaven and a new earth (Rev. 21:1), the kingdom will be complete and Satan will be cast out for ever.

Think about this parable and see how it applies to the Church and the world situation today. Jesus makes it clear that we are not to "pull up the weeds" because that will not happen until the end of the age.

"Sow for yourselves righteousness, reap the fruit of unfailing love, and break up your unploughed ground; for it is time to seek the Lord, until he comes and showers righteousness on you (Hos. 10:12).

STUDY
Read Philippians 2:9–11 and consider the absolute supremacy of Jesus, Lord and King.

Mustard seed and yeast
Matthew 13:31–33; Mark 4:30–32

There are two possible interpretations of these parables. The first is that both represent the small beginnings of the Church which spreads throughout the world. In this respect they inspire confidence and hope that the Word of God will triumph in the face of opposition.

The second interpretation is a warning. The parable of the mustard plant resembles Nebuchadnezzar's dream in Daniel chapter 4 (see vv. 10–12, 20–23, 26). It could be a picture of the Church spreading rapidly to become a visible world power (as happened in the Emperor Constantine's reign and during the Middle Ages). Such a large organisation becomes corrupt. Birds in the parable of the sower were symbols of evil and could be again here.

Leaven is consistently a symbol of evil in the Scriptures (see 1 Cor. 5:6–8).

"... like a mus- tard seed ..."

When the Church becomes large, comfortable and respectable, there is a danger of complacency. All kinds of evil can come in when we are off-guard.

"He replied, 'Because you have so little faith. I tell you the truth, if you have faith as small as a mustard seed, you can say to this mountain, "Move from here to there" and it will move. Nothing will be impossible for you' " (Matt. 17:20).

◤ THINK ABOUT IT
The persecuted Church in some parts of the world tends to be purer and more zealous than Christians in the West. Read Daniel 4:26 again and pray over it.

THE MUSTARD PLANT

The "mustard seed" Jesus referred to was the garden black mustard. It was very common in Israel in Bible times, and was really a plant or a bush with bright yellow flowers. The strange thing was that it grew to the size of a tree, often reaching a height of twelve feet with woodlike branches spreading far and wide. Birds found shelter from sun and rain in its leafy branches. Goldfinches and thistlefinches in particular were fond of the tiny black seeds growing in the pods on its branches. It still grows wild on the shores of the Sea of Galilee and along the Plain of Gennesaret.

Jesus compared the Kingdom of God to a tiny mustard seed – one of the smallest of all seeds. It was not quite the smallest – the seeds of the orchid or the cypress are tinier. But the mustard seed was so common that the Jews made a proverb out of it.

DAY 114

Jesus' use of parables
Matthew 13:34–35; Mark 4:33–34

The quotation in Matt. 13:35 is from Psalm 78 (v. 2), which goes on to speak of teaching children about the wonderful deeds and law of the Lord.

We are all like children. We like pictures – on TV, walls and

"So was fulfilled"

in books. Jesus used simple, often visible illustrations for His parables.

Every time His hearers saw a farmer sowing seed they would remember Jesus' words. When a woman baked bread she would remember how the leaven spread through the flour. Maybe light would dawn years later on some who heard Jesus' teaching and didn't understand at the time. If you are asked to give a talk (perhaps you are a seasoned preacher), remember Jesus' use of parables and illustrations. Often they are the only thing people will remember afterwards, but a vast amount of teaching can be given by this method.

What a thrill it must have been for the disciples to have Jesus to themselves sometimes. They must have been precious times of teaching, explanation, questions and answers. Do you make the most of your times alone with Him?

"A word aptly spoken is like apples of gold in settings of silver" (Prov. 25:11).

◤ FOR STUDY
Proverbs 2:1–6. The Lord does not withhold understanding from those who really seek Him.

DAY 115

Parable of weeds explained

Matthew 13:36–43

Here we have an intimate look into the teaching that Jesus gave His disciples when they were on their own. The weeds referred to would

"... so it will be ..." be darnel, a tough rye grass which looks very similar to wheat until the ear appears.

It would be impossible to weed it out without damaging the crop. There are those who attend church who are not wholly committed to the Lord, but it's not for us to judge or to weed them out. Our judgement is fallible – Jesus judges rightly. We would cause hurt and dissension – Jesus gives every chance for people to repent and be saved. At the end of the age, however, there will be a great weeding out and the unrighteous will be discarded (see Joel 3:13, 14).

We must help people to make the right decisions, knowing the terrible fate of those outside the Kingdom of God. What a contrast between the awful fiery furnace, and the glad sunshine of the righteous. We cannot sit on the fence – we need to do all we can to draw as many as we can into the Kingdom.

"... the Lord knows how to rescue godly men from trials and to hold the unrighteous for the day of judgment, while continuing their punishment" (2 Pet. 2:9).

▰ FOR MEDITATION
Daniel 12:3

DAY 116

Hidden treasure

Matthew 13:44–46

I remember reading a children's book to my family when they were small. It very graphically depicted how a pearl merchant found the greatest, most perfect pearl and then had to sell all his other pearls and all his possessions to buy that

"... like treasure hidden in a field ..." one pearl that he wanted above everything else.

The Kingdom of heaven is free to all, yet to enter it costs everything we have and are. The more we are prepared to give, the more we value that Pearl, and the more we value the Pearl, the more we are prepared to give.

"Christ is my meat, Christ is my drink,
My medicine and my health;
My portion, mine inheritance,
Yea, all my boundless wealth"
J. Mason.

Christ should mean everything to you. You need to be excited about Him, your heart dancing for joy at the thought of following Him and obeying His commands. If not, perhaps you haven't yet given your all for Him. Notice that in verse 44 the man *"in his joy"* sold all.

"What is more, I consider everything a loss compared to the surpassing greatness of knowing Christ Jesus my Lord, for whose sake I have lost all things, I consider them rubbish, that I may gain Christ" (Phil. 3:8).

▰ ACTION
If you have a hymn book, read through the words of "I've found the Pearl of greatest price" by J. Mason, and let your heart sing for joy.

The net
Matthew 13:47–50

We are the fishermen. We are responsible for evangelism, spreading the good news about salvation. Jesus has the responsibility of the final judgment. The

"This is how it will be at the end ..." different fishing methods used on Lake Galilee can be pictures of different types of evangelism.

1. The line and hook from the shore. One-to-one evangelism, speaking with a neighbour or workmate.

2. The cast net from the shore. This is the net that Peter and Andrew were using when Jesus called them (Matt. 4:18). It represents group evangelism – street work, coffee mornings, evangelistic Bible study groups, youth groups ...

3. The larger cast net from a boat. Wider outreach, evangelistic church meetings, Gospel concerts, tent meetings, open-air rallies ...

4. The drag net, involving two or three boats working together as a team at night. A picture of full-scale evangelistic campaigns.

Criticism has been levelled at these large campaigns because some of the people who come forward do not go on with the Lord. That, however, is Jesus' responsibility, although we must play our part in seeking to help them go on in the faith, encouraging them to study the Word of God and seek Him in prayer. We must fulfil our responsibilities as fishermen.

"For it is time for judgment to begin with the family of God; and if it begins with us, what will the outcome be for those who do not obey the gospel of God?" (1 Pet. 4:17).

▮ THOUGHT
When the Church stops seeking the lost it is lost.

* * *

The householder
Matthew 13:51–53

Jesus wanted to make quite sure that His

"Have you understood all these things?" disciples understood what He had been teaching them. It was to be very important in the Early Church that the leaders understood both the Old Testament truths and the instructions about the Kingdom that Jesus was giving them.

I wonder if the disciples understood when Jesus referred to them as "teachers of the law"? I don't think so.

They were simple men and probably had no pretensions to be leaders. But they were in a "Teacher training college", and Jesus was teaching them to teach. They listened attentively – they asked questions when they didn't understand.

We need that same eagerness to grasp hold of God's Word. Time must be spent comparing the Old Testament with the New asking questions, looking things up in a commentary, praying and meditating so that we understand what we read.

"But when he, the Spirit of truth, comes, he will guide you into all truth ..." (John 16:13).

◀ FOR STUDY
Look through Peter's sermon (Acts 2:14–36) and see how a simple fisherman brought out old and new treasures.

The storm calmed
Matthew 8:18, 23–27; Mark 4:35–41; Luke 8:22–25

Some of Jesus' disciples were experienced fishermen. They knew how to handle a boat in a storm. But this storm was of such intensity that it had them absolutely terrified.

"Quiet! Be still!" Although God controls nature, Satan is allowed, on occasion, to tamper with the weather (see Job 1:12, 16, 19). So this Galilean storm could have been the result of demonic activity.

Jesus was asleep, partly because He was tired, but also because He had complete faith in His Father's protection. He rested in His Father's arms knowing that He had no need to fear. The disciples didn't understand that because they had the Creator on board ship, they did not need to fear the creation. If fears and anxieties disturb your sleep, learn from Jesus – know that your Father takes care of everything.

The disciples demanded action from Jesus. Our Lord responded first by stilling the storm and then by asking them why they were afraid. Jesus gives us peace simply by His presence. He is able to still every storm – but if my faith is strong enough I can go through the storm with Him.

"And the peace of God, which transcends all understanding, will guard your hearts and your minds in Christ Jesus." (Eph. 2:14).

▌ MEMORIZE
Make a note of these Scriptures and memorize them for a time of need: Ex. 14:13; Joshua 1:9; Luke 12:32; Heb. 13:6.

Demons cast out
Matthew 8:28–34; Mark 5:1–20

The disciples were terrified of the Man Who could command the winds and waves, and they asked, "Who is this?" Yet the demons had no doubt about who Jesus was.

"Go!" They recognised Him from a distance and cried out in fear.

Mark gives us a very graphic description of the violence and strength of the possessed man – not a man we would wish to get close to!

Jesus had no fear of the storm – and neither was He frightened of this dangerously demented man. Jesus had absolute authority over the demons, and used it. We don't know why He allowed the destruction of the pigs. It could have been that the pig breeders were Jews breaking the law of Moses and that this loss of their livelihood was a punishment.

Isn't it sad that the people pleaded with Jesus to leave the district? They didn't want His miraculous power there. Jesus, however, had an answer: He left His ambassador there to preach the good news all round the ten towns of the district. There are people today who are afraid of supernatural power, afraid to meet Jesus face to face. How can you help them?

"And God placed all things under his feed and appointed him to be head over everything for the church" (Eph. 1:22).

▌ MY DECLARATION
Jesus is Lord! Hallelujah!

DAY 121

Reaching out to Jesus

Matthew 9:18–22; Mark 5:21–34; Luke 8:40–48

The woman who reached out and touched Jesus was suffering from a debilitating illness. Apart from the pain and discomfort, it also made her ceremonially unclean according to Jewish law. She would have been barred from the temple, and anyone who touched her would also become unclean for the day (Lev. 15:25-27).

"... your faith has healed you ..."

This, no doubt, explained her reluctance to make her presence known in that crowd of people. Yet, because she longed so much to be healed, she was willing to risk public disgrace and wrath to get near Jesus. Jesus had to find her in the crowd to allay her feeling of guilt for having touched Him. He was as concerned for her peace of mind as He was for her physical condition.

As with the leper (Matt. 8:3), uncleanness could not touch Jesus – His purity and wholeness flowed into the woman. It cost her a lot to confess before the crowd what she had done – she was terrified (Mark 5:33), yet she did it! Jesus commended her for her faith. He will commend you, too, for faith and boldness when you speak our for Him.

"Praise the Lord ... who forgives all your sins and heals all your diseases" (Psa. 103:2–3)

▌ QUESTION
Why is open confession necessary? (Rom. 10:9–11).

DAY 122

God is never late

Matthew 9:23–26; Mark 5:35–43; Luke 8:49–56

How frustrating! Jairus had pushed his way through the crowds to see Jesus and pleaded with Him to heal his daughter. Our Lord said He would come, but was then delayed by the woman with the haemorrhage. The delay must have seemed unnecessary and interminable to Jairus as Jesus insisted on finding the woman in the crowd.

"Don't be afraid; just believe"

I can imagine Jairus getting more and more anxious and frustrated as time went by. Then came the message: "It's too late!" Jesus, however, knew and understood what Jairus was going through. Look again at the comforting words that He spoke to the distraught father. Do you get frustrated by God's seeming delays? God is never late. He always has the perfect time for answering prayer and fulfilling His purposes.

Notice Jesus' authority. There was a huge crowd around Him, but He didn't let them follow Him. Taking only three disciples, Jesus ignored the derisive laughter of the professional mourners and evicted them. What a masterful presence Jesus must have had! There was something about Him that commanded obedience, even from people who had no faith in Him.

"Jesus said to her, 'I am the resurrection and the life. He who believes in me will live, even though he dies' " (John 11:25).

▌ THOUGHT
Fear not death, for the sooner we die the longer we shall be with Him.

Hailing the King
Matthew 9:27–31

"Son of David!" cried the two blind men. This is Jesus' Kingly Messianic title.

"According to your faith will it be done to you" Jesus never used this title Himself, preferring "Son of man," which emphasised His humanity and role of servant.

Jesus had not come at that time to reign on David's throne in Jerusalem. After His resurrection, Jesus took His place at His Father's right hand in heaven as ruler of the eternal Kingdom, a far greater and higher position than was visualised by the Jews at that time.

The two blind men recognised Jesus as the Messiah, but He made no comment on this, merely asking them if they really believed He could restore their sight.

Once again, faith was the prerequisite for healing.

If you have difficulty in believing God for miracles, not just for healing but for answers to prayer in impossible situations, the solution lies in recognising Jesus for who He is. He is the Creator, the giver of life, King of all kings, Lord of lords, loving, merciful, compassionate. Meditate on His glory, worship Him, then your faith will be strengthened.

"The Lord sets prisoners free, the Lord gives sight to the blind, the Lord lifts up those who are bowed down, the Lord loves the righteous" (Psa. 146:7, 8).

◢ REMEMBER
Faith is belief in action. Living without it is like driving in the fog.

Time for the needy
Matthew 9:31–34

It is difficult to see how the two blind men (yesterday's reading) could have kept quiet. But their disobedience to Jesus' instructions not to tell anyone about their healing may have made it harder for Jesus to minister to those who truly wanted to hear His teaching. Crowds will always gather when anything sensational happens – a fire, a road accident or a riot.

"The crowd was amazed ..."

The crowds gathered around Jesus at that time to see the signs and wonders He did. How many of them, we may well wonder, were later among the crowd at Jerusalem shouting "Crucify Him!" Yet some did respond – the sick, the oppressed, the spiritually hungry. Jesus always had time for needy people, despite the crowds pressing in on Him.

Bring your needs to Jesus today. He will listen and answer. The blind men received healing, the dumb man deliverance. Whatever our symptoms or outward circumstances are, Jesus knows and can deal with the root of the problem.

"Since the children have flesh and blood, he too shared in their humanity so that by his death he might destroy him who holds the power of death – that is, the devil" (Heb. 2:14).

◢ CHALLENGE
Even those of us who are not dumb find it difficult to speak out for Jesus. How about you? (Exodus 4:11 & 12).

OUTLINE HISTORY OF THE DISCIPLES

The original Twelve appointed by Jesus, Matt 10:2–4; Mk. 3:16–19; Lk 6:13–16.

	Name	Surname or Application	Home	Business	Bible History and Traditional Legends
The Inner Circle so called because they were accorded special privileges Mt: 17:1; Mk. 26:37; Mk. 5:37	Simon	Peter Cephas A Rock	Bethsaida and Capernaum	Fisherman	Evangelist and missionary work among the Jews, going as far as Babylon. 1 Pet 5:13. Tradition says as far as Rome, where he was crucified, head downwards (?)
	James (the Elder)	Sons of Thunder	Bethsaida Capernaum and Jerusalem	Fisherman	Preached in Jerusalem and Judea Beheaded by Herod, AD44 (?)
	John (The beloved disciple)			Fisherman	Laboured among the Churches of Asia Minor, according to tradition, especially at Ephesus. Banished to Patmos. Afterwards freedom and died a natural death
	Andrew (brother of Peter)		Bethsaida and Capernaum	Fisherman	Disciple of John the Baptist. Tradition: Preached in Scythia, Greece and Asia Minor. Crucified on a St. Andrew's Cross.
The Quiet Workers	Bartholomew	Nathanael	Cana of Galilee	Not known	According to tradition he was a missionary in Armenia and was flayed to death (?) Jerome says he wrote a gospel.
	Thomas	Didymus	Galilee	Not known	Tradition says he laboured in Parthia, Persia and India: suffering martyrdom near Madras, at Mt St Thomas (?)
	Matthew	Levi		Publican or Tax Collector	Tradition: is that he died a martyr in Ethiopia (?)
The Little Known	James (the Less or the Younger)		Galilee	Not known	According to tradition, preached in Palestine and Egypt. Was crucified in Egypt
	Jude	Thaddaeus	Galilee	Not known	Tradition says he preached in Assyria and Persia and died a martyr in Persia
	Simon	The Zealot	Galilee	Not known	Tradition says he was crucified
The Traitor	Judas	Iscariot	Kerioth of Judea	Not known	He betrayed Jesus for 30 pieces of silver and afterwards hanged himself. Mt 26:14–16; 27:3–5

Amazing unbelief

Matthew 13:54–58; Mark 6:1–6

Amazed. Only twice is this recorded of Jesus. He was amazed at the faith of the Roman centurion. He was amazed at the unbelief of His own friends and neighbours at Nazareth.

"... lack of faith ..." The people of Nazareth had watched Jesus grow up. They knew His family well and were not prepared to receive any fresh revelation about Him. They were too proud to do so! Search your own heart for pride. As we study these familiar stories of Jesus together, are you prepared for fresh revelation about Him – and about yourself?

We can never plumb the depths of Jesus or aspire to His heights in this life. One day we will see Him face to face, but meanwhile there is always more to learn. Day by day, even moment by moment, we are commanded to walk with Him and listen to His voice. As always it was the needy people, the sick, who received from Jesus at Nazareth. If you are prepared humbly to acknowledge needs, you, too, will receive from Him.

"Then the man said, 'Lord, I believe,' and he worshipped him" (John 9:38).

▮ MY DECLARATION
Lord, today I turn my back on unbelief and place my full confidence in Your ability.

- **Phoenicia** – Healing of Canaanite woman's daughter
- **Mount Hermon**
  - (probable) Transfiguration
  - (near) Epileptic boy healed
- **Caesarea Philippi** – Peter declares his faith
- **Bethsaida** – (near) Feeding of the 5,000
  - Blind man healed
- **Capernaum**
  - The woman with the issue of blood
  - Jairus' daughter healed
  - Two blind men healed
  - Dumb man healed
- **Sea of Galilee** – Walking on the water
- **Samaria** – 4,000 fed
  - A Samaritan village – Jesus rejected
- **Decapolis** – Deaf and dumb man healed
- **Jerusalem** – The Temple
  - Jesus declares Himself the water of life
  - The woman caught in adultery

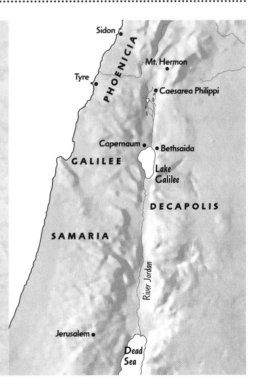

DAY 126

In His school

Matthew 9:35–38; 10:4; Mark 6:7; Luke 9:1–2

The disciples were enrolled in Jesus' training college, although they might not have realised it at the time. The Master was taking them through a course to prepare them for proclaiming the Gospel and building up the Church after Pentecost.

"... he had compassion on them ..."

In the midst of this, Jesus gave them some teaching practice. They had a threefold commission – to preach the Kingdom of God, heal the sick and cast out demons.

The three always go together in the New Testament. Together with the commission, Jesus gave them power and authority over demons. God never commands us to do something for Him without giving us the tools to accomplish the task. This was before the outpouring of the Holy Spirit on all believers, so the disciples received a special anointing for a particular task.

Jesus had another motive, too, for sending out the disciples – helpless crowds needed empowered workers, as Matthew vividly emphasises. Have you a heart of compassion for the crowds where you live, work and worship?

"Therefore go and make disciples of all nations, baptising them in the name of the Father and of the Son and of the Holy Spirit" (Matt. 28:19).

■ ACTION
Read again Matt. 9:38 and pray for willing workers in your area, remembering that you must be willing to be the answer to your prayer.

DAY 127

Sharing His life

Matthew 10:5–15; Mark 6:8–11, 30; Luke 9:3–5, 10

The commissioning of His disciples over, Jesus gave them detailed instructions about their mission. The 12 were completely inexperienced in preaching. They had, however, kept close to Jesus, absorbed His teaching and observed His dealings with all kinds of people and, because they had spent so much time with Him, they had received much.

Spent time each day alone with God. Some people say, "I pray all the time. I don't need special times." That's not the same – we all need a time and a place where we can unhurriedly learn and receive from God. We need to get alone with Jesus to enjoy a close relationship of love with Him, so that we can understand His commission and His specific instructions for each day.

The disciples' instructions were to go to the Jewish communities rather than the Greek cities in Galilee or to Samaria. They were to travel very simply to learn to trust God for His provision, and to choose carefully which of the generous Eastern hospitality they accepted. And out they went – bearers of Good News!

"Freely you have received, freely give"

"Again Jesus said,'Peace be with you! As the Father has sent me, I am sending you'" (John 20:21).

◣ QUESTION
How do we hear the Lord's instructions to us? Psalm 119:105, 133.

Wisdom we need

Matthew 10:16–33

Be alert! Be wise! The kind of wisdom we need to be effective disciples comes only from God (v. 16). Our Lord makes it clear that we are not to walk knowingly and foolishly into danger, but be on our guard.

"... you are worth more than many barrows ..."

Jesus alludes to the snake because of its habit of cautious watchfulness, of not inviting trouble. Doves illustrate purity. If we are truly led by the Holy Spirit, we are likely to experience persecution and times of hardship, even betrayal and rejection, but we are not to go out of our way to bring these things upon ourselves.

It must have been difficult for the disciples to take in what Jesus was saying to them. They had shared His rejection at Nazareth and were aware of the wrath of the Jewish leaders, but Jesus was still preaching and healing people openly without there being any attempt to stop Him. God's Son had, however, to prepare the 12 for the trouble to come.

As He did this, Jesus carefully emphasised how much God loved them, how valuable there were to Him. That's why He introduced sparrows. The little birds were sold for food at less than a halfpenny for a pair, yet God knew and cared for each of them. And your Father loves and cares about you. In all the trials we may face in the future, we must remember that.

"But the wisdom that comes from heaven is first of all pure; then peace-loving, considerate, submissive, full of mercy and good fruit, impartial and sincere" (James 3:17).

 MEDITATE
Ponder on verses 30 and 31 of today's passage.

WISDOM IS...

... the ability to use knowledge so as to meet successfully the emergencies of life. Men may acquire knowledge, but wisdom is a gift direct from God.

He is truly wise who gains wisdom from another's mistakes.

Wisdom is the right use of knowledge.

A wise man will not only bow at the manger but also at the Cross.

Meditate on Proverbs 16:16.

The Cross factor

Matthew 10:34–42; 11:1; Mark 6:12–13; Luke 9:6

A new factor is introduced to the disciples: the Cross. Jesus was facing it because He, the Father and the Holy Spirit were in constant close communion with each other so nothing was hidden between them.

Jesus was also in close communion with His disciples, so He did not hide the cost of discipleship from them.

Our Lord never led the 12 to believe that they would have an easy time as His followers – He told them exactly what they would have to face. We should have the same openness with those whom we seek to lead to the Lord, and with young Christians. They need to count the cost. That is the only way to grow strong in the faith. Jesus asks for

"... whoever loses his life for my sake will find it"

total commitment, even to the extent of giving up our lives for Him.

Love for Him must come before all other loves. If, however, our allegiance to Jesus costs everything, it also brings us great rewards. If we are willing to sacrifice the natural, or self-life, then we will find eternal life, to be forever in the presence of our glorious Lord and Saviour.

"I tell you the truth, unless a grain of wheat falls to the ground and dies, it remains only a single seed. But if it dies, it produces many seeds" (John 12:24).

◾ **FOR STUDY**
Compare verses 38 and 39 with Galatians 2:20.

DAY 130

Utterly selfless

Matthew 14:13–21; Mark 6:30–44; Luke 9:10–17; John 6:1–13

The four accounts of a marvellous incident give us a wonderful picture of Jesus' humanity, His compassion for others and the use of His spiri-

"... he gave thanks and broke the loaves ..."

tual power in a practical way. The feeding of the 5,000 happened just after our Lord had heard of the death of His cousin, John the Baptist. Sad and upset, He just wanted to go to somewhere quiet for a while. His excited disciples were just back from their preaching tour and wanted to tell Him of the wonderful things that had happened.

Instead of the peace and quiet that they all wanted, a huge needy crowd followed them. How would you have felt? Annoyed? Jesus wasn't. He was able to lay aside His own feelings and meet the needs of all those people. He ministered to their spiritual needs with teaching, their physical needs with healing and their bodily needs with food.

I think the greatest miracle in this story is Jesus' utter selflessness in giving Himself to all those people. Think about that the next time you feel harassed by other people's demands on your time, privacy and emotions. Draw strength from Him and go on giving.

"Every day they continued to meet together in the temple courts. They broke bread in their homes and ate together with glad and sincere hearts" (Acts 2:46).

◣ **CHALLENGE**
"Freely you have received, freely give." What have you received? What have you given?

DAY 131

Shining leadership

Matthew 14:22–23; Mark 6:45–46; John 6:14–15

It was typical of Jesus to send His tired disciples off first while He dismissed the crowd. It is a mark of good leadership to consider your juniors before yourself – to be first in and last out.

Jesus was a working leader, not a figurehead or a tyrant.

When His work for the day was finished, He turned to prayer – not sleep.

"... he went ... by himself to pray" Even though Jesus was the Son of God He needed that constant re-charging of His spiritual batteries that only close communion with His heavenly Father could give. His spiritual need always came before His physical need. How about you? Do you say "I'm too tired to pray," or "I'm too tired not to pray"? "I have so much work to do that I must spend extra time in prayer" or "I have so much work to do that I haven't time to pray"?

The Father loved to have fellowship with His Son, and He longs to have that same close fellowship with you.

Jesus also went into the hills to be alone with the Father to escape from the crowd who wanted to force Him to become Israel's earthly king, as John explains. Our Lord sought the Father and His will rather than personal acclaim and gain. So must we.

"One day Jesus was praying in a certain place. When he finished, one of his disciples said to him, 'Lord, teach us to pray, just as John taught his disciples' " (Luke 11:1).

STUDY
Compare Matthew 10:16b & 17a with John 6:15.

Walking on the water
Matthew 14:24–33; Mark 6:47–52; John 6:16–21

Real faith means stepping out and overcoming obstacles. It is the only way faith will grow. God always tests faith by allowing various obstacles to come in our way. It is up to us whether we use those obstacles as stepping stones or stumbling blocks.

We know the disciples were in the will of God on the lake because Jesus had told them to cross to the other side. But

"Take courage! It is I" they were having a hard time – not a sudden storm as before (Mark 4:39), but a strong head wind, making rowing difficult. Then, when they had thought He was miles away on the mountain, Jesus came near and they didn't recognise Him. He was about to pass by them, but their cries of fear caused Him to speak. Jesus is always near us when we are going through hard times, but He waits for us to cry out before He helps us.

Peter had the faith to step out of the boat, but it was an impetuous faith, not grounded on the facts of the Word of God. When he looked at his circumstances, he sank. Many of us are like that. We need a faith tested and tried by storms, head winds and the unexpected so that we can stand firm in any situation. Then we will know and worship the Son of God.

"Now faith is being sure of what we hope for and certain of what we do not see" (Heb. 11:1).

QUESTION
What is the end result of the testing of our faith? (James 1:2-4)

CROSSING THE WATERS

The Red Sea	Daytime, crowds of people, a scene of terror and doubt, their enemies pursuing them.	Enemies – the Egyptians.	Waters parted as Moses raised his staff and stretched out his hand.	Enemies drowned.	God said, "I will gain glory through Pharaoh and all his army."
The Jordan	Daytime, crowds of people, excitement and hope, their enemies before them in terror.	Enemies – the Ammonites and the Canaanites.	River stopped flowing when priests carrying the ark of the covenant stepped into the water	Enemies only partially destroyed.	God said, "I will begin to exalt you (Joshua) in the eyes of the people."
Jesus on Galilee	A windy moonlit night, alone on the water. The disciples terrified at seeing Him.	Enemy – Satan.	Jesus walked on the water.	Complete victory.	Jesus said, "Come", and Peter walked on the water in front of the other disciples.
Peter on Galilee	Twelve men in a rowing boat, battling against the wind. Peter excited at seeing Jesus.	Enemies – fear and doubt.	Peter's faith in Jesus enabled him to walk on water. Doubt caused him to sink.	Partial victory.	The disciples worshipped saying, "Truly You are the Son of God."

The children of Israel walked through the waters. Jesus had absolute authority over the elements and He and His disciples walked on the water.

Note that Peter did not step out of the boat presumptuously, he waited until Jesus called Him.

DAY 133

Cost of following Him
Matthew 14:34–36; Mark 6:53–56

It was between 3 and 6 am that Jesus came to the storm-battered disciples on the lake. None of them had any sleep and when they landed at Gennesaret, a fertile plain on the north-west coast of Lake Galilee, they must have been looking forward to a rest. But Jesus was instantly recognised and the disciples' hopes shattered.

It wasn't easy being a disciple of Jesus

"... all who touched him were healed"

– it was arduous, demanding, tiring, bewildering and sometimes frightening. No-one in his right mind would work without pay for a boss who demanded hard work in dangerous situations 24 hours a day, seven days a week. But Jesus' personality, His love, purity, peace and spiritual power, kept those 12 men with Him. Take time to look into His face just now, to become deeply aware of His presence, to really know Him and renew your allegiance to Him.

The scene at Gennesaret, the spontaneous spreading of the news of Jesus' arrival and the gathering of the sick, was repeated wherever He went. The people recognised their needs, and they recognised Jesus as One who could meet those needs. Praise Him!

"But for you who revere my name, the sun of righteousness will rise with healing in its wings. And you will go out and leap like calves released from the stall" (Mal. 4:2).

DAY 134

Running after Jesus

John 6:22-24

While the crowds were gathering around Jesus at Gennesaret, the people on the opposite shore were still looking for Him. They had seen the disciples go off in the one boat available the evening before and assumed that Jesus was still on their side of the lake. But they couldn't find Him. Jesus' original invitation to His disciples was "Follow me," not "Stay with me". God is always on the move, always doing something new. We cannot expect yesterday's blessings to last through today, or for today's instructions necessarily to apply to tomorrow.

"... in search of Jesus"

Following Jesus is an exciting journey, not a comfortable armchair. We need to look for Him in the right place. We must not expect Him to remain where we are spiritually, but to be where He is. These people who had been miraculously fed by Jesus were eager for more, and they took the first opportunity to cross the lake to search for Him.

Can you sense the excitement of those heady days? Everyone was eager to tell of the miracles they had seen, others to see for themselves. The whole area was buzzing with talk about Jesus. Oh, that it might be the same again today!

"Seek the Lord while he may be found; call on him while he is near" (Isa. 55:6).

📖 **MEMORIZE**
Matthew 7:7 & 8

BREAD ▮▮▮ ▮▮▮▮▮▮▮▮▮▮▮▮▮▮▮▮

One of the main tasks of the housewife was to prepare daily meals for her family. Bread was the most important part of any meal. In the Hebrew language, "to eat bread" meant "to have a meal."

The rich man's bread was made from wheat, the poor man's bread from barley. Women ground the grain between two millstones in the courtyard and then kneaded the dough in a trough. To make the dough rise, they used fermented dough left over from the last baking. Only a little yeast was needed for three pecks of flour – the usual amount used in baking for the family. But it leavened all the dough.

That is why Jesus said that the kingdom of God is like yeast. Only a little yeast is needed to permeate all the dough and work right through it. It only takes a few Christians to influence many people and spread the faith throughout the world. That is how the kingdom of God grows.

Getting motives right
John 6:25-33

The people flocked to Jesus again – but for the wrong reason. They wanted personal gain, not to know the Messiah.

"... the true bread from heaven" They didn't believe in Him as the Son of God, but as someone who had marvellous powers of supplying physical necessities.

Jesus saw this and had to explain to them that their real need was a spiritual one. That need was the one He had come to fulfil in Himself.

It is important to learn that our primary need is for Jesus Himself. He does supply our daily needs – food, clothing, money, homes, jobs – but if we are looking to Him only or primarily as a supplier of material necessities, He is likely to withhold these from us. "Seek *first* his kingdom and his righteousness, and all these things will be given to you as well" (Matt. 6:33).

The Galileans' next question (v. 28) reveals that they still haven't understood what Jesus is saying or who He is. The only thing they had to do was to believe in Him. But, sadly, they still weren't convinced.

"They all ate the same spiritual food and drank the same spiritual drink; for they drank from the spiritual rock that accompanied them, and that rock was Christ" (1 Cor. 10:3 & 4).

■ **COMPARE**
John 6:27b with Eph. 1:13 and 2 Cor. 1:22.

I am the bread of life
John 6:34-58

Jesus gave word pictures of Himself to show who He was and why He had come into our world. Over the next few days we shall be looking at our Lord's "I am's."

Through calling Himself "the bread of life," we begin to see more of the true significance of the feeding of the 5,000. The five loaves had to be broken to feed the crowd. After they were broken, they were distributed and then multiplied so that there was enough for all. Jesus, the living bread sent from heaven, had to be broken on the Cross, to die for us in order that we might share in His life.

He offered His body as a sacrifice and, unless we accept that sacrifice by faith, we cannot partake. His blood also was shed for us, so that we can be forgiven and cleansed from sin.

Many people have difficulty in understanding verses 53-56, but it becomes simpler as we look at the passage in the context of all Jesus' teaching, especially His sacrifice on the Cross.

"If anyone eats o this bread, he wil live for ever ..."

Jesus gave Himself wholeheartedly and unreservedly for me, for you and for the whole world. All we have to do is to partake of His sacrifice – and to give ourselves unreservedly to Him. Ponder on the significance of Holy Communion in the light of this passage.

"The Lord Jesus ... took bread, and when he had given thanks, he broke it and said, 'This is my body, which is for you; do this in remembrance of me' " (1 Cor. 11:23 & 24).

◪ **FOR MEDITATION**
Exodus 16:4; Matt. 14:19-20; John 6:54; Luke 22:19; 1 Cor. 10:16, 17.

I am the Good Shepherd
John 10:10-18

In one of the most comforting passages in the Bible, we learn that Jesus is our Shepherd and that we who obey Him are His sheep. He knows each one of us by name.

"... I have come that they may have life ... to the full"

He loves us, cares for us, heals us when we are sick or wounded, feeds and protects us. He laid down His life for us so that we might be His for ever. We know His voice – all we have to do is to listen and follow. What a sense of security this knowledge gives us!

The Jews knew that a shepherd and his flock symbolized the relationship between God and His people. There are many such references in the Old Testament. They were familiar, too, with the idea of delegated responsibility.

Moses, Joshua, and the true prophets were good shepherds who led God's flock according to His instructions. False shepherds were condemned by Jeremiah (23:1 & 2).

Jesus claimed to be the owner of the flock, not a hired shepherd. Because of this, and because He is the Son of God, He is willing to lay down His life for His sheep. Doesn't that give you a wonderful sense of belonging?

"May the God of peace, who through the blood of the eternal covenant brought back from the dead our Lord Jesus, that great Shepherd of the sheep, equip you with everything good for doing his will ..." (Heb. 13:20 & 21).

FOR STUDY
Read Psalm 23 in context with Psalms 22 and 24.

I am the Way, the Truth and the Life
John 14:1-7

"Way" can be used in two senses – a path, or a person's attitude and conduct. A public path goes in a certain direction and leads to a particular destination. Conduct reveals a person's inner motives, strengths and goal in life. Jesus is "the way" in both these senses – the way to the Father.

"Do not let our hearts be troubled ..."

"Truth" here means more than factual accuracy. It is reality, completeness, dependability. Jesus gives us reality in a world of falsehood. He is the only One who can make our lives complete, full, abundant. His words are absolutely dependable and reliable. When we commit ourselves to Him, He will never let us down. We can always trust Him.

"I am the Life." Jesus had already told His followers that He would give them life. Now He goes a step further – He gives us Himself. It is His life in us that gives us entrance to the place prepared for us in heaven. My life is nothing. His life in me is everything.

"Then you will know the truth, and the truth will set you free" (John 8:32).

THOUGHT
Jesus never taught men how to make a living – He taught them how to live.

I am the True Vine
John 15:1–8

The picture of the Good Shepherd shows us that we are owned and loved by Jesus. In the vine we see an even closer union. The branches are organically part of the vine – apart from the main stem they die. The same sap flows through both and the same fruit and leaves grow on both. In every respect the branches depend on the stem and are identical to it.

The vine was a symbol of peace and prosperity in the Old Testament and also of God's chosen people (Psa. 80:8). Jesus used vines and vineyards in many of His parables because His hearers were familiar with them – grapes were one of their main crops. They would have known how tenderly the gardener nurtured his vines – protecting, fertilising, pruning, cutting down and harvesting. His aim was that the vineyards should be profitable.

"Remain in me"

Your Father's aim is that you, too, should be profitable, bearing much fruit for Him. If you are firmly abiding in Jesus the True Vine, then you *will* bear fruit because the same Holy Spirit that empowered Jesus flows through you. That realisation takes the striving and straining out of life. So submit to your Father's will, abide in Jesus and be filled with the Holy Spirit.

"Whoever claims to live in him must walk as Jesus did" (1 John 2:6).

■ QUESTION
What fruit does the True Vine bear? (Gal 5:22–23).

I am the Light of the world
John 8:12–19

The Word of God is exciting! See how God gradually unfolds His truth to us. Genesis 1:3 tells us that He commanded, "Let there be light" – and light appeared. There was light even before the sun was created.

Psalm 119:105 declares: "Your *word* is a lamp to my feet and a light for my path." John 1:14 reveals: "The *Word* became flesh and made his dwelling among us" and (v. 9), "the true light that gives light to every man ..." Finally, Revelation 22:5 tells us: "There will be no more night ... for the Lord God will give them light."

"... Whoever follows me will never walk in darkness ..."

Jesus chose the Feast of Tabernacles to declare Himself as the Light of the world. Lighting the four great golden candelabra in the temple courts recalled the journey of the children of Israel through the wilderness guided by the pillar of fire.

Jesus, the Word of God, the Light of the world, illuminates our path, guiding us through the darkness of sin and unbelief into freedom and faith. Light is attractive, drawing people to itself out of the darkness. And darkness can never overcome light.

"For God, who said, 'Let light shine out of darkness,' made his light shine in our hearts to give us the light of the knowledge of the glory of God in the face of Christ" (2 Cor. 4:6).

■ ACTION
Ask God to show you someone upon whom you can shine His light.

NAMES FOR CHRIST IN THE GOSPELS

Baby	Lk. 2:12
Bread	Jn. 6:33
Bridegroom	Matt. 9:15
Capstone	Matt. 21:42
Child	Matt. 2:13
Christ	Matt. 16:16
Doctor	Matt. 9:12
Friend of sinners	Matt. 11:19
Gate	Jn. 10:7
God	Jn. 20:28
Gift	Jn. 4:10
Holy One of God	Mk. 1:24
Heir	Matt. 21:38
Immanuel	Matt. 1:23
Jesus	Matt. 1:21
King of Jews	Matt. 2:2
King of Israel	Jn. 1:49
Lamb	Jn. 1:29
Lord	Matt. 14:28
Man	Jn. 1:30
Master	Matt. 10:24
Messiah	Jn. 1:41
Nazarene	Matt. 2:23
One and Only	Jn. 1:14
Prophet	Matt. 13:57
Rabbi	Jn. 1:38
Rising Sun	Lk. 1:78
Ruler	Matt. 2:6
Shepherd	Jn. 10:11
Saviour	Jn. 4:42
Son of God	Matt. 14:33
Son of Man	Matt. 8:20
Son of David	Matt. 9:27
Son of Abraham	Matt. 1:1
Son of Joseph	Jn. 1:45
Word of God	Jn. 1:1

DAY 141

Before Abraham – I am
John 8:52–59

If Jesus' claim to be the Light of the world was extraordinary and bewildering to the Jews, His statement, "Before Abraham was born, I am," was crystal clear. He was either the Son of God or He was a blasphemer. And blasphemy was a capital offence, punishable by stoning to death (see Lev. 24:16).

"My Father ... glorifies me"

The two verbs in Jesus' statement are different in the Greek. "Before Abraham was" signifies "came into being" – Abraham was created at a specific time. But "I am" suggests an eternal being. Jesus always was and always will be "I am." The claim must have reminded the Jews of God's words to Moses (Exodus 3:14), and caused them to reach for stones to throw at Him. They needed no further excuse or proof that Jesus was a blasphemer. But it was they who were guilty of blaspheming, of insulting the Son of God.

Jesus is "before all things" (Col. 1:17). "He was with God in the beginning" (John 1:2). By Him "all things were created: things in heaven and on earth" (Col. 1:16). He is "the Alpha and the Omega, the First and the Last, the Beginning and the End" (Rev. 22:13). Jesus was not making an extravagant claim for Himself. He was stating the simple truth – truth that demanded, and still demands, a response from people who hear it.

"In the beginning was the Word, and the Word was with God, and the Word was God" (John 1:1).

▼ READ
Look again at the above Scriptures and read them in context.

I am the Gate

John 10:1–9

An Eastern sheepfold had one narrow entrance. The shepherd stood by the gate as he drove his flock in for the night, examining each sheep as it entered. Sick or wounded sheep would be cared for and those not belonging to his fold turned away. When they were safely in, the shepherd himself would often lie down across the entrance so that no sheep could escape and no marauder – animal or human – could enter. Jesus is the gate through which we enter the kingdom of God (see Acts 4:12).

"... whoever enters ... will be saved ..."

If you were the only sinner on earth Christ would still have died, just for you! There is no other way that you could come to God to be forgiven and cleansed.

The sheepfold, however, is not a holy huddle. Jesus says that each sheep "will come in and go out" (v. 9). That doesn't mean that we can slip out of the kingdom once we are in, but that we are free to go out into the world as He leads us and serve Him there. Jesus is the gate to a life of freedom in His service – if we listen to His voice and follow where He leads.

"Therefore, brothers, since we have confidence to enter the Most Holy Place by the blood of Jesus, by a new and living way opened for us through the curtain, that is, his body ... let us draw near to God with a sincere heart in full assurance of faith ..." (Heb. 10:19–22).

■ PRAYER

Thank You, dear Lord, for leading me into the sheepfold. Help me to go out and let You through me draw others to the Great Shepherd.

I am the Resurrection

John 11:17–27

Most Jews in Jesus' time on earth believed in the resurrection of the body at the last day – the raising up of the same body they had in their lifetime. The Sadducees didn't, however, believe in a resurrection. Martha believed it, but it did not help her in her present grief. Jesus then gave her this tremendous revelation about Himself: "I am the resurrection and the life."

"He ... will live, even though he dies"

Jesus Himself is the Life that Lazarus needed. He is the Resurrection that would restore the life into Lazarus' body. He is your Resurrection and Life, too. Before you became a Christian you were dead in sins, condemned to judgment and damnation. Jesus, by His death and resurrection, conquered sin and death, so that you could be raised from spiritual death to receive His glorious life for eternity. Martha was looking to the future, not the present.

Many Christians look to a vague happy prospect in heaven some time in the future, but Jesus is the Resurrection and the Life *now*!

"Now this is eternal life: that they may know you, the only true God, and Jesus Christ, whom you have sent" (John 17:3).

▲ THOUGHT

Life with Christ is an endless hope. Life without Him is a hopeless end.

All or nothing
John 6:59-71

The sorting out had begun. Many of the people who followed Jesus around only did so because of the healings, the miracles, the arguments about the new teaching, the general excitement of being part of a crowd.

"The words I have spoken ... are spirit and ... life" They were the ones who could not accept Jesus as the Son of God. They did not accept His word that He was sent from the Father. Jesus had made the most extraordinary claims about Himself which were quite unacceptable to good, religious Jews. He was either mad or a blasphemer – or He was truly the Son of God, the Messiah.

Do you accept everything that Jesus claimed for Himself, everything in the Word of God as true? There are many today who say "Yes I believe, but ...". Many compromise by saying, "I'll go so far, but no further. I accept that part of the Bible but not this part." It just doesn't work.

There is no halfway house. Jesus turned to the 12 and sought reassurance from them. They gave it – "We believe and know ...". Will you reaffirm your wholehearted faith in Him today?

"Sanctify them by the truth; your word is truth" (John 17:17).

◼ THOUGHT
Obedience to Christ is the greatest liberty.

Living faith – not rules
Matthew 15:1-9; Mark 7:1-13

Getting more and more concerned about Jesus and His teaching, the religious authorities in Jerusalem sent another fact-finding commission to try to trap Him. Again, it was the disciples they accused, not Jesus person-

"You ypocrites!" ally (see Mark 2:18-24). Yet the ritual of washing had little to do with cleanliness because cold water was merely poured over the hands. The accusers clearly inferred that Jesus' teaching was wrong and He was leading His followers astray because they ignored the traditions of the law.

Jesus played them on their own home ground by pointing out that *their* teaching was leading people away from the law of Moses. According to Pharisaical teaching, it was honourable to devote one's money to the temple and neglect elderly parents. This is clearly contrary to the spirit of the law. As the quotation from Isaiah emphasises, Christianity is not a set of rules, but a living faith in a Person. It is God we worship – not a code of practice.

God gives us His Word, the Bible, to reveal His Son, and for teaching, rebuking, correcting and training (2 Tim. 3:16). We need to take the *whole* Word of God as our guide, not to make doctrines out of a small portion of the truth.

"You hypocrite, first take the plank out of your own eye, and then you will see clearly to remove the speck from your brother's eye" (Matt. 7:5).

◼ QUESTION
What is the difference between the law and the Spirit of God? (2 Cor 3:6).

SCRIBES AND PHARISEES

The Scribes, also called lawyers or teachers (Rabbis), originated in pre-exilic times as government writers or copiers of the law. By New Testament times they had developed into a separate group with their own schools. They wore the long robes of nobility and were held in deep respect by the people. As they interpreted the law, however, they gradually added more details to it, making it impossible to keep.

The Pharisees were a strict religious sect with origins in the lay governing body of the temple in Maccabean times – a period between the end of the Old Testament and the beginning of the New Testament period. There were about 6,000 of them during Jesus' years on earth. They were legalistic and separatist, despising those who did not keep their burdensome laws. They built a fence around the law, excluding non-Pharisees from the benefits of the Torah. A number of them were godly men – Nicodemus, for example. Paul too, was a Pharisee.

DAY 146

The root of evil

Matthew 15:10–20; Mark 7:14–23

The Pharisees believed in the basic righteousness of man. To them the law existed for the preservation of that righteousness, and defilement came from outside sources.

"... things ... that come from the heart ... make a man 'unclean'"

By the meticulous keeping of the law they believed they could remain, rather than become, pure. Jesus knew the innate sinfulness of man since the fall of Adam and the ineffectiveness of the law to cure that sin. Both Matthew and Mark put "evil thoughts" at the top of the list of sins.

Evil thoughts produce evil words and actions. The disciples didn't understand what Jesus was saying. Jesus had not gone to the Cross and the Holy Spirit had not yet come, so they did not yet understand that Jesus had come into the world to deal with sin. They must have been completely bewildered by Jesus' apparent reversal of teaching they had believed from childhood.

It is easy to get frustrated and annoyed when non-Christians fail to understand when you speak to them of Jesus. Pray for the Holy Spirit's enlightenment for them, that the word of truth will take root in their lives.

"The heart is deceitful above all things and beyond cure. Who can understand it?" (Jer. 17:9).

PONDER
Peter needed further explanation and confirmation of this teaching later. Mark 7:19; Matt. 26:69–75; Acts 10:9-15.

DAY 147

Persistence pays off
Matt 15:21–28; Mark 7:24–30.

It was Jesus' first visit to the Tyre and Sidon region – a Gentile area. Possibly He wanted to avoid further clashes with the Jewish leaders, to spend time in private with His disciples and to secure time for rest and preparation for the last part of His ministry.

"... you have great faith!"

The Canaanite woman who approached Him had evidently hear of Jesus' miracles of healing and deliverance and had faith in His power. Jesus initially rebuffed her because, although He was to be "a light to the Gentiles," His earthly ministry was primarily to the Jews.

The woman, however, was persistent and, even when Jesus tested her humility, she came back with an answer. "Dogs" was the usual Jewish term for Gentiles. Jesus was not using it in a particularly derogatory sense, but making it clear that He was the Jewish Messiah and she was a Gentile. He was pleased with her answer.

God wants us to pray persistently, using the words of Scripture to hold as passports before Him.

"And without faith it is impossible to please God, because anyone who comes to him must believe that he exists and that he rewards those who earnestly seek him" (Heb. 11:6).

QUESTION
How is faith demonstrated? (James 2:1–26).

DAY 148

That wonderful voice
Matthew 15:29–31; Mark 7:31–37

Jesus walked on, first further north to Sidon and then southwards past Lake Galilee, crossing the River Jordan to the mountainous Decapolis region.

Predominantly a Gentile region (Mark 7:31), though there were many Jewish villages, it was there that the people had begged Jesus to leave after He had healed the demoniac at Gadara. Once again Jesus is surrounded by crowds of sick people, His fame having been spread by those who had flocked to Him in Galilee (Matt. 4:25) and by the healed demoniac (Mark 5:20).

Mark's moving story of the deaf mute so clearly shows the compassion and understanding that Jesus has for the handicapped. In the midst of the busy day, Jesus took time to take the man aside and explain by sign language what He was going to do for him. Then, away from the noise of the crowd, the man was able to hear for the first time a voice – the wonderful sound of Jesus' voice!

"... and he healed them"

There are so many spiritually deaf people who, if only they would come away from the crowds for a while and seek Jesus, would be able to hear His voice. Make sure you hear His voice clearly. It is only when we hear Him clearly that we can speak clearly for Him.

"But he was pierced for our transgressions, he was crushed for our iniquities; the punishment that brought us peace was upon him, and by his wounds we are healed" (Isa. 53:5).

MY DECLARATION
Lord, by Your stripes I am healed. Amen.

DAY 149

Only in His strength
Matthew 15:32-38; Mark 8:1-9

When the 5,000 were fed it was the disciples who were concerned for the people and Jesus who gently told them to feed them (Matt. 14:15 & 16).

"I have compassion for these people ..." But they stood back and let Jesus work the miracle. In Decapolis it is Jesus who initiates the concern. He gives His disciples a second chance to take hold of the power that He had given them so that they could feed the people. But they made the same excuse again, "We haven't enough" (14:17 and 15:33).

Do you ever feel powerless, inadequate to counsel, to pray for the sick, to lead someone to Christ? We all are in our own strength. But with Jesus standing beside us – as He was on that mountain – and the power of the Holy Spirit within us, we can do all things. The disciples made the mistake of looking at the material resources. Jesus, Son of God, looked to His heavenly Father's limitless provision.

The primary lesson of the two miraculous feedings is that God is not limited by man's resources. He can, and does, multiply what we give to Him. He wants us to be channels of His power to feed hungry people.

"Finally, all of you, live in harmony with one another; be sympathetic, love as brothers, be compassionate and humble" (1 Pet. 3:8).

■ STUDY
Look up the word "compassion" in a Bible concordance and read the references that apply to Jesus.

DAY 150

Demand for a sign
Matthew 15:39, 16:1-4; Mark 8:10-12

Before crowds could gather again the Pharisees and Sadducees waylaid Jesus and, with their stubborn unbelief, prevented Him from ministering in Magadan, which was probably near Tiberias.

"Jesus ... left them and went away"

Bitter opposition was being stirred up against Jesus by the Jewish leaders. Not content with the signs and miracles that Jesus had already performed, they demanded a special sign for themselves.

Jesus grieved in His heart over their hardness and spiritual blindness. Faith believes without seeing. Signs follow – not precede – those who believe. In the same way that Satan tempted Jesus in the wilderness to use His power to prove who He is, the Jewish leaders tempted Him by asking for a sign to prove that He was sent from God. But Jesus had already overcome that temptation. He also knew that even if they saw a sign they would not believe.

Jesus performed miracles out of His concern for the practical needs of the people – not for their own sake. The sin of unbelief hardens hearts. Don't grieve Him like those Pharisees did. Jesus is looking for those who will believe.

"Then the Lord said, 'My Spirit will not contend with man for ever, for he is mortal; his days will be a hundred and twenty years' " (Gen. 6:3).

■ THINK ABOUT THIS
The rewards of faith – John 20:29; Hebrews 11:1 & 2.

DAY 151

Beware of the yeast
Matthew 16:5–12; Mark 8:13–21

The disciples, including Matthew, were sometimes puzzled, slow to understand, forgetful, quarrelsome and self-seeking.

Yet Matthew faithfully recorded their failings, weaknesses and the rebukes the 12 received from Jesus. He glorified his Lord and Master in his writing – never himself or his fellow disciples.

"... be on your guard ..."

The yeast of the Pharisees and Sadducees was hypocrisy (Luke 12:1) which caused spiritual blindness. Herod's hypocrisy was probably worldliness. The Greek word translated "reasoning" or "discussing" (v. 7) is akin to "being of a doubtful mind" and is elsewhere translated "worrying". We are not meant to talk and worry over problems among ourselves, but to take them straight to our Father, who has all the answers. Jesus was trying to teach them again that He alone was the True Bread, the Giver of Life.

The types of baskets used for left-overs at the two feasts were different. The 12 baskets were small sacks carried by every travelling Jew and, no doubt, they belonged to the disciples. The seven baskets were large wicker containers used by Gentile merchants. The bread is for both Jew and Gentile – and there is enough to feed everyone.

"Your boasting is not good. Don't you know that a little yeast works through the whole batch of dough?" (1 Cor. 5:6).

■ PRAYER
Lord, may I not be slow to understand. Teach me your ways. Amen.

DAY 152

Healed – gradually
Mark 8:22–26

The episode with the blind man at Bethsaida is the only recorded instance of a gradual healing in the New Testament. And Mark is the only Gospel writer to note it. Jesus had to put His hands on the man's eyes twice before he was healed.

"He took the blind man by the hand ..."

Whether this means that the man lacked faith or there was hardness of heart among the people – as at Nazareth – we don't know. What we do know is that Jesus didn't give up until the man was seeing clearly.

When we pray for sick people we should believe that God will heal completely instead of being content with some improvement, a relief of symptoms. Everyone who was healed by Jesus was made *completely* whole. He is still the same Jesus today.

Notice again Jesus' tenderness and understanding. The blind man was brought to Jesus by friends, unlike Bartimaeus, who shouted to Jesus for himself. Perhaps this man didn't really understand what was happening, but Jesus led him gently by the hand away from the crowds and indicated what He was doing by applying cooling saliva to his eyes.

"But blessed are your eyes because they see, and your ears because they hear" (Matt. 13:16).

◆ PRAISE
I worship You, Lord, for once I was blind but now I see. Hallelujah!

DAY 153

Peter's declaration

Matthew 16:13–20; Mark 8:27–30; Luke 9:18–21

Peter's open declaration of the disciples' belief in Jesus as the Christ or Messiah is an important landmark in the Gospel narrative. After that our Lord began to speak openly to them of His coming death.

"Who do you say I am?"

Some people thought Jesus was merely a prophet – but He was far more than that. The Old Testament seers foreshadowed Jesus, each revealing facets of His character. Jeremiah wept in love and met with little response. Elijah was a miracle worker and fearless prayer warrior. Then there was John the Baptist, the stern ascetic, preaching repentance, who immediately preceded our Lord. Jesus, however, was and is Christ, the expected Messiah, Son of the living God. Jesus' heart was gladdened by the revelation given to Peter by the Father, and by his boldness in speaking out.

Peter was often the spokesman for the 12 and it is likely that he was so here. Peter became the leader and spokesman for the Church after Pentecost, though afterwards the leadership passed to James, brother of Jesus (Acts 15:13). The keys promised by Jesus were symbolic of authority. By his preaching Peter would open the door to the Kingdom of God to many.

"The Son is the radiance of God's glory and the exact representation of his being, sustaining all things by his powerful word. After he had provided purification for sins, he sat down at the right hand of the Majesty in heaven ..." (Heb. 1:3).

PETER

Simon Peter was the natural leader of the 12 disciples and one of three Jesus took everywhere with Him. He was a fisherman from Bethsaida and lived at Capernaum. He became known as Peter – or Cephas – because that was the new name the Lord gave him. It means "rock". A leader of the early Christians after Jesus' resurrection, he finally went to Rome where, according to tradition, he was crucified upside down. He died about AD 64 during the persecution by Nero. His symbol is a pair of keys (see Matt. 16:16–20).

Write a short biography of Peter from: Luke 5:1–11; Mark 3:16; Matt. 14:22–33; 16:13–23; Matt. 17:1–8; John 18:1–11; Luke 22:54–62; John 20:1–10; 21:1–19; Acts 1:15–26; 2:14–43; 3:1–11; 4:1–22; 8:14–24; 9:32–35; 36–43; 10:1–48; 12:1–17.

STUDY
The foundation of the Church (1 Cor. 3:11; Eph. 2:20; Rev. 21:14). Further study of this passage with a good commentary would be very rewarding – there is so much more in it!

The way ahead

**Matthew 16:21–23;
Mark 8:31– 33; Luke 9:22**

Having become certain of their Master's identity, it was important that they learned the true nature of Jesus' mission on earth. The Jewish conception of their Messiah as a king coming to overthrow their natural enemies was far from the truth.

"..he must ... after three days rise again"

Jesus has a heavenly kingdom, and by His death and resurrection, would overthrow the spiritual enemy of the kingdom, Satan.

Matthew uses the work "explain" (16:21) and Mark "teach" (8:31). The preparation for Calvary had begun. Jesus was to speak of His death many times after that, patiently teaching the disciples that what was going to happen would not be a mistake, but was pre-planned. The disciples, however, did not want to accept what Jesus was saying, so they were slow to learn. How like us!

There are parts of God's Word that we readily accept – the blessings, the encouragements, the love. But what about the persecution, suffering, self-denial and fasting? Peter, in particular, could not bear to hear of his beloved Master dying. What a contrast between Jesus' commendation of Peter and His rebuke! His spiritual revelation was commended, but his fleshly thoughts were rebuked.

"Jesus answered them, 'Destroy this temple, and I will raise it again in three days' " (John 2:19).

**✎ COMPARE
Romans 7:18 and 8:6 & 10.**

Self-denial

**Matthew 16:24–28; Mark
8:34–38; Luke 9:23–27**

It was hard for the disciples to grasp that Jesus was going to suffer and die. It was equally hard for them to understand the concept of complete self-sacrifice of themselves.

We, looking back on Calvary, can understand. Try to imagine what it was like for those men still hoping to see Jesus triumphantly reigning in Jerusalem during their lifetime.

"... he must ... ke up his cross nd follow me"

To "take up" his cross (Mark 8:34) has a stronger meaning than in Matthew 10:38 – it implies a lifting up on high for everyone to see. Our willingness for self-denial and complete submission to God's will must include willingness for public humiliation, persecution, suffering even unto death for His sake. The expression, "Everyone has a cross to bear" is often misconstrued. A cross means death – death to the old life, death to self.

Jesus then spoke for the first time of His Second Coming and again of the rewards we will receive from Him. What we give up for His sake is nothing compared with what we gain.

"I have been crucified with Christ and I no longer live, but Christ lives in me. The life I live in the body, I live by faith in the Son of God, who loved me and gave himself for me" (Gal. 2:20).

**▮ ACTION
Ask the Lord to show you any areas of your life which you have not allowed the Cross to touch – and then surrender them.**

DAY 156

Transfigured
Matthew 17:1–8; Mark 9:2–8; Luke 9:28–36

It was quite an amazing sight that greeted Peter, John and James after Jesus had singled them out a second time (see Mark 5:37), and taken them up the mountain at night to pray. Luke muses (v. 32) on what the disciples would have missed if they had succumbed to sleep! But he is at pains to explain that they were fully awake and certainly did not dream the experience.

"Get up ... Don't be afraid"

It may have been that the disciples' faith was beginning to waver after Jesus' teaching about His suffering and death, and they were allowed to see His glory to restore their confidence in Him. The face that Moses and Elijah – representing the law and the prophets – were speaking of Jesus' forthcoming death proved that it was planned from the beginning. It was not to be an accident or a mistake.

Voluble Peter said the first thing that came into his head – to put up shelters or tabernacles was a sign of respect to distinguished people. What a tremendous privilege, to see the glory of the Lord, to hear the voice of the Father, and yet they were forbidden to speak of it! God trusted them. He still needs people whom He can trust.

"There is no fear in love. But perfect love drives out fear, because fear has to do with punishment. The one who fears is not made perfect in love" (1 John 4:18).

■ COMPARE
The transfiguration with Exodus 24:15, 33:9, 40:34; Luke 3:22.

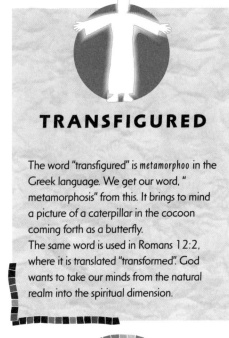

TRANSFIGURED

The word "transfigured" is *metamorphoo* in the Greek language. We get our word, " metamorphosis" from this. It brings to mind a picture of a caterpillar in the cocoon coming forth as a butterfly.
The same word is used in Romans 12:2, where it is translated "transformed". God wants to take our minds from the natural realm into the spiritual dimension.

DAY 157

Moving on
Matthew 17:9–13; Mark 9:9–13

The disciples had learned much in their course at Jesus' training college. They were firm in their belief that He was the promised Messiah.

That belief had been tested when He began to speak of His forthcoming suffering and death. The idea was completely contrary to their original concept of a Messiah. Peter, James and John had then seen Him transfigured in glory and received confirmation from the Father Himself that this was indeed His Son. Now they were ready for further teaching on a deeper level.

They wanted to understand, to relate

"... the Son o Man is goin to suffer ..

Jesus to the teaching of the law and the prophets. We, like the disciples, will receive both testing and encouragement from the Lord as we walk with Him. He will give deeper teaching and understanding as we are able to receive it.

Jesus used Malachi 4:5 & 6 to take them to this deeper level. Elijah had come in the person of John the Baptist but, because the Jewish leaders didn't recognise him, the way had been opened for his rejection, arrest and execution by Herod Antipas. So it was with Jesus, the Messiah, whom John had been sent to prepare the way for. He, too, went unrecognised, was rejected and put to death. But Jesus knew this – nothing ever takes God by surprise.

"He was despised and rejected by men, a man of sorrows, and familiar with suffering. Like one from whom men hide their faces he was despised, and we esteemed him not" (Isa. 53:3).

THOUGHT
To have suffered much is like knowing many languages. It gives the sufferer access to many more people.

....

DAY 158

Sorting it all out
Matthew 17:14–21; Mark 9:14–29; Luke 9:37–43

Mark hints (v. 15) that some of the glory of the transfiguration was still evident in Jesus' appearance as He came down the mountain (compare with Exodus 34:29). That was in stark contrast to down below – there scribes were arguing with the crowd, disciples were frustrated, an epileptic boy was unhealed

... you can say to this mountain, 'Move ...' "

and his father at the end of his tether.

Jesus rebuked His followers for their lack of faith. Then He rebuked the demon – and it left. Jesus can sort out any situation. We tend to try in our own strength, get discouraged and frustrated, lose the faith that we had and the enemy appears to triumph. But when we turn the difficulty over to Jesus and leave go of the controls, He has the victory.

God loves an honest confession and asks only for our willingness (Mark 9:24). Driving out demons is not easy and Jesus teaches the disciples a further lesson. They had received authority to do so, but they also had to learn the necessity of constant prayer, a life totally in submission to God. Then the devil would not be allowed any possible foothold in their lives.

"Every valley shall be raised up, every mountain and hill made low; the rough ground shall become level, the rugged places a plain" (Isa. 40:4).

MY CONFESSION
Lord, so often I feel weak and helpless. I confess my weakness to You and declare, with the apostle Paul, that I can do all things through Christ who strengthens me.

*Men don't believe in the devil now, as their fathers used to do;
They reject one creed because it's old for another because it's new;
But who dogs the steps of the toiling saint, who spreads the net for his feet,
Who sows the tares in the world's broad fields, where the Saviour sows His wheat.
They may say the devil has never lived, they may say the devil has gone,
But simple people would like to know —
who carries his business on?*

Preparing for the Cross

Matthew 17:22-23; Mark 9:30-32; Luke 9:44-45

Jesus had twice mentioned His rising from the dead. He had spoken of Jonah to the scribes and Pharisees (Matt. 12:39-42). He told Peter, James and John as they were coming down the mountain.

"... he will be raised ..."

Now He tells all 12 disciples together. But they didn't understand and were afraid to question Him. They were used to asking and having their questions answered by Jesus, but this time not even Peter opened his mouth.

Perhaps they had a sense of foreboding about the future, and didn't really want to know the worst. Matthew tells us they were filled with grief. It was a time of intensive teaching for them as Jesus walked with them back through Galilee to Capernaum and prepared for His final journey to Jerusalem. He needed time alone with the to prepare them for what was to come.

There is a sense of loneliness about Jesu during this time. Even though He was in constant communion with His heavenly Father, humanly speaking He needed friends who would love and support Him through the difficult time ahead. But the disciples didn't understand – they were incapable of helping Him. We all face diff culties and loneliness at times. It is a comfort to know that, as we go through these experiences, we can seek comfort from On who has known depths deeper than we ca ever reach.

"Praise be to the God and Father of our Lord Jesus Christ! In his great mercy he has given us new birth into a living hop through the resurrection of Jesus Christ from the dead" (1 Pet. 1:3).

▌ ACTION
How can we encourage those who are going through difficult times? Do it today!

The tax lesson

Matthew 17:24-27

Every Jew over 19 years old was expected to pay an annual tax to the temple for the upkeep of its services. The amount, a Jewish half-shekel, was equivalent to the Greek 2 drachma. As the 2 drachma coin was rare in Jesus' time, it must have been usual for two people to get together and pay with the common 4 drachma coin. Jesus, hearing about the tax collectors' request to Peter, used the opportunity to teach an important lesson.

"What do you think ...?"

The Son of God is Lord of the temple and as such, exempt from taxes, together with His followers. Rather than offend, however, He sends Peter for the money. Where a principle is at stake we should be absolutely uncompromising, yet we should not offend unnecessarily.

There may be laws and customs that, as Christians, we have freedom to ignore. Yet if we follow Jesus' example, we will obey them. When I take my Bible into a Muslim household I will cover it with a cloth and be careful never to place it on the floor, for this will offend them. But I will not bow down to their or any other gods.

"... Then he said to them, 'Give to Caesar what is Caesar's, and to God what is God's' " (Matt. 22:21).

▌ LOOK UP
For a similar circumstance see Acts 16:1-3.

Humility needed

Matthew 18:1–5; Mark 9:33–37; Luke 9:46–48

The argument about who was the greatest probably started as a result of the selection of Peter, James and John to go with Jesus up the mountain, plus the evident emergence of Peter as leader among the disciples.

"... whoever humbles himself ..."

Jesus took the child and told the quarrelling disciples that if they didn't have a complete turnaround in their lives, a willingness to repent and become utterly submissive to their Father God, they would never enter the Kingdom of Heaven.

Strong words! We need to be continuously childlike in our relationship with God, humble, totally dependent on Him, and willing to take the lowest place. Jesus loves children, and He still longs for them to be welcomed into the Church fellowship, taught and made to feel at home.

Only one who is humble can get alongside children. They will not respond to arrogance or one-upmanship. Pray for leaders, youth leaders, midweek children's clubs, and above all, parents.

"The greatest among you will be your servant" (Matt. 23:11).

◀ EXAMINE
Look at Philippians 2:5–8. Is the humility Christ displayed apparent in your life?

Sin destroys!

Matthew 18:6–9; Mark 9:42–50

Jesus felt strongly about people who would trip up or hinder believing children, which is why He did not mince His words.

The millstone He referred to was a large one driven by an ass, not a small handmill. Let us be very careful how we speak or behave towards, and in front of, children. There is so much in the world these days to lead them astray. Moral values have plummeted, with violence, occultism, blasphemy and sexual immorality littered over TV, books and comics. Our children need our uncompromising example, teaching and love to keep them safe and secure.

"Woe ..."

Jesus then turned His attention in even stronger language to the believer himself. Hand, foot and eye are symbols of action, conduct and desire. The eye may be used for scorn or for lustful desire. The language is pictorial, but the message is clear: we should cut off our sinful thoughts and desires before they come to birth as sin, harming both ourselves and others.

Gehenna is the local form of the name of the valley near Jerusalem where the city refuse was burnt. Jesus gives a picture of the everlasting unquenchable fire of hell which is the final destination of those who have sinned.

"Then they will go away to eternal punishment, but the righteous to eternal life" (Matt. 25:46).

▼ THOUGHT
Sin is a clenched fist shaken in the face of a loving God.

DAY 163

The lost sheep
Matthew 18:10–14

With the little child still standing amongst them, Jesus told the parable of the lost sheep to teach that we should not look down on children and that we should be just as concerned as our heavenly Father is that none of them should be lost.

"... your Father ... is not willing that any ... should be lost"

The world today is a difficult place for children and young people. At school they are subjected to humanistic teaching and asked to take part in religious festivals of other faiths. Growing up in an atmosphere of divorce, one-parent families and step-parents, they suffer rejection and insecurity. They come across drugs, sex, violence and the occult. So unless they are firmly rooted and grounded in Christ, it is very difficult for them to say "No" to these things.

Christian children are mocked and persecuted at school as never before. Our heavenly Father is not willing for any of them to be lost. If you have contact with children, be diligent in prayer for them, set them an example, feed them with the Word of God and, above all, love them as your Father does.

"Jesus said, 'Let the little children come to me, and do not hinder them, for the kingdom of heaven belongs to such as these' " (Matt. 19:14).

■ **ACTION**
Make a list of the children you are in contact with, then pray for them today and regularly.

DAY 164

On the same side
Mark 9:38–41; Luke 9:49–50

John was strongly rebuked by Jesus for hindering a man who was working in Jesus' name against the powers of darkness.

"... in my name ..."

We need to be very careful not to criticise or hinder in any way people from other churches with different ways of worship, different methods, different ways of looking at things from ourselves. Jesus said, "By their fruits you shall know them."

The man in this passage was successful in driving out demons in Jesus' name. He was being fruitful for Christ – in contrast to the seven sons of Sceva, who were taking Jesus' name in vain and the evil spirit overpowered them (Acts 19:13–16).

Let us not judge other Christians, but pray for one another, have fellowship where we can, combine together with other churches for prayer, outreach and celebration. Let's encourage those who are struggling and draw strength from those who are stronger than ourselves. Jesus prayed that we might be one as He and the Father are one. Paul proclaimed that we are all one in Christ Jesus (Gal. 3:26–29). Let's play our part in maintaining the unity of Christ's Body.

"And I will do whatever you ask in my name, so that the Son may bring glory to the Father" (John 14:13).

◤ **STUDY**
1 Cor 1:11–18. What was the Corinthians' problem?

Forgiveness and prayer

Matthew 18:15-20

We maintain our unity in Christ by being open with one another, not allowing resentments and hurts to build up and cause division. If a small drop of water in a crevasse freezes, it will crack the rock.

... there am with them"

Warmth will disperse the water – coldness causes it to freeze. Jesus gave very practical teaching about sin between brothers. Read verse 15 again with Proverbs 9:8 & 9. Make sure, if you are on the receiving end of a rebuke, that you are wise. If you are on the giving end, be careful to be warm and loving.

The authority already given to Peter (16:19) is extended to all the disciples in verse 18 of this passage. Sandwiched between the instructions about sin in the Church and the assurance in verse 20, it emphasises the authority of a company of believers with Christ in the midst.

One of the greatest promises recorded about prayer in the Gospels comes in verse 19. The requirements are that the two or more are met in Jesus' Name, and that they are in perfect agreement. That's why it is invaluable to meet regularly for prayer with someone you know well.

"For if you forgive men when they sin against you, your heavenly Father will also forgive you" (Matt. 6:14).

◢ QUESTION
What other requirements are there for answered prayer? 1 John 5:14; James 1:6; 5:16.

Unforgiveness

Matthew 18:21-35

An unforgiving heart is a desperately sick condition. When Jesus said we must forgive seventy-seven, or seventy times seven, He meant "always." The contrast between the two debts in the parable is vast: millions of pounds compared with about £3.

... seventy-seven times "

The debt I owe to Jesus, who suffered and died on the Cross, giving His life as a ransom for my sin, is a debt that can never be repaid. He has totally wiped out my sin and let me go free. How can I possibly, then, not forgive the far more trivial, or even imaginary, sins of my brothers and sisters towards me?

An unforgiving spirit raises a barrier between us and God, causing hardness of heart, lack of peace and joy, and a gradual falling away from the Lord. How sad it is to see Christians in this state. Far more serious is the punishment to be received from the Father.

"Be kind and compassionate to one another, forgiving each other, just as in Christ God forgave you" (Eph.4:32).

▼ EXAMINE
Search your heart – is there any unforgiveness in you towards anyone?

FORGIVENESS

"He who cannot forgive others breaks the bridge over which he must pass himself.   **George Herbert**
"Doing an injury puts you below your enemy; revenging one makes you but even with him; forgiving it sets you above him."   **Benjamin Franklin**
"Forgiveness is man's deepest need and highest achievement."   **Horace Bushnell**
"Forgive and forget. When you bury a mad dog, don't leave his tail above the ground."   **Charles Spurgeon**
"Forgiveness is more than the remission of penalty; it should mean the restoration of a broken fellowship."   **(Unknown)**

Not the fiery way
Luke 9:51–56

Jesus had been welcomed when He had travelled through Samaria previously (John 4:40, 41). Now, because He was heading towards Jerusalem instead of away from it, His presence **"... the Son of** aroused the old animosity **Man did not** and rivalry between Samaritan and Jew.

come to James and John lived up **destroy ..."** to their nickname, "Sons of thunder," by making their fiery suggestion, only to be rebuked by Jesus.

No doubt hurt by the discourtesy and inhospitality shown by the Samaritans towards their beloved Master, they react-

ed in completely the wrong way. Belligerence and vengeance are not acceptable ways of winning people to Christ, however provoked or deserved those reactions may be.

Solomon said, "A gentle answer turns away wrath, but a harsh word stirs up anger" (Prov. 15:1). God says, "It is mine to avenge; I will repay" (Deut. 32:35).

Jesus will judge in due time and all will receive their just rewards. It is not for us to avenge even insults to Jesus, whom we love.

"The thief comes only to steal and kill and destroy; I have come that they may have life, and have it to the full" (John 10:10).

■STUDY
Look up Acts 8:14–17. It is good to read of John's opportunity to bless the Samaritans some time afterwards.

At the feast
John 7:1–13

The Feast of Tabernacles, in September or October, commemorated the Israelites' journey through the wilderness and was also cele-**"The right** brated as a harvest **time for me** thanksgiving.

has not yet The people made booths of branches and **come ..."** lived in them during the seven-day event. Many travelled from all parts of Judea to celebrate in Jerusalem. Jesus' brothers encouraged Him to go because they did not believe Him to be the Messiah and probably felt if He did demonstrate His powers in Jerusalem it would help to prove His identity and authenticity.

Jesus, however, never rose to the bait

of "proving" Himself in public. His crucifixion was six months away, so He, wisely, did not want to place Himself at the mercy of the Jewish leaders before the time appointed by His Father. He travelled privately to Jerusalem, not with the public caravan.

Notice the different atmosphere. In Galilee the news of Jesus' presence had been proclaimed publicly and crowds gathered openly, but in Jerusalem they whispered about Him because they feared the Jewish leaders. The events at Pentecost changed all this (Acts 2:14). Fear went out of the window and Jesus' name was proclaimed boldly in the power of the Holy Spirit.

"... and Jesus ... looked towards heaven and prayed: 'Father, the time has come. Glorify your Son, that your Son may glorify you ...' " (John 17:1).

▌QUESTION
What dispels our fear of speaking openly for Jesus?

The real Bible teacher

John 7:14–24

Congregations had been astonished at the authority in Jesus' teaching at Capernaum (Mark 1:22) and Nazareth (Mark 6:2). Now, right in the temple at Jerusalem where the most learned rabbis taught, the Jewish leaders themselves were amazed at His teaching, especially as He had not attended a rabbinical school. Jesus was quick to disclaim any self-glory – He had been sent from God, and His teaching came direct from the heavenly Father.

"Stop judging by mere appearances ..."

Theological colleges, Bible Schools and religious instruction can be valuable teaching and training, but unless we allow the Holy Spirit to illuminate and interpret the Scriptures to us it will be of little value. It is vital, too, to put into practice what we learn so that we fulfil God's will in our lives. Otherwise our learning will be mere head knowledge and lacking in authority.

The miracle that Jesus referred to (v. 21) was the healing of the man at the Pool of Bethesda (John 5:1–15). The Jews had rebuked the healed man for carrying his bed on the Sabbath. Jesus gave them irrefutable evidence on their own legalistic terms to show how ridiculous their judgement was. If we are in tune with the Holy Spirit, we will "demolish arguments and every pretension that sets itself up against the knowledge of God" (2 Cor. 10:5).

"But when he, the Spirit of truth, comes, he will guide you into all truth. He will not speak on his own; he will speak only what he hears, and he will tell you what is yet to come" (John 16:13).

✦ PRAYER

Come, Holy Spirit, Teach me, that I might know the hidden treasures of the Father's heart. Amen.

Seen but unknown

John 7:25–36

No wonder the people were bewildered! Here was a Man whom the Jewish leaders were trying to kill because, supposedly, He was a blasphemer. Yet He was speaking openly in the temple, not only teaching the common people, but opposing with authority the rulers themselves. Perhaps the rulers really knew that He was the Christ. Yet Jesus came from Galilee and the Messiah was expected to come suddenly from an unknown place. On the other hand, Jesus had performed so many miracles

"... he sent me"

that it was hard to conceive of the "real" Messiah doing more. It was all very confusing.

The key to the confusion lies in verse 28, "You do not know him [the Father]". The people did not know their God. How sad that is. God had revealed Himself to His people through the law and the prophets, signs and miracles, His protection and His just punishment ever since Adam, and yet they still didn't know Him and did not recognise the One sent from Him, Jesus, the Messiah.

There is only one key to knowing God – faith. We will never understand Him completely in this life, but by faith we can accept Him. Only then will He open our eyes to see Him.

"And without faith it is impossible to please God, because anyone who

comes to him must believe that he exists and that he rewards those who earnestly seek him" (Heb. 11:6).

The water of life
John 7:37–39

"How many of you are thirsty for Jesus?" a preacher once asked a large congregation. Practically every hand was raised. "Then there is something wrong with you," he responded. "Jesus said, 'Come to Me and drink.' Why haven't you done that?" During the Feast of Tabernacles, water from the Pool of Siloam was poured out each day from a golden vessel to commemorate the provision of water for the children of Israel in the wilderness. Jesus proclaimed Himself to be the water of life (see also

"If anyone is thirsty, let him come to me ..."

John 4:13–14), and everyone who drinks from Him will himself become a source of that same life-giving water.

As you grow in Christ you will give as well as receive. Any pool of water that has no outlet becomes stagnant. Christians are not meant to be stagnant ponds, but clear channels for the life-giving Spirit.

The Holy Spirit was poured out at Pentecost for every believer. He will fill your life day by day if you ask Him. As you receive, you will give to others, and receive again more and more abundantly.

"Everyone who ... drinks the water I give him will never thirst. Indeed, the water I give him will become in him a spring of water welling up to eternal life" (John 4:13, 14).

■ COMPARE
Isaiah 12:3; Zechariah 13:1; 1 Cor. 10:4.

No one like Him
John 7:40–44

Jesus is indeed the "prophet" spoken of by Moses in Deuteronomy 18:15, as Peter confirmed later (Acts 3:22). He is also the Christ. It was also true that the Christ was to come from Bethlehem, born of David's line and not from Galilee, where the people supposed that Jesus was born. So everybody was right – and yet there was still division and confusion. Head knowledge is not enough. The only way to recognise Jesus for whom He is, is by direct revela-

"He is the Christ"

tion from the Father, by the Holy Spirit (Matt. 16:17). The same is just as true today as it was when Jesus lived on the earth.

From the bewilderment of the crowd John then turns to the frustration of the Pharisees. Their own temple guards refused to arrest Jesus, saying they'd never met anyone like Him before. It must have been an amusing situation for onlookers! That's so true, for no-one ever has or ever will meet anyone like Jesus.

Jesus is unique, the one and only true Son of God. He is wonderful, majestic, compassionate, authoritative, kind, stern, loving – praise Him! Nothing and no one could touch Him until the time appointed by His Father to go to the Cross to fulfil His purpose to redeem mankind from slavery to sin.

"For by him all things were created: things in heaven and on earth, visible and invisible, whether thrones or powers or rulers or authorities; all things were created by him and for him" (Col. 1:16).

MEDITATE
Our times are in His hands (Eccl. 3:1–8).

DAY 173

The trap which failed
John 8:1–11

The gaiety and joyfulness of the Feast of Tabernacles, the crowds and the freedom of living in booths rather than houses probably lent itself to licentious behaviour. This woman had been caught.

"... neither do I condemn you" However, it was not her sin that concerned the self-righteous Pharisees, but the opportunity to set a legal trap for Jesus.

Under Roman law it was illegal for any other than the Roman authority to pronounce a death sentence. Stoning those who had committed adultery had long since fallen into disuse. What was Jesus to do? If He upheld the law of Moses He would be challenging the Roman authority. If He didn't, He would be denying His own words (Matt. 5:17, 27, 28).

In His infinite wisdom, Jesus removed the problem from its legal setting and placed it in its right perspective – the moral one. His words hit home to the hypocritical hearts of the accusers and they melted away. The fact that the woman stayed indicated her willingness to repent. She, too, could have walked away, but she remained with Jesus – and He did not condemn her. I'm sure she never sinned in that way again. We can rejoice if we heed the apostle John's words (1 Jn. 1:9): "If we confess our sins, he is faithful and just and will forgive us our sins and purify us from all unrighteousness."

"This then is how ... we set our hearts at rest in his presence whenever our hearts condemn us. For God is greater than our hearts, and he knows everything" (1 John 3:19, 20).

STUDY
Look up 1 John 3:17–18; Rom. 8:1. What condemns?

DAY 174

Rushing into judgments
John 8:12–20

The contrast between Jesus and the Pharisees is striking. Jesus is the Light of the world. He knew exactly who He was, where He came from and where He was going to. He was absolutely clear about His mission on earth and commission from the Father. He was clear-cut in His judgments.

"... my testimony valid ..."

The Pharisees, on the other hand, were walking in darkness and muddled in their thinking, even about their own laws. They did not know the Father and they did not know who Jesus was. Yet they condemned Him. Pure wisdom can only come from God – we should never make a presumptuous judgment or make a decision from our own human understanding, which can only be superficial.

This principle applies both to our own lives, and even more importantly, when counselling others.

"This is my Son, whom I love; with him I am well pleased. Listen to him!" (Matt. 17:5).

QUESTION
How can we assess judgment? James 3:13–17.

Door to heaven
John 8:21-30

Faith in Jesus opens the door of heaven to every believer. Unbelief, lack of recognition of who He is, closes the door. Jesus' statement to the Jewish leaders, "Where I go you cannot come," must have been said with great sadness.

"... I always do what pleases him"

Jesus loved those men. He longed for them to recognise Him, to repent and believe in Him. But they were too hard, too entrenched in their own beliefs and laws.

We meet people like that from time to time, so let us learn from Jesus how to deal with them. He did not use clever arguments, but continued very simply on the same theme. He spoke humbly, directing their attention beyond Himself to the Father. He was absolutely clear in what He believed, but He did not get angry with their stubbornness.

A teenage girl who had been a Christian for two weeks once met a very intellectual man who had been arguing against Christianity for years. He knew the Bible very well – she knew about three verses. She countered every argument that he brought up with: "I'm sorry, I don't know about that, but what I do know is ..." That man received Christ as a result.

"It is written: 'I believed; therefore I have spoken.' With that same spirit of faith we also believe and therefore speak, because we know that the one who raised the Lord Jesus from the dead will also raise us with Jesus ..." (2 Cor. 4:13, 14).

■ **ENCOURAGEMENT**
Let verse 30 increase your faith in the power of the spoken word of God.

True freedom
John 8:31-38

The first time I really grasped the truth that "if the Son sets you free, you will be free indeed," I felt like shouting it from the house-tops. Jesus really sets us free from the slavery to sin! Do you know the reality of that statement?

"... you will know the truth ..."

Before accepting salvation from Jesus a person cannot help sinning. He is a sinner, born into sin, right in Satan's domain. After accepting Jesus' sacrifice on the Cross and committing one's life completely to Him, the prison doors are open, the shackles broken and we are completely free. That is not to say that we never sin again. We can choose to sin if we wish, but we can also choose not to (see 1 Cor. 10:13). Satan has no further right to our lives and no power over us.

The picture in this passage is of the son of a household buying a slave and then setting him free. A price has to be paid for a slave. The Son of God paid the price for you with His own life, so that you are no longer a slave but a member of the family, a child of God with all the rights and privileges that status gives. Enjoy your freedom and give Him thanks.

"Therefore, there is now no condemnation for those who are in Christ Jesus, because through Christ Jesus the law of the Spirit of life set me free from the law of sin and death" (Rom. 8:1,2).

▮ **REJOICE**
Meditate on Galatians 5:1.

DAY 177

Their greatest need
John 8:39–41

A disciple follows the teaching of his master and a son takes after his father, taught Jesus. The Jews neither followed the truth that Jesus declared, nor did they take after their father Abraham.

"... you are determined to kill me ..."

Jesus implied, therefore, that their father was the devil. They didn't understand that they needed to be set free – they were thinking of political slavery.

Although they had been under oppression from Babylon, Egypt, Persia and Rome, they had not submitted to slavery since Moses led them out of Egypt towards the Promised Land. In their opinion, they were children of Abraham and, therefore, free.

Many people rely on family tradition, national religion, ceremonies and rites or moral goodness to save them. But these things only serve to blind them to the truth – that their greatest need is salvation through Jesus. Only those who can see their need will accept the truth. The Jewish leaders thought they were children of God – but they were not. Doesn't this create an even greater longing in your heart for neighbours, relatives and friends to see the truth that can only be found through accepting Jesus and His salvation?

"He came to that which was his own, but his own did not receive him" (John 1:11).

PRAY
Read Acts 4:12 and pray for those you know who look elsewhere for salvation.

DAY 178

Only two sides
John 8:42–47

After implying that the unbelieving Jews were children of the devil, Jesus now spells it out. If they were children of God, then they would love the Son of God. But they did not, so they must be on the other side. There are only two families on earth – God's family and the devil's. We all belong to one or the other.

"... he is a liar ..."

There is no middle road. We are either slaves of the devil or sons of God. If you recognise this fact and let it sink deep down in your heart you will be far more diligent in obeying Jesus' command, "Go into all the world and preach the good news ..." (Mark 16:15).

Jesus described the devil as a murderer and a liar. He was responsible for the death of Abel (Gen. 4:8) and for every murder since then. He cannot tell the truth – it is not his nature. He takes truth and twists it, bringing out little bits of truth in the wrong context so that they are, in fact, lies. But Jesus is the Truth. All His words are true and He would never deceive us. Will you tell your neighbours that? Will you help them to hear what God says?

"Submit yourselves, then, to God. Resist the devil, and he will flee from you" (James 4:7).

MEDITATE
Ponder on Acts 5:40–42.

DAY 179
Staying cool
John 8:48–59

It's marvellous how Jesus kept His temper and humility in the face of the lies and insults that were being hurled at Him! It must have so frustrating for Him that these people, who believed themselves to be sons of God, could not and would not accept the truth that He was telling them.

Our Lord showed no anger and no impatience. He continued to show them the truth and to glorify His Father rather than Himself. He did not reply with soothing words, softening the truth, but followed through with logical arguments, parrying their lies with deeper truths.

"... before Abraham was born, I am!"

There was a rabbinical tradition that when God made His covenant with Abraham (Gen. 15:17–18), Abraham had a vision of the coming of the Messiah. Although not in Scripture, it was probably this that Jesus was referring to in verse 56. God had a very special relationship with Abraham, and Jesus speaks of him as if He, too, knows him well. When He said, "Before Abraham was born, I am" it was the last straw for the Jews. They began to stone Him as a blasphemer. Yet nothing could thwart Him from carrying on to His appointment at Calvary.

"I am the Alpha and Omega, the First and the Last, the Beginning and the End" (Rev. 22:13).

STUDY
Hebrews 11:8, 10, 39 & 40.

SAMARIA

Jesus travelled south through Samaria. This was the direct route from Galilee in the north to Judea in the south, but very few Jews went that way. They took the longer route by the River Jordan. For centuries there had been enmity between the Jews and the Samaritans. No good Jew would have anything to do with them, if he could avoid it.

This friction emanated from the time when the kingdom was divided into Judea and Samaria under Jeroboam. The Samaritans, or northern kingdom, intermarried with other local communities, and were not, therefore, accepted as pure Jews. They also intermingled their religious beliefs and did not stick strictly to the Jewish faith as did the southern kingdom of Judah.

Jesus was rejected by the people of one village, but at another He healed ten lepers. Only one came back to say "thank you", and he was a Samaritan.

Jesus had travelled through Samaria at least once before. He had sat and talked with a Samaritan woman at Jacob's Well, which can still be seen today.

DAY 180
Pressing on
Matthew 8:19–22; Luke 9:57–62

Contrast the excuses of those would-be followers of Jesus with our Lord's own attitude (Luke 9:51): "Jesus *resolutely* set out for Jerusalem." Jesus was aware that, for Him, Jerusalem spelt death, yet He did not falter in His determination to go there.

"Follow me ..."

We cannot make feeble excuses for our lack of commitment, apathy, laziness and worldliness when He gave everything for us.

He suffered not only physically, but

spiritually because the weight of sin upon Him on the Cross separated Him from His Father. Following Jesus means trusting Him for the necessities of life, leaving home if He calls us to, putting Him before home and family. It takes determination, courage and single-mindedness. I cannot summon up these attitudes from my own human resources, but I can set my will to follow Jesus. All He asks is a willingness. He will do the rest.

Now you are almost halfway through the year with the Life of Christ, are you determined to finish the course? Pray for Christians who are experiencing difficulties.

"Then Jesus said to his disciples, 'If anyone would come after me, he must deny himself and take up his cross and follow me' " (Matt. 16:24).

◢ QUESTION
Look up Phil 3:8. What was Paul's attitude?

Spreading the Good News
Luke 10:1–16

The 72 were sent out with the same instructions as the 12 (Luke 9:1–6). Jesus' time was now growing short, so there were more of them to spread the news of His coming more widely and more quickly.

"Peace to this house"

There is an air of urgency about the commission: "Do not greet anyone on the road." Eastern greetings were polite, formal and very long. "Do not move around from house to house": they were not to waste time accepting everybody's hospitality. Neither were they to waste time in cities that did not want the news they brought. One of Satan's ploys against Christians

is time-wasting. We need to be very sure of our Father's will for us so that we don't spend time on good works that He hasn't called us to do.

Nevertheless, the instructions were to tell even those who didn't want to know that the Kingdom of God was near (v. 11). Everyone should have an opportunity of accepting or rejecting Jesus. We can often give a short word, even a single sentence, to someone we meet in the street where a long testimony would not be appropriate or acceptable.

"Therefore do not be foolish, but understand what the Lord's will is" (Eph. 5:17).

■ EXAMINE
Sit down for a few minutes today and evaluate your use of time. Then ask yourself how much time is spent for the Master.

Joyful return
Luke 10:17–20

There is joy in going out to preach the Gospel! This writer can testify of going out every other Sunday evening with the church fellowship on to a large housing

estate. After praising God in song in the open air half the group went in pairs to knock on doors and tell people about Jesus while the other half continued praising God.

On returning to church afterwards the joyful praise and worship almost raised the roof. Some people responded to the message we brought, others rejected it. But the exultant joy of being witnesses continued.

Jesus, however, gave a timely warning to His enthusiastic disciples. Rejoicing in success can lead to pride, so our joy should spring only from the fact that we are His forever – His obedient people. We go out and reap at His command, but the harvest is His – not ours. Demons are subject to us because of the authority that Jesus gives us. They tremble and flee at the name of Jesus – not our names.

"... your names are written in heaven"

Rejoice today that your name is written in heaven, with indelible ink: permanent, irremovable.

"Him who overcomes I will make a pillar in the temple of my God ... I will write on him the name of my God and the name of the city of my God, the new Jerusalem, which is coming down out of heaven from my God; I will also write on him my new name" (Rev. 3:12).

■ **FOR STUDY**
Compare verse 18 with Isa. 14:12–15; Rom. 16:20; Rev. 20:10.

Rapturous welcome
Luke 10:21–24

Jesus was exultant. He rejoiced as He met His disciples when they returned from their mission and heard their reports of what they had done and seen. Those 72 men had realised who Jesus was and willingly obeyed His command to be His witnesses. The Greek verb translated "rejoiced" or "full of joy" (v. 21) is very strong, meaning "exultant" or "rapturous" joy.

"Blessed are the eyes that see ..."

The Lord still rejoices over each of His servants who go and preach the Gospel at His command. He rejoices over *you* every time you receive a fresh revelation from Him. He rejoices over every step of faith and obedient response, every word you speak for Him, every time you pray for a sick person to be healed or cast out a demon. He rejoices over childlike faith, over ears that hear His voice and hearts that love Him. Is He rejoicing over you today?

What a privilege it is to know and love Jesus, to understand, through the Holy Spirit, the things that are revealed to us about the Father.

"I have told you this so that my joy may be in you and that your joy may be complete" (John 15:11).

■ **PRAYER**
Lord Jesus, please forgive me for the times I have grieved You. I want to give You great joy today. Amen.

The right choice
Luke 10:25–37

A Christian friend offered to come and do some ironing and housework for me once, when I was pregnant, ill and unable to cope. I really looked forward to her visit, but that morning she 'phoned and said that she wasn't coming after all because she felt she should go to a prayer meeting instead. They would pray for me, she added.

It is so easy for us all to fall into the trap and be like the priest in Jesus' story who, hurrying down the road from

Jerusalem to Jericho, had no time to help the wounded man on the roadside.

I do not condemn my friend and have no resentment about the incident – we are still good friends! But it did make me think about my own attitudes when Christian meetings clashed with practicalities. Both are good – and necessary. How we need the Holy Spirit's guidance to discern God's priorities in any given situation!

"... he took pity on him"

God will test our love for Him by bringing to our notice helpless, unlovely, demanding and time-consuming people. It may be easy to give prayer time and money to help the needy, but it isn't so easy to give oneself. That, however, is what Jesus did.

"Finally, all of you, live in harmony with one another; be sympathetic, love as brothers, be compassionate and humble" (1 Pet. 3:8).

THOUGHT
A friend is one who comes in when others go out.

I cannot choose; I should have like so much
To sit at Jesus' feet – to feel the touch
Of His kind, gentle hand upon my head
While drinking in the gracious words He said.

And yet to serve Him! – Oh, divine employ –
To minister and give the Master joy,
To bathe in coolest springs His weary feet,
And wait upon Him while He sat at meat!

Worship or service – which! Ah, that is best
To which He calls us, be it toil or rest –
To labour for Him in life's busy stir,
Or seek His feet, a silent worshipper.

Caroline Atherton Mason

The day Martha snapped
Luke 10:38–42

What a contrast between two sisters! Martha and Mary lived at Bethany, about two miles from Jerusalem along the road to Jericho.

Their home was a hive of activity the day Jesus arrived. Martha, the practical one, was cleaning the house, making beds, preparing an elaborate meal – and getting thoroughly flustered. Mary, the quiet one, honoured their Guest by sitting at His feet and listening to Him.

"... one thing is needed"

Both women were doing what they considered right. Suddenly Martha snapped. She couldn't cope on her own any longer. Jesus must have been aware of the approaching crisis before, but He waited until Martha reached the end of her tether before calmly and wisely pointing out the truth of the situation.

God cannot help us if we are too busy to ask for help. One senses a previous tension in the relationship between the two sisters. If their relationship had been right they could have quickly prepared a simple meal together and then both sat at Jesus' feet. Ask yourself if you are too busy to spend sufficient time with Jesus? Take your tensions, anxieties and worries to Him and ask for His peace.

"Cast all you anxiety on him because he cares for you" (1 Pet. 5:7).

QUESTION
What was the better part Mary chose?

DAY 186

Healing priority
John 9:1-15

The blind man's condition was a priority case for Jesus. He was not prepared to discuss the doctrine of sin in relation to sickness with His disciples. He made one simple statement in answer to their question and then got on with the healing.

"... I am the light of the world"

Many people today ask, "If there is a God, why is there so much suffering in the world?" To Jesus, however, the important questions about suffering are not the "why's?" but, "What are we going to do about it?"

Jesus always has compassion for sick and suffering people. He is able to for- give their sin, comfort, heal and supply every need. Notice the individual attention that He gave to the blind man. Jesus did not have a *method* for healing – He has the *power* to heal.

The saliva, clay and the walking to the pool to wash were all, no doubt, an aid to the man's faith. Jesus' command and authority to heal, given to His disciples then, are still valid for Christians today. Take the authority and obey the command.

"The Spirit of the Lord is on me, because he has anointed me to preach good news to the poor. He has sent me to proclaim freedom for the prisoners and recovery of sight for the blind, to release the oppressed ..." (Luke 4:18).

■ MEDITATION
Mark 16:18b; Acts 28:8, 9.

DAY 187

Light and dark
John 9:16-41

The once-blind man was obviously intelligent and unafraid. See how his faith grew. He knew he was blind; he knew he could then see; he recognised Jesus as a prophet (v. 17); he acknowledged that He came from God (v. 33); he stood up to the Pharisees, boldly asserting his faith (v. 30); he worshipped Jesus, calling Him Lord (v. 38).

"One thing I do know. I was blind but now I see!"

Many Christians find that faith grows as they speak out for Jesus. Have you experienced that?

The Pharisees, in contrast, went steadily downhill during this incident. They quibbled over Jesus healing on the Sabbath (v. 14); some of them then refused to believe that a healing had taken place (v. 18); they accused Jesus of being a sinner (v. 24); they even scoffed at the healed man (v. 28); they threw him out of the synagogue (v. 34); they refused to acknowledge their own spiritual blindness (v. 40).

The essential difference was that the man knew he was blind while the Pharisees didn't. He received his sight, but for the Pharisees the darkness grew darker that day. When you recognise and confess a need, Jesus will answer. Never let pride stand in your way.

"He also told them this parable: 'Can a blind man lead a blind man? Will they not both fall into a pit?' " (Luke 6:39).

◆ FOR STUDY
Re-read the man's unanswerable argument (vv. 30–33) and also look at Prov. 2:6.

Your Journey with Jesus...

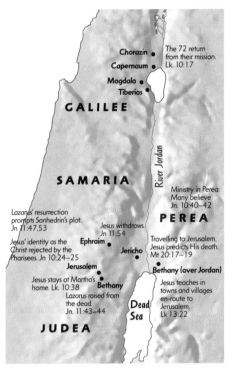

Chorazin
Capernaum
The 72 return from their mission. Lk. 10:17

Magdala
Tiberias

GALILEE

River Jordan

SAMARIA

Ministry in Perea: Many believe Jn. 10:40–42

Lazarus' resurrection prompts Sanhedrin's plot. Jn 11:47,53

PEREA

Jesus withdraws. Jn 11:54

Jesus' identity as the Christ rejected by the Pharisees. Jn 10:24–25

Ephraim

Jericho

Travelling to Jerusalem, Jesus predicts His death. Mt 20:17–19

Jerusalem

Jesus stays at Martha's home. Lk. 10:38

Bethany

Bethany (over Jordan)

Lazarus raised from the dead. Jn. 11:43–44

Jesus teaches in towns and villages en-route to Jerusalem. Lk 13:22

Dead Sea

JUDEA

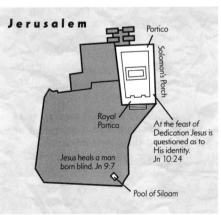

Jerusalem

Portico

Solomon's Porch

Royal Portico

At the feast of Dedication Jesus is questioned as to His identity. Jn 10:24

Jesus heals a man born blind. Jn 9:7

Pool of Siloam

Knowing Him
John 10:1–6

The shepherds gathering their sheep into a common fold each evening was a custom in the East. A hired watchman would then guard the sheep for the night. When the shepherds came to collect their sheep in the morning the watchman would recognise them and let them through.

"... they know his voice"

The sheep also recognised their own shepherd and followed him out of the fold. It was impossible for a thief to get past the watchman, and even if he had got in over the wall, the sheep wouldn't follow him.

The illustration is both a solemn warning and an encouragement. A warning to those who, like the Pharisees, try to lead God's children astray with false doctrines, legalism or unbelief. There are many such false cults and sects today.

For us, however, it is a beautiful picture of security. We, His sheep, His children, are fully safeguarded. Jesus is both the gate and the shepherd. No-one can steal us away from His care or lead us astray. If we listen to His voice we will never be deceived by anyone else.

"When he saw the crowds, he had compassion on them, because they were harassed and helpless, like sheep without a shepherd" (Matt. 9:36).

◢ THOUGHT
If you lie in bed at night and cannot sleep, talk to the Shepherd, don't count the sheep.

DAY 189

Giver of life
John 10:7-21

Jesus, our Shepherd, laid down His life on the Cross for you and me so that we can have the same fulness of life He has. There's a big difference between existence and life.

In biological terms, some of the characteristics of life are growth, respiration, movement, feeding and the ability to reproduce.

"I have come that they may have life ..."

Think about it in spiritual terms. A Christian should be growing in grace, becoming more mature daily. He or she should be constantly experiencing renewal by the Holy Spirit, moving on according to His directions, being fed and energised by the Word of God and adding to the Church by leading others into salvation. What's your spiritual life like?

Jesus gives a sense of purpose to life. He gives us joy and peace. Our lives should never be dull, but an exciting adventure with Him. Sometimes life will be tough, difficult to understand, at times sorrowful, sometimes joyful, but always bearing fruit. If you are not experiencing this fulness of life that Jesus offers, ask Him for it now.

"Jesus said to her, 'I am the resurrection and the life. He who believes in me will live, even though he dies' "(John 11:25).

▌ THOUGHT
Life with Christ is an endless hope. Without Him life is a hopeless end.

DAY 190

God in control
John 10:22-39

God's supreme control is so evident in this incident. Jesus' ministry on earth was nearing its end so He spoke about Himself more plainly to the Jewish leaders.

"... the Father is in me, and I in the Father"

His Messiahship had been clearly revealed to those who followed Him. Those who wanted to see had had their spiritual eyes opened already, but the leaders, although outwardly still questioning (v. 24), had already hardened their hearts toward Him (v. 26). So to them Jesus said again, "I and the Father are one." They tried to stone Him and seize Him but couldn't.

Nothing and no-one could touch Jesus until He voluntarily gave Himself into their hands.

The Feast of Dedication, or Hanukkah, commemorated the restoration of the temple services by Judas Maccabeus in 165 BC. Each evening of the eight-day feast the Jews lit lamps and put them in their houses and synagogues. Yet they didn't recognise the Light of the world as He walked among them. We must be wary of symbols replacing reality, even in our Christian worship. Are there any symbols, rituals or traditions that are more important to you than Jesus Himself?

"For you did not receive a spirit that makes you a slave again to fear, but you received the Spirit of sonship. And by him we cry, 'Abba, Father' "(Rom. 8:15).

▌ THANKSGIVING
Thank You, Father, that You have revealed Yourself to me in the Person of Your Son. Now I can truly cry "Abba, Father!"

THE GOOD SHEPHERD SERMON

JOHN 10:1–28

"The thief comes only to steal and kill and destroy; I have come that they may have life, and have it to the full. I am the good shepherd."

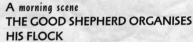

A morning scene
THE GOOD SHEPHERD ORGANISES HIS FLOCK
He is the only true Shepherd 10:1, 2
He is recognised by the watchman 10:3
He calls His sheep by name 10:3
He leads them out of the fold 10:3–6

A midday scene
THE GOOD SHEPHERD FEEDS HIS FLOCK
The gate and food of salvation 10:9
The gate of sanctification 10:10

An evening scene
THE GOOD SHEPHERD PROTECTS HIS FLOCK
He gives his life for the sheep 10:11
He knows the sheep and the sheep know him 10:14, 27
He gathers his sheep 10:16
He is raised again for the sheep 10:18
He gives his sheep eternal life 10:28, 29

A true prophet
John 10:40–42

What a striking contrast to Jerusalem! In the place where John the Baptist had prepared the way for Jesus, many believed in Him.

"... many believed in Jesus"

How thrilled John would have been to see that! We don't always see the results of our prayers, our work and witness, but we do know that our God is faithful and will always bring fruit out of our obedience to Him.

What a wonderful epitaph for John in verse 41: "All that John said about this man was true." John spent his life preaching and teaching about Jesus and many, many people tested his words, found them to be true and put their faith in Jesus. He was a bridge over which people could walk to find the true Messiah, Christ Jesus. I long for that to be true of me, don't you?

People listen to what we are as well as what we say. John's lifestyle was quite different from Jesus', but he was consistent in everything he did and said in obedience to God's will for him. Think about the results of John's dedication, his constancy, and zeal, and resolve to let your life point others to Jesus, too.

"They replied, 'Believe in the Lord Jesus, and you will be saved – you and your household' " (Acts 16:31).

▼ COMPARE
Today's reading with 2 Kings 13:20, 21.

DAY 192

Learning to pray

Luke 11:1–13

A young Christian once said, "I know that now I'm a Christian I ought to pray,

"Ask ... seek ... knock ..."

so I kneel by my bed for a while every morning. But I don't know what to say."

Jesus understood that feeling. He taught His disciples to pray when they asked Him, repeating a shortened version of the pattern prayer He had first given in the Sermon on the Mount.

Think about this pattern again. Praise comes first, then prayer for God's kingdom before prayer for personal needs. This is followed by a reminder that we must first forgive before we ask God's forgiveness and, as we pray for protection from temptation, so we must remember our own responsibility to stay away from tempting situations. Jesus then taught two lovely things about His Father:

1. He will always answer persistent prayer.

2. He *knows* how to give good gifts to His children – the best of which is His Holy Spirit.

God loves us to be consistent, persistent, and expectant when we pray.

"Then Jesus told his disciples ... that they should always pray and not give up" (Luke 18:1).

▌ THOUGHT

When it's hardest to pray we ought to pray hardest.

THE MODEL PRAYER
Matthew 6:9-13

Teaching	Language
A personal relationship with God and other believers	"Our Father in heaven,
Faith	
Worship	hallowed be your name,
Expectation	your kingdom come,
Submission	your will be done on earth as it is in heaven.
Petition	Give us today our daily bread.
Confession	Forgive us our debts, as we also have forgiven our debtors.
Dependence	And lead us not into temptation, but deliver us from the evil one."

Spot-on answers
Luke 11:14-26

Jesus was always master of the situation. He never tried to argue and wriggle His way round awkward questions, but always silenced the opposition with a wise statement.

He who is not with me is against me ..." When He is again accused of being in league with the devil, He refutes the charge firstly by common sense: "If Satan is divided against himself ..." Then Jesus turns the question back to His accusers: "By whom do your followers drive them out?"

We can learn from His example. Truth does not need defending – it can stand up for itself. Seek a word of wisdom from the Lord when you are verbally attacked, then He will be glorified.

The strong man (v. 21) is a picture of Satan. But Christ is stronger (v. 22). Grasping hold of this truth takes away all fear of Satan and his kingdom. He can have no power over those who are in Christ. We need to make sure, however, when we are delivered from the power of Satan or his demonic agencies, that we are then filled with the Holy Spirit. Fully committed to the Lord Jesus, we will leave no possible foothold for the powers of darkness to return.

"He who does what is sinful is of the devil, because the devil has been sinning from the beginning. The reason the Son of God appeared was to destroy the devil's work" (1 John 3:8).

DECLARATION
Satan, you are a defeated foe through the atoning death of Christ on the Cross. And I am a recipient of the resurrection life of Christ who is the Lord of glory.

Fulfilled lives
Luke 11:27-28

We are called to obey God's commands instantly and totally. **Blessed ... are those who hear the word of God and obey it"** That demands our complete commitment to Him, a willingness to die to self and to live for our Lord Jesus 24 hours a day, week in, week out.

The old hymn puts it simply:
*"Trust and obey, for there's no other way
To be happy in Jesus, but to trust and obey."*

Actually putting those words into practice is, however, a lot harder! To be able to obey Him we need to know what His commands are. In the Army there are two kinds of orders – standing and daily. The Christian's standing orders are found in God's Word. So take time to study the Bible, learn to know God, understand His plan for mankind and get to know His ways.

Daily orders are received by listening to the Holy Spirit. We have to learn to recognise His voice (which always agrees with Scripture) and then obey. Anything less than hearing and obeying results in a life short of blessedness – unfulfilled.

"If you love me, you will obey what I command" (John 14:15).

MEDITATION
Psalm 1:1-3

Demand for a miracle
Luke 11:29–32

Probably the greatest revival of all took place when Jonah was sent by God to Nineveh to warn the people in the heathen city to either turn from their wickedness or suffer the Almighty's wrath (Jonah 1:2; 4:11). All 120,000 of them repented. Yet the Jews of Jesus' time would not listen to a Prophet greater than Jonah because their hearts were so hard.

"This is a wicked generation"

The Queen of Sheba travelled a great distance to taste Solomon's wisdom herself and she praised God for the wisdom and wealth she found (1 Kings 10:7–9). Yet the Jewish leaders listening to Jesus' teaching refused to even acknowledge that He came from God. The Ninevites and the Queen of Sheba will stand in judgment against the proud and unrepentant generation of Jesus' time on earth – and also against those in our own generation who refuse to listen to God's warnings.

We in Britain are so blessed with opportunities to hear the Gospel and read the Word of God. All of us, in the churches (especially those in leadership) as well as outside them, need to take heed, otherwise God's judgment will fall on a rebellious people.

"Jews demand miraculous signs and Greeks look for wisdom, but we preach Christ crucified: a stumbling-block to Jews and foolishness to Gentiles" (1 Cor. 1:22, 23).

◗ PRAY
For our nation, leaders and all those in authority.

Using our light
Luke 11:33–36

It is important that we use the light God gives to us. We are not to hide or smother it, but are to let it be seen by others so that they can be helped in coming into a personal relationship with Jesus Christ themselves (v. 33). Can others see your light in today's dark world?

".. full of light ..."

The "eye" (v. 34) is used as a symbol of spiritual vision – ambitions, goals, motivation in life. Think about your own spiritual goals, the vision you have for your own life. If your aims are pure and clear your whole life will be in order and pleasing to God. If you harbour selfish ambitions or are confused in your goals, you will not be living as God wants you to.

When a torch is beamed into a dark cupboard it reveals the dust and cobwebs that couldn't be seen before. Allow the light of Jesus and the Word of God to shine into the recesses of your heart and mind to chase away sin, wrong motives, attitudes and ambitions. Then Christ's light can be reflected clearly and brightly in you and will be seen by desperately needy society around us.

"The true light that gives light to every man was coming into the world" (John 1:9).

◗ FOR MEDITATION
John 3:15–21 and 1 John 1:7.

Blind guides

Luke 11:37–54

Justice and the love of God, or meaningless religious rituals? Inner cleansing or outward cleansing? The Pharisee was surprised that Jesus didn't observe the routine ritual pouring of water over the hands before a meal.

"Woe to you ..." Jesus did not usually offend people deliberately, but perhaps on this occasion He wanted to provoke these questions.

Both the Pharisees and the legal experts (scribes) were guilty of an outward show of religion and of burdening the people with needless petty rules and restrictions. We can laugh at the absurdity of washing only the outside of a cup, counting the leaves on the garden mint and giving exactly a tenth away, but think about some of the traditions that have grown up in the Church today.

Do we saddle our children and young people with unnecessary burdens? "Thou shalt attend church twice on Sundays, the housegroup on Wednesdays, the youth group on Fridays and the prayer meeting on Tuesdays." "Thou shalt not wear lipstick, listen to rock music or go to the theatre." Are we concerned with inward peace and joy or outward show? We need to examine, with God's help, whether we are helping or hindering.

"Woe to you, teachers of the law and Pharisees, you hypocrites! You are like whitewashed tombs, which look beautiful on the outside but on the inside are full of dead men's bones and everything unclean"
(Matt. 23:27)

◢ CONSIDER
Sit quietly for five minutes and ask the Holy Spirit to reveal any inconsistencies between outward behaviour and inward reality.

We can't hide anything!

Luke 12:1–3

There weren't any crash barriers in those days! Thousands of people were jostling and pushing to get near Jesus, but first He spoke quietly to His disciples: "Hypocrisy will get you nowhere." To adapt a remark by Abraham Lincoln, "You can fool some of the people some of the time, but you can't fool God any of the time." An outward show of religion is an abomination to God.

"Be on your guard against the yeast ..."

God knows our innermost thoughts and motives, the words spoken to a friend in private, our attitudes towards our families when no-one else is there, our personal prayer life. These are the things that matter to Him, not our routine attendance at church, our long prayers at meetings, our outward respectability.

"But mark this: There will be terrible times in the last days. People will be ... without love, unforgiving, slanderous, without self-control ... having a form of godliness but denying its power ..." (2 Tim. 3:1–3, 5).

▮ PRAYER
Please forgive my hypocrisy, Lord. Cleanse my thoughts and wipe out those which are not pleasing to You. Amen.

DAY 199

In His care
Luke 12:4–7

Jesus yearned for His disciples to have a sense of peace and security. Our Lord Himself was never afraid of men because He knew that nothing could happen to Him unless it was His Father's will.

"Don't be afraid ..." Unrepentant sinners have reason to fear both man who can harm and kill, and God Himself, who has no option but to cast them into hell. However, we who have committed our lives into His care need not be afraid.

The Master loved His disciples. They were all very different from one another – unruly, foolish and contentious at times – but Jesus patiently taught them, explained when they didn't understand and cared for them like a shepherd. It was all preparation for their future work and the persecution to come.

Jesus loves you like that. Your heavenly Father knows every detail about you. You are so precious to Him that He sent His Son into the world so that you might know how much He loves you. Receive His love and rest in the security of His care for you.

"How great is the love the Father has lavished on us, that we should be called children of God! And that is what we are! The reason the world does not know us is that it did not know him" (1 John 3:1).

◀ **THANKSGIVING**
I praise You, Lord, that You are interested in the smallest details of my life.

DAY 200

All-important choice
Luke 12:8–12

Countless men and women over the centuries have suffered persecution and martyrdom rather than deny Jesus. They have experienced imprisonment, torture, separation from their families and painful death.

"... whoever acknowledges me before men ..." martyrdom rather than deny Jesus. They have experienced imprisonment, torture, separation from their families and painful death.

In the West today standing up for Jesus may mean ridicule, the loss of a job or petty irritations. How much are we prepared to suffer for His sake?

The believers in the Early Church suffered tremendous persecution. Most of the original 12 disciples were killed for their faith, but they didn't deny Jesus.

Prayerfully read verses 8 and 9 again. God is not pleased with secret disciples, those who say, "My faith is a very personal thing – I don't talk about it."

Many of us find it difficult to choose words to explain our relationship with Jesus, particularly to people like our bosses at work. But help is available, for the Father sent the Holy Spirit to give power and boldness to witness. Ask Him for that help when you need it.

"Give us today our daily bread" (Matt. 6:11).

◀ **FOR STUDY**
John 14:26; Acts 1:8; Acts 4:31.

Fooled by riches
Luke 12:13–21

A rich lady died and went to heaven, so a story goes. She was shown round the various beautiful mansions there, one of which had been prepared for her maid.

"You fool!" Then she was shown to a small hovel, with her own name on it. "But why has my maid got a beautiful mansion and I only have a hovel?" she protested. "There must be some mistake." "No," said the angel, sadly, "We can only build with the materials you send up from earth. You kept your riches for yourself there, but your maid gives all she has away."

If we seek after our own comfort in this world, that's what we shall get. Jesus left the glory and splendour of heaven. He relinquished His position at His Father's side for a while to come to this earth and devote His life to others. He was willing to die and descend to the depths of hell, so His Father promoted Him to the highest position in heaven.

There is no other Name higher than the Name of Jesus. Take time today to think about priorities – the relative importance of possessions and position in this world, and your standing with God.

"The fool says in his heart. 'There is no God.' They are corrupt, their deeds are vile; there is no-one who does good" (Psa. 14:1)

♦ PONDER
Philippians 2:5–11

A FOOL IN A FIX
Luke 12:16–21

1. A rich farmer makes the following decisions after a bumper crop

a) I have no place to store my crops.
b) I will tear down my barns and build bigger ones.
c) I will store all my grain and my goods.
d) I will seek only pleasure for I have plenty of good things laid up for many years.

2. A sovereign God also makes some decisions concerning the foolish farmer.
a) "You fool! This very night your life will be demanded from you ...
b) ... Then who will get what you have prepared for yourself?"
The man was a fool because he thought he could satisfy his eternal soul with materialistic goods. Note this statement: "and I'll say to myself, 'You have plenty of good things laid up ...'" (12:19). See Jesus' statement in Matt. 4:4, 16:26. The only real soul food is the Word of God. The man was a fool because he smugly assumed he would live to a ripe old age. (See Prov. 27:1, 29:1; Psa. 90:12; Isa. 14:13-15).

His timetable – not ours
Luke 12:22–31

Jesus called for a complete reversal of worldly attitudes by His disciples. It is easy to become preoccupied with everyday necessities. Most of us go through periods when there doesn't seem to be time for anything other than making ends meet, looking after our families, coping with work and demanding schedules – all essential things that have to be done. Jesus said, however, that though the pagans worry about these things, we should not.

"... seek his kingdom ..."

Our one essential priority should be God's kingdom. Put God first, spend time with Him as early in the day as possible, seek His will and allow Him to reign in every detail of your life. Seek to extend His kingdom through encouraging Christians and by bringing others into the kingdom. If we do this, Jesus said, our Father will take care of our needs.

One of the great promises in the New Testament is in verse 31. Memorise it and lean on it when you are perplexed about priorities. God will give you time for your work and your family – and, in fact, supply *every* need.

"Do not be anxious about anything, but in everything, by prayer and petition, with thanksgiving, present your requests to God" (Phil. 4:6)

Fret not – He loves you (John 13:1)
Faint not – He holds you (Psa. 39:10)
Fear not – He keeps you (Psa. 121:7)

DAY 203

The real treasure
Luke 12:32–34

Treasure. What does the word mean to you? Gold nuggets discovered in a faraway land, fabulous jewels in an eastern cave, family heirlooms or money in the bank? Countless lives have been lost in seeking and defending treasure. The stories make exciting reading, but all the effort involved was not worth it.

"... there your heart will be ..."

Jim Elliott, martyr of Ecuador, wrote as a young man, "He is no fool who gives what he cannot keep to gain what he cannot lose." Earthly treasure is a worry and only of passing worth. The treasure that our heavenly Father gives us is priceless, glorious, thief-proof, rust-proof and eternal.

I know which I would rather have. All our earthly possessions should be held loosely in open hands, available to God, to be given or used as He directs. Concentrate on your heavenly treasure, the greatest of which is the pearl of greatest price – Jesus Himself.

"What is more, I consider everything a loss compared to the surpassing greatness of knowing Christ Jesus my Lord, for whose sake I have lost all things. I consider them rubbish, that I may gain Christ" (Phil. 3:8).

 THOUGHT
The rich are not always godly but the godly are always rich.

DAY 204

Watching and waiting
Luke 12:35-40

Occasionally I find an irate visitor on our doorstep muttering, "I've been knocking are ringing for *ages*. Didn't you hear me?" Obviously I've been preoccupied with something and wasn't paying attention. But when I'm expecting someone to come, I listen. When someone very special is coming I watch at the window, ready to open the door and greet them before they even arrive on the doorstep.

Are we ready for Jesus? Are we watching? Read verse 37 again. God is good and it is His desire to give good things to His servants. He longs to bless you, to overwhelm you with His goodness. When

THE RAPTURE

Christ comes in the air (1 Thess. 4:16, 17).

He comes for His saints (1 Thess. 4:16, 17).

The rapture is a mystery, ie: a truth unknown in Old Testament times (1 Cor. 15:51).

Christ's coming for His saints is never said to be preceded by signs in the heavens.

The rapture is identified with the day of Christ (1 Cor. 1:8; 2 Cor. 1:14; Phil 1:6, 10).

The rapture is presented as a time of blessing (1 Thess. 4:18).

The rapture takes place in a moment, in the twinkling of an eye (1 Cor. 15:52). This strongly implies that it will not be witnessed by the world.

The rapture seems to involve the Church primarily (John 14:1–4; 1 Cor. 15:51–58; 1 Thess. 4:13–18).

Christ comes as the bright Morning Star (Rev. 22:16).

Jesus comes again He longs to find you ready to receive Him, so that He can serve you with good things from His table.

You ... must e ready ..."

God is a generous and giving Father. Jesus is coming to receive us to Himself, to bless us with His own presence. Don't grieve Him by not being ready when He comes. Be watchful.

"So you also must be ready, because the Son of Man will come at an hour when you do not expect him" (Matt. 24:44).

CHALLENGE
If Jesus returned today would He find you ready and serving Him?

Ready for His return
Luke 12:41–48

A firm belief in the return of the Lord Jesus to this earth is of great practical importance, because it affects the way

From every- one who has been given much, much will be lemanded ..."

we live today. We don't know when Jesus is coming back. Many Christians believe that it will be soon, but however long or short it may be before He appears, Jesus wants to find His servants ready.

His coming will be sudden (v. 46). We will not have time then to put our affairs in order, make up for previous slackness,

THE RETURN

He comes to the earth (Zech. 14:4).

He comes with His saints (1 Thess 3:13; Jude 14).

The return is not a mystery - it is foretold in many Old Testament prophecies (Psa. 72; Isa. 11; Zech. 14).

Christ's coming with His saints will be heralded by celestial signs (Matt. 24:29, 30).

The return is identified with the day of the Lord (2 Thess. 2:1–12).

The main emphasis of the return is on judgment (2 Thess. 2:8–12).

The return will be visible worldwide (Mt. 24:27; Rev. 1:7).

The return involves Israel primarily, then the Gentile nations as well.

Christ comes as the sun of righteousness with healing in His wings (Mal. 4:2).

forgive our enemies ... A faithful servant is just as diligent when his master is absent as when he is present. Jesus prepared His disciples thoroughly for their duties as His servants, then gave them the responsibility of looking after His affairs on earth until He returns.

We have been entrusted with those same responsibilities. Each one of us has a ministry, a special responsibility as a servant of Jesus. Take time today to ask Him if you are fulfilling your role diligently and to His satisfaction.

"Whoever can be trusted with very little can also be trusted with much, and whoever is dishonest with very little will also be dishonest with much" (Luke 16:10).

◢ PRAYER
Lord, help me to be faithful with what You have committed to me, so that I might be found to be a faithful steward. Amen.

Jesus the divider
Luke 12:49–53

We can sense the deep emotion in Jesus' voice as He speaks of His coming suffering at Calvary. His dread, however, was not primarily of physical suffering, but of the overwhelming anguish He must have felt in taking the sins of the world upon Himself.

"I have come to bring fire on the earth ..."

Jesus felt very deeply, too, for His disciples. He knew the persecution and suffering that they would endure for His sake.

Jesus knew, and still knows, the agonising choices facing some of His servants between unbelieving families and His service. Our Lord is the prince of peace, but the peace that He gives us now is a deep inner peace that does not depend on circumstances. His reign of peace on earth is still to come.

Jesus never deceived His disciples into believing that serving Him would be easy. We can expect the fire that cleanses and purifies, persecution, mocking, deprivations and division. Trust Him who has been through it before you. He will go through it with you.

"All men will hate you because of me, but he who stands firm to the end will be saved" (Matt. 10:22).

◢ THOUGHT
People are not persecuted for doing wrong but for doing right.

Signs of the times
Luke 12:54–59

The crowd at Jerusalem were familiar with Messianic prophecies, yet they couldn't see their fulfilment right in front of their eyes. They had put their own interpretation on Old Testament Scriptures and closed their minds to reality.

Jesus' admonition (v. 56) needs to be taken to heart by us today, for the Lord is coming again soon.

We need to study the Scriptures relating to His second coming and watch for the signs in the world today, otherwise we will be caught unawares. Watch what is happening in and around Israel particularly, and relate it to biblical prophecy.

God does not leave His children uninformed. He tells us His plans and His purposes – if we are willing to listen and understand.

Knowing that the time is growing short, grasp the urgency of preaching the message of reconciliation to the world around you. People in your neighbourhood will be judged and "thrown into prison" unless they are reconciled to God now. Have you told them?

"Jesus replied, 'I tell you the truth, everyone who sins is a slave to sin'" (John 8:34).

◢ ASK YOURSELF
Am I discerning the times I live in? Read Matt. 24:4–28 and compare the passage with daily events.

"How is it that you don't know how to interpret this present time?"

Repent or perish
Luke 13:1–9

I can never point a finger at someone else and think "That's a worse sinner than me." "All have sinned and fall short of the glory of God" (Rom. 3:23).

"... unless you repent ..."

Sin is sin in God's eyes and will be judged unless true repentance brings forgiveness and cleansing through the shed blood of Jesus. Think about your very privileged position in Christ and never judge those who are without Him. Tell them, as Jesus did, of their need for repentance and the consequences of failing to do so.

The parable of the fig tree brings home to us again the importance of fruitfulness. The message was directed firstly at the nation of Israel. God was giving them one last chance, in the person of Jesus, their Messiah. They rejected Him and were cut down by persecution, lost their homeland and were scattered throughout the world.

The parable applies to the life of every Christian, too. God requires us to be productive, bearing good fruit for Him.

"In the past God overlooked such ignorance, but now he commands all people everywhere to repent" (Acts 17:30).

◼ REMEMBER
Repentance is not just being sorry for sin – it is being sorry enough to stop sinning.

Compassion foremost
Luke 13:10–17

The synagogue ruler was angry because Jesus had broken the rules. The woman was overjoyed because He had broken the power of Satan in her life.

Near Jerusalem, just as in Galilee, the fixation the Jewish leaders had about their traditions and laws blinded them to the presence of God in their midst. This is the last recorded visit of Jesus to a synagogue and, far from being put off by previous denunciations of His healing on the Sabbath, He again demonstrated His love, compassion and power by setting this woman free from her infirmity.

The ruler's suggestion (v. 14) sounded plausible in one sense – the woman had

"... immediately she straightened up ..."

been ill for 18 years so one more day wouldn't have made any difference. But Jesus timed it to perfection. He wanted to teach an important lesson: it is part of God's nature to heal and He is not subject to man-made rules. We may come to Jesus for healing any time, for any kind of sickness.

"... the people all tried to touch him, because power was coming from him and healing them all" (Luke 6:19).

■ MEMORISE
"Praise the Lord, O my soul, and forget not all his benefits – who forgives all your sins and heals all your diseases" (Psa. 103:2 & 3).

God's kingdom has come
Luke 13:18–21

Jesus returned again and again to one theme in His teaching – the kingdom of God, or kingdom of heaven. He taught in word what He was demon-

"... the kingdom of God ... is like ..."

strating in power by His actions. Jesus the King showed His authority over Satan and his demonic forces. The kingdom of God had broken into, and superseded, the kingdom of Satan.

The parables of the mustard seed and the yeast both illustrate how small beginnings can grow into great things. First, Jesus, then 12 disciples, then 3,000 converts at Pentecost (Acts 2:41). Now Christianity has reached almost all the world, but it has taken nearly 2,000 years to do so. That's because the kingdom of God is only as effective as the extent to which Jesus the King is allowed to rule in individual lives.

Crown Him as King in your life, allow Him to have absolute sovereignty over your mind, heart and actions. Then the kingdom of God will grow within you and around you.

"And lead us not into temptation, but deliver us from the evil one" (Matt. 6:13).

▮ FOR MEDITATION
Luke 10:18 & 19

The safety door
Luke 13:22–30

My son was playing a computer game, steering a car through a variety of haz-

"... those who are last ... will be first ..."

ards when it was flashed on the screen, "Steer to the left, bridge ahead blocked."

There was nothing else on the screen at that moment to indicate any danger, but shortly afterwards a very narrow opening appeared on the far left – the only way to escape from falling into a broad expanse of water. It reminded me of Jesus' parable of the narrow door.

Heeding the warning in time ensures safety, but if you dither you are lost for ever. Knowing about Jesus does not make you safe, but entering His kingdom through the narrow door of the Cross does.

What a responsibility we have to warn people of their danger! Think about verse 25 again. Realise the awfulness of being locked out of the kingdom of God for ever and pray for a spirit of urgency and compassion for those still outside. Take every opportunity to tell people about Jesus, the door to the kingdom of God.

"But small is the gate and narrow the road that leads to life, and only a few find it" (Matt. 7:14).

■ **ACTION**
Share Jesus with someone today.

A special place
Luke 13:31–35

Herod Antipas, who was responsible for the death of John the Baptist, was worried about the large crowds following Jesus. He feared a revolt among the Jews, so the obvious answer was to kill their popular leader.

.. how often I have longed to gather your children together ..."

Yet Jesus' sense of purpose never wavered. His only desire was to go on fulfilling His Father's will until His work was completed by His death in Jerusalem.

The city had had a special place in Jewish history since David captured it, built his palace and brought the Ark of the Covenant there. Solomon's temple established Jerusalem as the centre of Jewish worship – the city of God's dwelling place. How God loved, and still loves, Jerusalem! Jesus' heart cried out with longing for the people who had had so many chances to hear and experience God, yet threw them away.

Our Lord's words (v. 35) were prophetic. In AD 70 the Romans destroyed Jerusalem, a million people were killed and 100,000 others taken to Egypt to work in the mines. Will you pray for Jerusalem and for the Jewish people, whom God still loves and longs for?

"As he approached Jerusalem and saw the city, he wept over it" (Luke 19:41).

■ **PRAYER**
Psalm 122:6 & 7

Mercy – not rules
Luke 14:1–6

There was a spy in their midst. The man with the dropsy was "planted", it seemed, to provide the Pharisees with further evidence against Jesus. Jesus pre-empted them by asking a direct question. They wouldn't answer: the laws about healing were complicated and the Pharisees had

"... he healed him ..."

been humiliated before by Jesus (13:17). That incident had happened in front of crowds of people, but this was a private dinner party.

It was an occasion when the Pharisees might have felt free to argue their point with Jesus in front of their friends, but His question silenced them completely. So, after healing the sick man, Jesus proceeded further to show how far astray they were in their thinking, attitudes and rules. A rescue from a well is an act of mercy – a lawful Sabbath activity. Healing is also an act of mercy.

God is a merciful God and His nature

does not change with the days of the week. Think about your own attitude to Sundays. How do you and your family show God's love, compassion and mercy to others on His special day?

"One man considers one day more sacred than another; another man considers every day alike. Each one should be fully convinced in his own mind. He who regards one day as special, does so to the Lord. He who eats meat, eats to the Lord, for he gives thanks to God" (Rom. 14:5 & 6).

■ **ACTION**
Have you written to your local MP about the Sunday trading issue?

Go low!
Luke 14:7-14

The Pharisees were noted for their pride and self-importance, so it was to this trait that Jesus appealed in His gentle rebuke to them.

"... he who humbles himself will be exalted"

Loss of face is a disgrace in the East, but if you take the lowest place you cannot fall further. It was a wise argument that would not have offended them.

Jesus humbled Himself to the very lowest place on earth – the Cross – and God exalted Him to the highest possible place of honour at His right hand in heaven. God will only exalt you as far as you are willing to humble yourself.

Hospitality was taken for granted in biblical times. It was normal to give food and shelter to travellers and the poor and needy. Some people, however, were evidently selective about the guests they invited to their homes. Think about this in the light of Matthew 10:42 and Romans 12:13. It is easy to fall into the habit of inviting only compatible friends to one's home. It is more pleasing to God when you invite needy people.

"Humble yourselves before the Lord, and he will lift you up" (James 4:10).

◣ **ASK YOURSELF**
Am I guilty of exalting myself in any way? What sort of people do I invite most often to my home?

Invited to the feast
Luke 14:15-24

"Sorry I can't come to your wedding – there's a football match on that day." If you have been the recipient of that kind of flimsy excuse, you will understand how angry and hurt the man in Jesus' parable was.

God prepared a banquet of salvation for His chosen people, the Jews. He sent John the Baptist to tell them to get ready. He sent His Son to be the sacrificial lamb for the feast. Generally the people weren't interested. They were not hungry. They were satisfied with what they had and what they were doing. Those Jews who did flock to hear Jesus were the "poor" – the sick, blind and lame, publicans and sinners. Even then there was room, and servants were sent out to "the country lanes" – the Gentile nations.

Paul Yonggi Cho, pastor of the largest church in the world in Seoul, South Korea, told his house group leaders to

"... they ... began to make excuses ..." search out needy people in their neighbourhoods and preach the Gospel to them first. They are the ones who will listen and respond – not those who are self-satisfied.

"Yet you refuse to come to me to have life" (John 5:40).

THE THREE FOOLS

Three men are invited to a great feast. All refuse for various reasons.

The first fool: "I can't come, for I must go and look at a field I have just bought." Only a fool would buy a field without seeing it first.

The second fool: "I can't come for I must try out some oxen I have just bought." Only a fool would buy untried oxen!

The henpecked husband: "I can't come, as I have just married." No comment necessary.

DAY 216

Meeting the conditions
Luke 14:25-35

Christians who stand firm in the face of trouble or persecution are those who have counted the cost when making their first commitment.

A young man joining the armed forces in time of war knows that he may be required to give his life. A soldier in Jesus' army can do no less.

"... if it loses its saltiness ..."

Being a soldier, or disciple, of Jesus means being willing to give up worldly comfort, face hardship and persecution, die daily to selfish desires and submit one's will completely to the Father's will. Jesus was willing for these things. Can He count on you to follow Him?

Three times Jesus says "he ... cannot be my disciple" (vv. 26, 27, 33) if a person doesn't meet those conditions. Think about your discipleship:

1. Do you love Jesus more than your partner and your family (v. 26)? 2. Are you humbly submitting your will to His will (v. 27)? 3. Are you prepared to give up anything that He asks you to (v. 33)?

"I have been crucified with Christ and I no longer live, but Christ lives in me. The life I live in the body, I live by faith in the Son of God, who loved me and gave himself for me" (Gal. 2:20).

🔖 **THOUGHT**
When Jesus called His first disciples He used only two words: "Follow me." And they did!

DAY 217

Seeing their need
Luke 15:1–10

The tax collectors and sinners flocked to Jesus. They knew they were unrighteous and had a need. The self-righteous Pharisees criticised. This parable illustrates the lengths and depths that Jesus, the good shepherd, will go to to rescue a sinner.

"... I have found my lost sheep"

No-one is beyond His help, nor too sinful or too horrible for Him to love. The only criterion is that the sinner admits his need and repents. We need to grasp hold of this truth to enable us to reach out to needy people for Jesus.

The ten silver coins were a symbol of marriage, given by the husband in the same way as a wedding ring is today. The loss of one of them was thought to show the wife to be unfaithful. No wonder she searched hard to find it!

We should have that same diligence in our faithfulness to God. Allow the Holy Spirit to search your heart today and show you if there is any area of unfaithfulness in your relationship with the Lord.

"For you were like sheep going astray, but now you have returned to the Shepherd and Overseer of your souls" (1 Pet. 2:25).

◼ THOUGHT
He who loses his money loses much. He who loses a friend loses more. But he who loses his soul loses all.

DAY 218

Sin of self-righteousness
Luke 15:11–32

Whatever the elder brother was doing while the young profligate was away, he was evidently not praying for him, longing for his return or keeping a place in the family open for him. Otherwise he would have rejoiced with his father when his younger brother eventually came back, sorrier and wiser. The elder brother had, in fact, written him off.

"... he was lost and is found"

Consider your own attitude to Christians who "backslide" or fall into some kind of sin. Self-righteousness is an abomination to God. Not one of us can say, like the elder brother, "*I've* never dis-

obeyed your orders" (v. 29). Pray for those who fall away, take every opportunity to love them in practical ways – and rejoice when they come back.

It is very difficult for a backslider to return to a church fellowship. Things have changed – new people and issues being discussed which the "prodigal" doesn't know about. He or she can still be out in the cold, so make sure you welcome such people warmly and whole-heartedly help them to re-adjust and to feel part of God's family again.

"When you were dead in your sins and in the uncircumcision of your sinful nature, God made you alive with Christ. He forgave us all our sins" (Col. 2:13).

◀ REMEMBER
"There, but for the grace of God, go I."

Using money wisely

Luke 16:1-13

The estate manager had, no doubt, been "cooking the books" for years and was horrified at the thought of losing his job when he was found out. To understand Jesus' commendation of this wily character, we need to see that He was praising his wisdom, not his dishonesty. The manager's own money could have been used to make friends, but not his master's.

"No servant can serve two masters"

We are managers for Jesus. Everything that a Christian has – money, home, possessions, even family – is held in trust for Him and will one day have to be accounted for. To use them wisely is honest, to use them for selfish luxuries is dishonest.

Jesus commends the right use of worldly wealth (v. 8). It is not wrong to be rich or to be successful in business (as some Christians think), provided that the money is used for God's kingdom. Money given to Christian missions, famine relief and for the distribution of Bibles and Christian literature will gain us friends for eternity.

"But if serving the Lord seems undesirable to you, then choose for yourselves this day whom you will serve, whether the gods your forefathers served beyond the River, or the gods of the Amorites, in whose land you are living. But as for me and my household, we will serve the Lord" (Josh. 24:15).

▼ EXAMINE

Prayerfully consider your relationships to others. Are you making any unjust demands to meet your own needs?

MONEY IS A GOOD SERVANT, BUT A POOR MASTER Bonhours

Money will buy –
A bed but not sleep,
Books but not brains,
Finery but not beauty,
Food but not an appetite,
A house but not a home,
Medicine but not health,
Luxuries but not culture,
Amusement but not happiness,
A church but not heaven.

It is better to have your bank in heaven than to have your heaven in a bank.

Above: First and Second Century coins from Israel

Don't be deceived

Luke 16:14–17

Jesus was never deceived by self-righteousness. The Pharisees were rich and they made a great show of giving to the poor but their hearts were not right. Think about your own attitude towards money. Money may be used for either good or evil.

"... God knows your hearts ..."

God loves willing, cheerful givers – those who give themselves as well as their money. Those who give in secret win God's approval, but those who give openly merely gain man's approval.

Jesus went on to reiterate His teaching about the new age that had begun at His birth. The age of the kingdom of God began when the King came to the world, following on from the age of the law and the prophets, and the teaching of the kingdom expanded, rather than diminished, the law. Paul expanded on this teaching (Gal. 2:15–21). When you allow Christ to reign in your life, His righteousness in you is in accord with the perfect law of God.

"We do not dare to classify or compare ourselves with some who commend themselves. When they measure themselves by themselves and compare themselves with themselves, they are not wise." (2 Cor. 10:12).

🔲 **FOR MEDITATION**
Galatians 3:24 & 25

Reality of hell – and heaven

Luke 16:19–31

A story of contrasts! The rich man in his luxurious comfort is compared with the starving sick beggar at his gates. A far greater contrast, however, is the picture of Lazarus relaxing at Abraham's side in heaven while the former rich man is in agony and anguish amidst the fire of Hades, the place where the departed await the final judgment day.

"... a great chasm has been fixed ..."

This is a very graphic illustration of the result of the wrong use of riches in this world. It also teaches us of the reality of Hades and the great uncrossable gulf between heaven and hell. Think about the torment of being able to see

into heaven but not being able to reach it! The holiness and love of God is completely separate from the evil of Satan's domain.

Only one person has crossed that gulf – Jesus. After His death He descended into hell and preached to the spirits there before rising again and ascending to heaven. Yet even then people were not convinced, they still wouldn't listen. A realisation of the reality of hell's torment will add urgency to your telling people of the way of escape from it.

"But the cowardly, the unbelieving, the vile, the murderers, the sexually immoral, those who practise magic arts, the idolaters and all liars – their place will be in the fiery lake of burning sulphur. This is the second death." (Rev. 21:8)

🔲 **PRAYER**
Father, help me to realise the reality of eternal torment and damnation, so that I might share with others Your love and saving grace. Amen.

DAY 222

Carrying on His work
Luke 17:1–10

Jesus was constantly giving His disciples insight to prepare them to carry on His work when He left them. He taught them:

1. Responsibility towards others – taking care not to cause anyone to stumble into sin.

"... forgive him"

2. The importance of unlimited forgiveness, however often a brother sins against you.

3. Quality of faith is more important than quantity. Genuine, life-producing faith will produce miracles.

4. Humility in service. As servants of God it is our duty to obey Him, to serve Him faithfully at whatever cost to ourselves. To do so gives us no reason for pride.

It is what we committed ourselves to when we first turned to Jesus. Do you see yourself as that kind of servant, with no other concern but to serve your Master?

"Be kind and compassionate to one another, forgiving each other, just as in Christ God forgave you" (Eph.4:32).

◢ COMMITMENT
Lord, I re-dedicate myself today for Your service, whatever it costs me. Amen.

DAY 223

Raised from death
John 11:1–16

Jesus raised three people from death during His ministry. Two of them were people He had been asked to heal but had been delayed in reaching them before they died (Mark 5:22–43 and today's passage).

"Lazarus is dead ..."

The third incident (Luke 7:11–17) was a special act of mercy in restoring a breadwinner, the only son of a widowed mother.

Lazarus and his two sisters were very dear to Jesus. He had been often in their home, possibly making it His base for His ministry in Judea. It seemed strange, therefore, that He did not immediately return to His friend when He heard he was sick. But Jesus knew what He was doing. His purpose was a greater one than just healing Lazarus.

On the two previous occasions the people had died only a short while before Jesus raised them. It could have been argued that a mistake had been made, that they had not really been dead. But no mistake could be made about a corpse, dead for four days and already decomposing. God always has a purpose in His seeming delays. Trust Him, have patience and know that His timing is always perfect.

"I tell you the truth, unless a grain of wheat falls to the ground and dies, it remains only a single seed. But if it dies, it produces many seeds" (John 12:24).

◢ COMPARE
Verse 16 with John 20:24

LIKE SLEEP

The episode with Lazarus is the first occasion where the death of a believer is likened to sleep (compare John 11:11 with Matt. 9:24; 27:52 (AV); Acts 7:60; 1 Cor. 11:30; 15:51, 1 Thess. 4:14). Jesus waited until Lazarus had been dead for four days. He may have done this because of superstition among the Jews that after death the spirit hovered over the body for three days and a resurrection up to that time was at least possible. But after three days there was not even a semblance of a chance of this occurring.

Comfort in grief

John 11:17–27

Martha was overwhelmed with grief. She was puzzled and shocked, yet she went out to meet Jesus. Her greeting was a heart-rending mixture of rebuke and hope. Her faith in the Master was very real, although she couldn't quite believe what He said to her (vv. 23, 24). Jesus understood her emotional turmoil and turned her attention directly to Himself (v.25) with gentle, comforting words.

"I am the resurrection and the life ..."

We need to remember that when people are deeply upset, by bereavement or any other kind of emotional shock, their minds do not function as clearly as usual. That is not the time for deep counselling, new teaching or doctrinal arguments. We help them best by turning their eyes to Jesus, who understands and will comfort and sustain.

Martha was relieved of her anxiety and immediate burden. She believed in Jesus implicitly. Everything would be all right because He was there. Turn your eyes to Jesus in any difficulty – He is the answer.

"And if the Spirit of him who raised Jesus from the dead is living in you, he who raised Christ from the dead will also give life to your mortal bodies through his Spirit, who lives in you" (Rom. 8:11).

QUESTION
Did Martha understand and answer Jesus' question? (vv. 25–27)

Jesus wept

John 11:28–37

"Lord, if you had been here ..." Mary uttered the same words as Martha had. How many times must the two sisters have said those words during the previous four days. But "if" never solves any problem.

"... how he loved him!"

Jesus was deeply moved with compassion at Mary's grief, and wept with her. His tears, however, were caused by an even deeper emotion. That He "was deeply moved in spirit and troubled" (v. 33) suggests an indignation against the powers of darkness themselves that were the cause of death. Compare it with Jesus' travail in the Garden of Gethsemane when faced with the overwhelming burden of bearing the sin of the world.

Jesus was faced outside Bethany with two grief-stricken sisters who were dear to Him, a group of hypocritical and cynical Jews, the death of a much-loved friend and the seeming triumph of Satan in the situation. Even though Jesus had absolute authority as the Son of God and knew the triumphant end of the matter, He still wept. Remember Jesus' compassion when you are in trouble – He weeps with you.

"I no longer call you servants, because a servant does not know his master's business. Instead, I have called you friends, for everything that I learned from my Father I have made known to you" (John 15:15).

CHALLENGE
When was the last time you wept with someone in the midst of their crisis because your heart was moved with compassion?

IF THOU HADST COME

"If Thou hadst come, our brother had not died."
  Thus one who loved, to One who came so late;
  Yet not too late, had she but known the fate
Which soon should fill the mourners' hearts
  with tide
Of holy joy. Now she would almost chide
  Her awful guest, as though His brief delay
  Had quenched her love and driven faith away.
"If Thou hadst come," oh could we only hide
  Our heart's impatience and with meekness stay
To hear the voice of wisdom ere we speak.
  We mourn the past, the tomb, the buried dead,
  And think of many a bitter thing to say,
While all the time True Love stands by so meek,
  Waiting to lift anew the drooping head.

George Matheson

Victorious – over everything
John 11:38–44

It was Martha, ever practical, who pointed out the objection to moving the stone

"Lazarus, come out!" away. She still hadn't grasped the reality of Jesus' promise, "Your brother will rise again." How often we leave obstacles in the way of God's sovereign power to answer prayer. We pray – but! "Lord I believe you can do this, *but* there's that in the way." God can do anything – there are no "buts".

Notice that Jesus had already interceded with His Father for Lazarus (v. 41). He knew His Father's will, what He should do and the outcome. We don't know how many hours Jesus had spent in prayer before He called Lazarus from the grave, but the Scriptures make it clear that it wasn't an easy, off-the-cuff matter. Jesus "was deeply moved in spirit".

We can sometimes be too glib in our praying, particularly in healing and deliverance. The secret of victory is knowing our Father's will, doing battle with the powers of darkness in prayer and fasting, *then* confidently speaking the word of authority, as Jesus did.

"Where, O death, is your victory? Where, O death, is your sting?" (1 Cor. 15:55).

◆ **FOR MEDITATION**
Romans 8:2

A miracle divides
John 11:45–54

As happened so often in Jesus' ministry, the wonderful miracle of Lazarus proved to be divisive. Many believed, but others plotted against Him. The fear of the Sanhedrin is comparable to that which faces many churches in Communist-controlled countries today – whether to compromise with the ruling power and remain safe or to go all out for their faith and face reprisals.

"... performing many miraculous signs" The Jews chose to play safe and please the Romans rather than recognise the Son of God, their Messiah. They didn't gain anything, for some 35 years later the Romans demolished Jerusalem. How sad that Caiaphas, the high priest, should be the chief instigator of Jesus' death and, at the same time, utter the prophecy that Jesus would die for the Jewish nation and for the Gentiles, making them one people for God. It is one of the examples in Scripture of the Spirit speaking through an unwitting prophet.

Jesus withdrew 12 miles away because it was not yet time for His death. God's timing is always perfect – in your life as well as in His Son's.

"Then Jesus came to them and said, 'All authority in heaven and on earth has been given to me' " (Matt. 28:18).

STUDY
John 19:8–12; 10:17 & 18.

Faith tested
Luke 17:11–19

The lepers stood at a distance from Jesus, as required by the law, and shouted to Him. On a previous occasion a leper had knelt at Jesus' feet, so near that Jesus could touch him (Mark 1:40). He had a greater faith in Jesus' power to heal – and was healed instantly. The ten had their faith tested. They had to start walking towards the priests for confirmation of their healing before they actually received their healing.

"... your faith has made you well"

It was a test of faith and obedience, and they all passed the test. Only one, however, came back to say, "Thank you" and to praise and glorify God.

It would seem that the nine had no strong faith in Jesus, but were willing to try anything that might help them. When they were healed they took it as a matter of course and still did not recognise Jesus for who He is. Healing is evidence of God's power and glory, so we should never take it lightly. Thank Him now for your life and your health. Give praise openly before men when you experience His healing power.

"... give thanks in all circumstances, for this is God's will for you in Christ Jesus" (1 Thess. 5:18).

THANKSGIVING
List 10 things the Lord has done for you, then give your thanksgiving praise and gratitude to Him.

Sudden return
Luke 17:20–37

The suddenness of Jesus' return to this earth will test our readiness. Will we be concerned for worldly goods (v. 31) or will we be so used to trusting Him completely that we will think of nothing but the joy of His presence? Although verses 20 and 21 record Jesus talking to the Pharisees, His teaching about His second coming was given only to the disciples (v. 22ff.) It will be a sudden, universal event seen all over the world at the same time. Elsewhere in Scripture we are given various signs of the imminence of Jesus' return, but Jesus here teaches that, as in Noah's time, most people will be indifferent to the signs and will be carrying on their normal lives.

"... the kingdom of God is within you"

It will be hard for Christians in those times. We will be longing to see Jesus again (v. 22) and praying for His return. Think about your own readiness. Are you prepared to go at a moment's notice, or are you entangled in worldly affairs? Are you looking forward to Jesus' return?

"For the kingdom of God is not a matter of eating and drinking, but of righteousness, peace and joy in the Holy Spirit ..." (Rom. 14:17).

STUDY
Look up in a Bible concordance the references to the kingdom of God.

Persistence pays
Luke 18:1–8

Do you remember Robert Bruce and the spider? Robert had been defeated in battle so many times that he was discouraged and about to give up. He was hiding in a barn one night and saw a spider patiently trying over and over again to attach its silk thread between two beams. Finally it succeeded. Robert went into battle again the next day and won.

"... always pray, and not give up"

Jesus chose to use a widow to illustrate His message of patient persistence. In those days widows were the most weak and defenceless of people. She desper-ately needed help from the judge to survive and, because of her persistence, she received that help. We need to realise our own weak state and that, from the position of utter helplessness, we can plead with our heavenly Father, knowing that He hears and loves to answer. The answer might be delayed, but it will come.

The second part of verse 8 has puzzled people. I offer one interpretation: "When I come, will I find that kind of persistent faith among you?" Pray that He may find it in you.

**"... pray continually ..."
(1 Thess. 5:17).**

CHALLENGE
How much time do you spend in prayer? Are you persistent or do you easily give up?

Pour it out to Him!
Luke 18:9–14

I was in a meeting at the Albert Hall, London, some years ago when the speaker invited us to kneel and spend a few moments in personal prayer. Behind me an elderly West Indian gentleman started to pour out his heart to the Lord. I couldn't concentrate, so I gave up and just listened.

"... have mercy on me, a sinner"

His utter humility and honesty as he confessed his faults to the Lord really blessed me. He pleaded to be changed, prayed for his family and thanked and praised God for His goodness to him. I learned more about prayer in those five minutes than I had done in years – and I've never forgotten it.

Jesus was really blessed by the prayer of the tax collector, who was completely oblivious of his surroundings and concentrated solely on his communion with God. We must resist the temptation to play to the gallery in prayer meetings but concentrate on Jesus instead of the people around us. Then we will truly bless the Master.

**"For by the grace given me I say to every one of you: Do not think of yourself more highly than you ought, but rather think of yourself with sober judgment, in accordance with the measure of faith God has given you"
(Rom. 12:3).**

THOUGHT
Swallowing pride seldom leads to indigestion. If we do not learn humility we will learn humiliation.

A perfect family plan

Matthew 19:1–12; Mark 10:1–12; Luke 16:18

It was another trap. There were two current schools of thought about divorce: one that it should only be permissible on the grounds of unfaithfulness, while the other allowed divorce on almost any excuse. Jesus would have offended whichever viewpoint He had spoken in favour of.

"... what God has joined together ..."

But with great wisdom the Lord referred the Pharisees back even beyond Moses' law to the Garden of Eden. God's perfect plan was that a man and a woman should be united for life.

Because of subsequent sin and human weakness Moses permitted divorce in certain circumstances (Deut. 24:1-4), but it was never in the original, perfect will of God.

In today's complicated society we are straying further and further away from God's purpose for marriage and we often find tangled situations to sort out, even in the Church. Jesus was unequivocal about divorce and remarriage. God's plan was for stable marriages and family security. Pray for a return of these values in this nation.

"Are you married? Do not seek a divorce" (1 Cor. 7:27).

❚ FOR STUDY
Ephesians 5:22 & 23

Children welcome

Matthew 19:13–15;
Mark 10:13–16; Luke 18:15–17

The disciples were tired. Following Jesus in Judea involved physical danger and anxiety on top of the sheer exhaustion caused by the ever-present crowds. Jesus'

"... for the kingdom of heaven belongs to such as these"

teaching was growing deeper, too. Often His disciples didn't understand and found it hard to follow what He meant. They didn't want to be bothered with a lot of children.

Mistakenly, the 12 tried to protect Jesus from the added burden, too. But, to Jesus, children were never a burden. He welcomed them, loved them and blessed them. How careful we need to be

to follow His example. Children remember not only words, but attitudes. A rejection may go on hurting for years, while loving encouragement will bring that little one closer to Jesus.

To enter the kingdom of God as little children, we need to be trustful, guileless, uncomplicated, loving and completely open. God is your Father – you are His child. He loves you.

"Jesus, knowing their thoughts, took a little child and made him stand beside him. Then he said to them, 'Whoever welcomes this little child in my name welcomes me; and whoever welcomes me welcomes the one who sent me. For he who is least among you all – he is the greatest' " (Luke 9:47 & 48).

◗ THOUGHT
Train up a child in the way he should go, and go that way yourself.

Worldly or heavenly riches

Matthew 19:16–30;
Mark 10:17–31; Luke 18:18–30

He was an eager young man. He ran to Jesus and knelt at His feet. He was rich but, not satisfied with his worldly security, he wanted eternal security as well. Jesus had to show him that he must first be willing to give up his worldly security in order to be sure of treasure in heaven.

"... come, follow me"

Jesus' instructions to sell all that he had were not a general command to all His followers, but to this man in particular. His wealth was his god. So he had to decide which was more important to him – money or eternal life.

The amusing illustration of the camel and the needle's eye brought the point home to the disciples. If a merchant arrived at a city after dark he would find the main gates shut. The only way to get in was to unload his camel and push the protesting beast through the narrow pedestrian's entrance, colloquially known as the "eye of the needle". Obviously a time-consuming and frustrating business! Like the camel, none of us will enter the kingdom of heaven with a load on our back. We can only come, humbly, with nothing.

"Then Jesus said to his disciples, 'If anyone would come after me, he must deny himself and take up his cross and follow me' " (Matt. 16:24).

■ QUESTION
Which commandment is omitted from the list Jesus gave to the rich young man? How did this relate to the request Jesus made to him?

Unmerited reward
Matthew 20:1–16

Peter was confused. Jesus had just commended the disciples for their willingness to give up everything for Him, and had then made the extraordinary statement in Matthew 19:30. He told this parable to explain the statement and to answer Peter's question (19:27).

"... the last will be first, and the first will be last"

The reward for a servant of God is the same for all – the gift of eternal life. It is unmerited, depending *only* on our faith in Christ's redeeming work on the Cross. Therefore the gift does not depend on how hard we work

or for how long. The old man who turns to Jesus on his death-bed receives eternal life just as surely as the one who has worked in the mission field for 60 years.

It is through God's grace that we receive our reward, not of our own striving or merit. This understanding nullifies the implication in Peter's question of, "What's in it for me?" God is gracious, generous and just.

"For who is greater, the one who is at the table or the one who serves? Is it not the one who is at the table? But I am among you as one who serves" (Luke 22:27).

■ THOUGHT
The service that counts is the service that costs. We are saved to serve, not to be served.

The vital appointment

**Matthew 20:17–19;
Mark 10:32–34; Luke 18:31–34**

Try to imagine how you would feel if someone you loved dearly told you he was going to a certain place to be murdered.

"On the third day he will be raised to life!"

Luke tells us that the disciples didn't understand. The Father, mercifully, hid the true meaning of the words from them at that time, but afterwards they remembered and understood.

When you don't understand, don't fret and fume – God will make things clear at the right time. Jesus knew exactly what was awaiting Him in Jerusalem. He knew the time was drawing very near now as He led the way, completely unafraid, from Perea to the city, where He was to die.

God hid the truth from the disciples because of their weakness. He revealed it to His Son because He was unyielding in His resolve to do His Father's will. Jesus knew the Old Testament prophecies and how they would be fulfilled. He was prepared to suffer all that for you! Worship Him now.

"Jesus answered them, 'Destroy this temple, and I will raise it again in three days' " (John 2:19).

▌PRAYER
Lord Jesus, I am so unworthy that You should suffer for me. I love You, Lord. Amen.

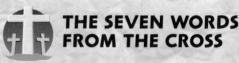

THE SEVEN WORDS FROM THE CROSS

First Word
Luke 23:34

Second Word
Luke 23:39–43

Third Word
John 19:25–27

Fourth Word
Mark 15:34

Fifth Word
John 19:28–29

Sixth Word
John 19:30

Seventh Word
Luke 23:46

Left: The hill in Jerusalem thought to be Golgotha, the Place of the Skull

Holy Spirit-inspired
Psalm 22:16; Luke 23:33; John 20:25

Over the next few days we shall be focusing on some of the Old Testament prophecies concerning Christ's death and their fulfilment. David poured out his heart to the Lord in Psalm 22 during some terrible experience, unaware that he was prophesying his Messiah's agony on the Cross. Crucifixion was not practised in David's day – death was by stoning. David's prophetic words in verse 16, therefore, were by inspiration of the Holy Spirit rather than by any knowledge of that form of death. "Dogs" is a Jewish term for Gentiles – the Roman soldiers who surrounded Jesus on the Cross.

... they have pierced my hands and my feet"

The Roman method of crucifixion was to lay the criminal naked on the crossbar, then nail or tie his hands or arms to the wood. The bar was then lifted and fixed to the upright stake, and a large single nail driven through the victim's feet.

We know from John's account of Thomas' experience that nails were used on Jesus rather than ropes, thus fulfilling David's prophecy. Think about the total submission of the Son of God as He allowed the soldiers to drive these nails through His limbs.

"Look, he is coming with the clouds, and every eye will see him, even those who have pierced him; and all the peoples of the earth will mourn because of him. So shall it be! Amen" (Rev. 1:7).

◼ I RESOLVE
Lord Jesus, I resolve now to be more like You, in total submission to the Father's will. Amen.

Rescued!
Isaiah 53:12; Mark 15:27–30; Luke 22:37

Imagine an air-sea rescue. A man is drowning in icy, rough seas, completely unable to help himself. A helicopter winches down a rescuer, but the rescuer is himself overcome by the conditions. The drowning man manages, however, to cling to him and both are winched to safety and revived. To rescue us from sin Jesus came right down to the depths of human sin.

Jesus was pure and sinless but He identified Himself with your sin, my sin

"... he poured out his life unto death ..."

and the whole sum of the world's sin, taking it on Himself and allowing Himself to be crucified between two common criminals as a sacrifice to God. Have you really grasped the enormity of what Jesus did for you?

Not only was Jesus treated as a criminal by the Roman authorities but by His Father also (see 2 Cor. 5:21). The crucifixion was an outward illustration for the world to see. The deeper truth is that God the Father "numbered His Son with the transgressors" and accepted His sacrificial death.

"Two robbers were crucified with him, one on his right and one on his left" (Matt. 27:38).

◆ FOR STUDY
Luke 23:40–43. List five things the dying thief did.

Thirst for God

Psalm 22:14,15; John 19:28

"I am thirsty". Recording Jesus' words, John gives no conception of the agonising thirst that consumes a person suffering as Jesus did. His circulation would have been impaired, His heart enlarged and fluid would have built up in His lungs and tissues, causing His whole body to cry out for water.

"... I am thirsty"

Even greater than His physical thirst, however, was His thirst for God, His Father. Psalm 42:1 & 2 gives a prophetically vivid picture of Jesus separated by the weight of sin from His Father. His spiritual thirst, the agony of rejection and separation caused Him even greater suffering than the physical deprivation.

Sin separates us from God. Even the smallest sin in the life of a Christian causes a cloud between us and His glory and purity. As we mature more in Him unconfessed sin will increasingly cause us to cry out in agony for a restoration of the flow of His living water.

"For I will pour water on the thirsty land, and streams on the dry ground; I will pour out my Spirit on your offspring, and my blessing on your descendants" (Isa. 44:3).

▼ FOR MEDITATION
John 4:13 & 14; Isaiah 55:1 & 2

Offer accepted

Psalm 69:21; John 19:29

Jesus received what was offered to Him – sour wine. This was the ordinary drink of the Roman soldiers. It would not have quenched His raging thirst, but the fact that someone, at least, took pity on Him and sought to alleviate His suffering would have brought comfort to Jesus in His dying moments. He accepted gratefully.

"... vinegar for my thirst"

Just as the gold, frankincense and myrrh brought by the wise men after His birth were acceptable and accepted, so was the spongeful of sour wine just before His death. Jesus still accepts what we have to offer, however poor and unworthy we think our offerings are. The words, "I am thirsty," probably came in an agonised whisper (only John, standing near the Cross, records them). After the "poor offering" of sour wine Jesus was enabled to shout His last words – "... Father, into your hands I commit my spirit" (Luke 23:46).

Whatever you are, whatever you have, offer to Jesus today. He will accept and use your gift.

"Come, all you who are thirsty, come to the waters; and you who have no money, come, buy and eat! Come, buy wine and milk without money and without cost" (Isa. 55:1).

◆ PRAYER
"Were the whole realm of nature mine, That were an offering far too small; Love so amazing, so divine, Demands my soul, my life, my all."

THE CALVARY PRAYERS

First prayer (Luke 23:34)
"Father , forgive them, for they do not know what they are doing."

Second prayer (Matt. 27:46; Mark 15:34)
"My God, my God, why have you forsaken me?"

Third prayer (Luke 23:46)
"Father, into your hands I commit my spirit."

Prophecy fulfilled

Psalm 22:18; John 19:23–24; Luke 23:34

The soldiers didn't know they were fulfilling Scripture, and probably wouldn't have cared if they had known. The clothes of their victims were the legal "perks" of the unpleasant job they had to perform.

"... that the scripture might be fulfilled ..."

The outer garment, or tallith, was torn into four parts and divided among them. The under garment, or citoneth, was woven in Galilean fashion with no seam and to tear it would have ruined it.

This prophecy and fulfilment gives a picture, too, of Jesus' work as our high priest offering Himself as one perfect sacrifice for sin. In Exodus 28:31 & 32 we see that the high priest's garment should be woven so that it would not tear.

God's ways are wonderful. The more we look into Scripture and realise how clearly everything fits in together from the beginning to the end and for all eternity, the more we can marvel and give praise to our God. He knows all things and does all things well. Not a single detail of His plans is out of place. Praise Him!

"When they had crucified him, they divided up his clothes by casting lots" (Matt. 27:35).

■ THANKSGIVING
Thank You, Lord, that You rule over the affairs of men, and that what You promise is guaranteed to be fulfilled.

Left: A small wooden cross erected beside the Sea of Galilee

DAY 242

No bones broken
Psalm 34:20; Numbers 9:12; John 19:33–36

Some victims had their shoulders dislocated before crucifixion as a merciful act to hasten death. Not so with Jesus. Most also had their legs broken by the soldiers after some hours on the Cross, to hasten death and to fulfil the Jewish law that bodies must not be allowed to remain on the Cross after sunset. When the soldiers came to break Jesus' legs they found Him already dead, having voluntarily given up His spirit.

"... they did not break his legs"

The legs of the criminals each side of Jesus were broken but Jesus, the sacrificial lamb, remained intact. Once again we see God's attention to detail. The outward physical signs corresponded with the deeper spiritual meaning of Jesus' offering of Himself as the perfect Passover lamb.

It is a symbol of wholeness. Just as a whole lamb was offered for each household at Passover, so Jesus offered His whole self for us. Can we do less for Him? Offer your whole life to Him, not the bits and pieces that you can spare from other concerns.

"In bringing many sons to glory, it was fitting that God, for whom and through whom everything exists, should make the author of their salvation perfect through suffering" (Heb. 2:10).

▌ REJOICE
That you are completely saved from your sins by Jesus the perfect Passover lamb.

DAY 243

Jesus' need met
Isaiah 53:9; Matthew 27:57–60

In death, as in life during His earthly ministry, Jesus had no home. It was usual Jewish practice to have a family grave – a place already prepared to receive the corpse after death. Jesus had no such luxury. As a common criminal, His body would probably have been buried under a pile of stones, if it had not been for Joseph of Arimathea.

Joseph was a member of the Sanhedrin, a good and upright man, a secret disciple of Jesus. He also possessed exactly what Jesus needed at that time – a new tomb. He gave it gladly, risking scorn and ridicule to ask for the body of Jesus.

"... placed ... in his own new tomb ..."

We never know when Jesus may require us to give something we have. We need to be ready at any time to relinquish even a most treasured possession if someone else has greater need of it. Jesus died as a destitute common criminal and He was buried as a rich man. He rose and ascended to be the glorious King of kings and Lord of lords.

"So Joseph bought some linen cloth, took down the body, wrapped it in the linen, and placed it in a tomb cut out of the rock" (Mark 15:46).

▌ CHALLENGE
Ask the Lord to show you if there is someone who has a need you can meet.

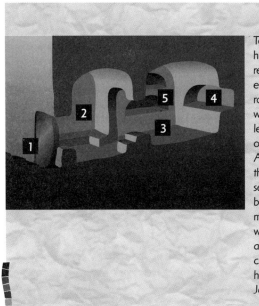

Tombs were cut in the soft limestone on the hillside. A trench was dug in the earth to reach a good depth and steps cut. A low entrance was hewn in the limestone and a round stone cut to cover it. **1** A chamber was made to serve as an anteroom, with a ledge all around for the mourners to sit on. **2** Then the burial chamber was cut. **3** A cavity was cut in the wall and it was in this that the body was laid. **4** Sometimes several cavities were hewn out of the same burial chamber to provide resting places for more bodies. **5** After a time the remains were buried in the ground to make room for a new burial. But the Gospels say very clearly that the tomb in which Jesus was laid had never been used before (Matt. 27:60; John 19:41).

DAY 244

Ambitions dealt with

Matthew 20:20–28;
Mark 10:35–45

Jesus' thoughts were on the suffering that lay immediately ahead of Him. But

"... to serve ..."

James and John, with Salome their mother, could only think of their own selfish ambition for future power and position.

For Jesus the only way to glory was through death. For James and John and for you and me the only way to enter the kingdom is through identification with His death.

Jesus knew that His disciples would, after His resurrection, drink from the same cup of suffering and go through the same baptism of fire as He Himself experienced. That's why He was gentle in His dealings with them.

Their ambition was wrongly placed, but Jesus knew that when the test came they would be willing to pay the price, not for greatness in His kingdom, but for being His servants. Consider your own aims and ambitions in Christ's service. Jesus came "... to serve, and to give His life ..." (v. 28). Can His followers do less?

"... but made himself nothing, taking the very nature of a servant, being made in human likeness" (Phil. 2:7).

MY RESOLVE
To serve You, Lord, in whatever capacity You choose for me.

Blindness removed
Matthew 20:29-34

The blind men were nuisances! They were annoying people by creating a disturbance. We call it "attention seeking" nowadays. Often in our churches and

"Immediately they received their sight ..."

fellowships, we behave just like that crowd and tell such people to be quiet and listen instead of asking awkward questions and pestering people. Yet we must be careful never to hinder any genuine seeker from approaching Jesus, however noisy or unacceptable their behaviour might be.

There was only one thing preventing those two men from following Jesus – their blindness. As soon as they received their sight they followed Him. There are many spiritually blind people around us. Pray for Jesus' compassion for them. Take authority, in Jesus' Name, against the powers of darkness that are blinding them from the truth. Ask the Holy Spirit for the right words to speak to them about Jesus, that they may see Him and be set free to follow Him.

"The Spirit of the Lord is on me, because he has anointed me to preach good news to the poor. He has sent me to proclaim freedom for the prisoners and recovery of sight for the blind ..." (Luke 4:18)

█ PRAYER
Thank You, Lord, for opening my eyes. May I be the instrument of grace in Your hands in helping others also to see.

THE KEY IS JESUS

As all roads in Roman times were said to lead to Rome, so does every road in the Bible lead to Jesus Christ. This is not to say that every biblical passage is Christological or Messianic but all Scripture, since its primary aim is to:

a) REVEAL God and
b) REDEEM man,

has Jesus Christ as its central key.

THE KEY: JESUS

5 Books of Law		Revelation	
12 Historical Books	A N T I C I P A T I O N		Types
5 Poetic Books			Experiences
17 Prophetic Books			Prophecies
4 Gospels		Manifestations	
1 Acts		Realisation	
21 Letters			
1 Revelation		Coronation	

A transformed life
Mark 10:46–52; Luke 18:35–43

There were many blind beggars in the time of Jesus but Bartimaeus is the only one who is given a name by the Gospel writers. This suggests that he continued on to become a disciple and was well known in the Early Church.

Jesus heals because He has compassion on the sick and because, as the God of creation, His desire is for wholeness and perfection in His creation. What we do with our healing is our own responsibility. Bartimaeus had faith in Jesus. "Son of God" is a Messianic title and shows that Bartimaeus believed that this

.. your faith has healed you"

Jesus of Nazareth – whom he knew only by hearsay until then – was truly the expected Messiah.

Hearing about Jesus led Bartimaeus to faith in Him. Meeting Jesus produced a change of life. Bartimaeus was no longer blind. He was no longer a beggar but a servant of the living God. He no longer had to shout to Jesus, but could speak with Him normally. Think about the changes that Jesus has brought about in your life and thank Him for them.

"Now faith is being sure of what we hope for and certain of what we do not see" (Heb. 11:1).

◢ POSITIVE CONFESSION
"Jesus You are changing me, by Your Spirit, You're making me like You."

True repentance
Luke 19:1–10

Zacchaeus was an eager, energetic little man. Keen to see Jesus, he ran ahead of the crowd and climbed a tree, which was not very dignified for a man in his position! Anxious to serve Jesus, he climbed down and welcomed Him as a guest in his house. Eager to repent and to truly please Jesus he was willing to relinquish his ill-gotten wealth.

Compare Zacchaeus with the rich young ruler who found it too hard to let go of his riches to enter the kingdom of God. When we come to Jesus we must lay everything that we

"... he looked up ..."

have and are at His feet, holding nothing back.

Ask the Holy Spirit now to reveal to you if you are holding on to something in your life and are unwilling to give it up if Jesus should require it of you. Consider the extent of Zacchaeus' repentance (v. 8) and ask yourself if you have wronged anyone. Perhaps you have said, "Sorry," but have you taken steps to put things right?

"What do you think? If a man owns a hundred sheep and one of them wanders away, will he not leave the ninety-nine on the hills and go to look for the one that wandered off?" (Matt. 18:12)

◢ ACTION
Prayerfully consider the last sentence and determine to take the appropriate action - with God's help.

TAX COLLECTORS

Roman taxes were of two kinds. First were direct taxes, collected by the Roman authorities themselves. There was one on land amounting to nearly a quarter of what the land produced and another on a man's money.

Indirect taxes were rather like our customs duties, but the Romans did not collect these themselves. Every five years the right to collect taxes was auctioned at Rome to the highest bidder. Out to make a good profit himself, he hired local men to collect the taxes for him, and they too had to make their profit. Thus everyone cheated under this dreadfully corrupt system.

The local tax-collectors were termed "publicani" in Latin, the reason they were called "publicans" in the Authorised Version of the Bible. They sat in their customs-houses throughout Palestine in the market-place, at the cross-roads, and by the bridge with, perhaps, a Roman soldier standing by for protection.

The Jews deeply hated paying taxes to Rome, hated being cheated and hated most of all the traitor Jews who collected the taxes for the Romans. "Tax collectors" are always linked with "sinners" in the Gospels. They were outcasts of Jewish society, rich in their ill-gotten wealth, but poor in friends.

DAY 248

Fruitlessness – through fear

Luke 19:11–27

Fear is a paralysing emotion. The servant who hid the money entrusted to him was afraid. He was so afraid of making a mistake, afraid of losing the money, of having it stolen, that he was not competent enough to use it wisely. His master was very angry with him for being so miserably negative in attitude and action.

"... work ... until I come back"

Jesus is the master in this parable. Before He left this earth to go back to His Father's side He entrusted His disciples with the good news of His kingdom, to be spread throughout the world and to bear fruit for Him.

Just as the servants in the parable were all given the same amount of money, so we are all entrusted with the same Gospel (1 Tim. 1:11; 1 Thess. 2:4). We have the responsibility of spreading it. Take care that fear does not prevent you. Ask God to remove any fear of man from your heart and to fill you with His Holy Spirit, who gives power and boldness to witness (Acts 1:8). Know that God is with you, that His power within you is greater than the evil power of the world. Have confidence!

"Now it is required that those who have been given a trust must prove faithful" (1 Cor. 4:2)

■ MEDITATION
Psalm 56:3 & 4

DAY 249

God reigns

John 12:1, 9-11

Many Jews were gathering in and around Jerusalem in preparation for the Passover. The buzz of conversation as relatives and friends greeted one another often turned to the major news item of the day: "Have you heard about Lazarus?" "Have you met this Jesus?" Everyone was interested, many wanted to see for themselves, and so a large crowd gathered at Bethany.

... whom he had raised from the dead"

For the chief priests, already angered by the unorthodox teaching and large following of Jesus, this was the last straw. They thought that by removing the insti-gator, Jesus, and the evidence, Lazarus, they would cool the situation and all would return to normal. How wrong they were!

They were working in a natural realm – but God works in a spiritual realm. All through the ages evil men have killed Christians in attempts to stop the spread of God's kingdom. They haven't succeeded. Praise God today that *He* reigns and that His plan of redemption will not be thwarted!

"And if the Spirit of him who raised Jesus from the dead is living in you, he who raised Christ from the dead will also give life to your mortal bodies through his Spirit, who lives in you" (Rom. 8:11).

▼ THOUGHT

Our Lord has written the message of resurrection not in words alone but in every leaf in springtime.

DAY 250

Love poured out

John 12:2-8

Martha was still serving and Mary still sitting at Jesus' feet (see Luke 10:40) but this time there is no mention of tension between the sisters. We can learn to respect the ministries of others even though different from our own.

"You will always have the poor among you ..."

Mary's worship, however, had deepened. Whereas previously she had sat and listened to Jesus, now we find her actively showing her love and adoration for Him, pouring the expensive perfume lavishly over His feet. It didn't matter to Mary what anyone

SPIKENARD

Spikenard was an oil with an exquisite scent. It was made from the roots and leaves of a plant which grows on the slopes of the Himalayan mountains. To import it from so far away made it rare and costly. The precious drops were kept in small phials made of alabaster. Spikenard was brought by ship up the Red Sea, and then overland by the camel trains of Nabatean merchants.

The perfume was decanted drop by drop, into the tiny narrow-necked alabaster jars. By breaking the neck Mary was able to let the perfume drop on to Jesus' head. It was the custom for guests at a feast to have their hands anointed (see Luke 7:46) with cool and refreshing ointment. The perfume Mary used would have cost a year's wages for a working man.

else thought of her – she was concerned only with Jesus. What wonderful worship services we would have in our churches and fellowships if we had Mary's attitude! What precious times each of us would have if we poured out our love for Him like that in our prayer times.

Mary loved Jesus and she wasn't ashamed to show it. The pouring out of the expensive perfume was an outward expression of the love that she felt in her heart. Compare your own expressions of love, worship and adoration with Mary's.

"Now it is God who makes both us and you stand firm in Christ. He anointed us ..." (2 Cor. 1:21).

▮ WORSHIP
"Worship the Lord in the beauty of holiness".

Above: In Jerusalem's Old City

DAY 251

Hailing the King

Matthew 21:1–11; Mark 11:1–11; Luke 19:29–44; John 12:12–19

"At last," the people must have thought, "Jesus is riding into Jerusalem to establish His kingdom and free us from the Roman oppression." They added "King of Israel" and "Son of David" to the psalm traditionally sung by pilgrims to Jerusalem (Psa. 118:26). They were extravagant in their praise, waving palm branches and sacrificing their clothing to smooth the way before Him.

"... the Lord needs them ..."

For the first time Jesus did not refuse the honour shown to Him. It was necessary for Him to ride into Jerusalem to ful-fil the Scripture (Zech. 9:9) and Jesus did not rebuke the crowds for praising Him, even though He knew that their conception of His kingship was false.

If only they knew who was among them! If only they would recognise their King of peace. But they didn't, and they wouldn't. So even as the shouts of praise and adulation were ringing in Jesus' ears, He wept over Jerusalem. He weeps for people today who do not, or will not, recognise Him for who He is – Saviour, Lord and coming King.

"... which God will bring about in his own time – God, the blessed and only Ruler, the King of kings and Lord of lords" (1 Tim. 6:15).

▮ ASK YOURSELF
Is my praise of Jesus consistent in a hostile environment? Do I fade away into the rest of the crowd? Matt. 27:22–26.

Continual cleansing needed

Matthew 21:12–17; Mark 11:11, 15–19; Luke 19:45–48

Jesus had cleansed the temple courtyards three years previously (John 2:13–16), but the money lenders and stall-holders had crept back, with their animals. We, whose bodies are the temple of the Holy Spirit (1 Cor. 6:19), need to be continually watchful that old sins, habits and worldly attitudes do not creep back into our lives after our initial cleansing by the blood of Jesus at conversion. The Word of God will keep us daily washed and clean if we

'My house will be called a house of prayer' ..."

heed and obey it (Eph. 5:26).

The contrast between "a house of prayer" and a "den of robbers" is a very strong one. The incense in the temple was a symbol of the prayers of God's people ascending as a sweet fragrance to Him. This fragrance was contaminated naturally by the smell of the many animals and spiritually by the deceit, lies and hypocrisy of the people.

If our lives are contaminated, the only prayer God will hear is that of repentance. Then, from a cleansed temple, our prayers will ascend to Him as a pleasing fragrance. God desires your life and your home to be a house of prayer.

"Very early in the morning, while it was still dark, Jesus got up, left the house and went off to a solitary place, where he prayed" (Mark 1:35).

■ MEDITATION
Ephesians 5:26-27

Looking for fruit

Matthew 21:18–19; Mark 11:12–14

Like the fig tree, like the temple, like the nation. The fig tree and the vine are both symbols of Israel. Jesus looked for fruit on the fig tree (the early figs, as it was not the main cropping season) but did not find any.

He looked for the fruit of prayer in the temple but found corruption instead. He looked for acknowledgement of His Messiahship in Israel but received rejection instead.

"Immediately the tree withered"

The fig tree was cursed, the temple destroyed in AD 70 and the nation of Israel completely suppressed by the Romans four years later.

Jesus still looks for fruit in His Church and in our individual lives. He Himself will bring forth that fruit if we fulfil certain conditions. We should be rooted in Him (Col. 2:7); watered with living water (John 4:14); nourished by the Word (Matt. 4:4); pruned regularly (John 15:2). Ask Jesus if He is pleased with the fruit in your life. Listen and learn from His answer.

"The axe is already at the root of the trees, and every tree that does not produce good fruit will be cut down and thrown into the fire" (Matt. 3:10).

◢ FOR CONSIDERATION
Matt. 7:19; Galatians 5:22, 23

Greater than our faith

Matthew 21:20–22;
Mark 11:20–26

Peter was astounded that the fig tree should wither at Jesus' command. He didn't yet understand that it was by the word of Jesus that the whole world was created. The withering of one fig tree was a small thing in comparison. When we consider prayer the question should not be "How great is my faith?" Rather, it should be "How great is my God?"

"... it will be done"

When we begin to realise the infinite power of the God of creation, the majesty and glory of the God of heaven, the inestimable love of our Father whose love reaches to every person who is, or ever has been, on this earth, when we appreciate Jesus' compassion on the Cross and understand what He accomplished at Calvary, then we will not need to strive after faith. We will know our God.

So know what He *is* God, that He is your Father and that you are His child. He will hear you when you talk to Him and He will give you what you ask. It is as simple, and as profound, as that.

"Every valley shall be raised up, every mountain and hill made low; the rough ground shall become level, and rugged places a plain" (Isa. 40:4).

▉ MEMORISE
Isaiah 45:2 & 3

THE FIG TREE

A fig tree that was well cared for produced its fruit for ten months of the year. There were three crops:

(1) The main crop called 'late' or 'autumn' figs, from August to winter. They grew on the new wood.

(2') Green or 'winter' figs which did not ripen and stayed on the branches through winter. They were eaten when the wind blew them down.

(3) 'Early' or 'first-ripe' figs, which were best of all for flavour. They remained on the tree and ripened in June. The Bible speaks of all three crops: (1) Isaiah 28:4; (2) Jeremiah 29:17; (3) Song of Songs 2:13 and Jeremiah 24:2.

Jesus once looked for fruit on a fig tree at Bethany when He was hungry (Mark 11:12–14). It was not the season for either late autumn figs or early first-ripe figs.

He expected to find green or winter figs, for the tree had plenty of leaves, but there was no fruit. This too was a parable of the Jewish people – full of religion, but bearing no fruit of faith and goodness.

DAY 255

Jesus' offer spurned

Matthew 21:23–27;
Mark 11:27–33; Luke 20:1–8

Attack and counter-attack! Jesus was never on the defensive even though His life was in danger. He did not need to explain His actions and His teaching to the "enemy" in the form of the Jewish officials, because all that He did was in direct obedience to the highest authority, His Father. Yet Jesus gave these stubborn men further opportunity to humble themselves if they would confess that the powerful preaching of John the Baptist could have come from God.

"I will also ask you one question"

They hesitated. "If we say this ... if we say that"! They were not seeking a truthful reply, but an expedient one, and their wilful refusal to give a straight answer to Jesus' question provoked a flat refusal from Him to answer theirs.

Jesus can only deal with truth because He is the truth. He will always answer our honest questions, doubts and fears, but He cannot help us when we try to deceive, cover up or wriggle out of the truth.

"Then Jesus came to them and said, 'All authority in heaven and on earth has been given to me' " (Matt. 28:18).

◆ FURTHER STUDY
Matt. 7:29, Mark 1:27, John 5:27. To whom were the people comparing Jesus when they made their observation?

DAY 256

No half measures!

Matthew 21:28–32

Every parent will identify with the feelings of the father after he had told his son to tidy his room. "OK, I'll do it after I've watched this programme/finished my homework/phoned my friend ..." It never gets done. Obedience is not obedience unless it is instant obedience.

"What do you think?"

There is no room for half-heartedness in God's kingdom. The priests and elders in Jerusalem pretended obedience to God. They obeyed His laws according to their own standards. They were outwardly religious, saying "Yes" to God but not, in fact, doing His will.

Can you understand the Father's heart in this situation? Can you enter into His grief and anger over these religious men who would not acknowledge His Son and obey Him? Pray for such people today, that God would melt their hearts and reveal the truth to them. Also watch that you yourself do not fall into the same trap.

"But Samuel replied: 'Does the Lord delight in burnt offerings and sacrifices as much as in obeying the voice of the Lord? To obey is better than sacrifice, and to heed is better than the fat of rams' " (1 Sam. 15:22).

◆ FOR STUDY
With a concordance study the "immediatelys" in the Gospels.

Warning unheeded

**Matthew 21:43–46;
Mark 12:1–12; Luke 20:9–19**

The chief priests and Pharisees knew Jesus was talking about them but, tragically, they did not heed the warning and repent. In the parable the tenant farmers killed the son of the owner *because* they recognised him for who he was, not out of ignorance.

"Haven't you read this scripture ..."

The priests who were plotting against Jesus' life *did* recognise that His power and authority came from God, although they pretended not to. Their sin, therefore, was even more grievous and culpable.

Jesus adapted this parable from Isaiah 5:1-2, the meaning of which would have been very clear to Jewish scholars. The owner of the vineyard is God the Father, the tenants the Jewish leaders, the servants the Old Testament prophets and the Son, Jesus Himself. The Jewish leaders had persecuted the prophets and refused to listen to them – now they were about to kill the Son.

God's judgment is very severe on those who knowingly reject the claims of Christ, but those of us who throw ourselves on His mercy find Him to be a rock of salvation.

"These things happened to them as examples and were written down as warnings for us, on whom the fulfilment of the ages has come" (1 Cor. 10:11).

**MEMORISE
2 Tim. 2:15**

Our Father

**Matthew 6:6–9; John 15:16;
16:23**

We are going to spend a week studying the prayer life of Jesus and His teaching on prayer.

A man once went for an interview with a very important person. He washed and dressed very carefully, determined to make a good impression. He presented himself at the reception desk early and was asked to wait. He was then taken along polished corridors to the man's private secretary and asked to wait again. Finally he entered the office and stood in front of the interviewer's desk before being invited to sit down. Nervously, he

"This ... is how you should pray ..."

was attempting to ask and answer questions correctly when, suddenly, the door burst open and a small boy ran in, jumped on the man's knee and cried, "Daddy, my engine's broken! Please will you mend it?" He did.

Jesus taught His disciples to say, "Our Father." Your whole attitude to prayer hinges on whether you really see God as your Father and can come to Him as that little boy did: trustingly and without fear.

"Then Jesus told his disciples a parable to show them that they should always pray and not give up" (Luke 18:1).

**PRAYER
My Father, I'm so glad I'm Your child. I come to You now, knowing that You love me. I love You, Father. Amen.**

Praise, worship and thanks

Matthew 6:9; John 4:23; 6:11; 11:41

A small child worships his father. Dad can do no wrong in his eyes and is better than anyone else's Dad. Even mature Christians need to remain as little children in this respect, continually worshipping the great God whom we serve, remembering who He is.

"... worship the Father in spirit and truth ...

True worship requires purity of spirit and humility. As we come before Him in prayer, we should first bow down and worship. Jesus was full of joy as He praised His Father, recognising His greatness as Lord of heaven and earth (Luke 10:21). Praise is a joyful thing. On our own and with others we can sing God's praises, dance and clap before Him. Praise Him for who He is, for all the aspects of His character and for the wonderful things that He has done. Jesus praised His Father in public, letting all around Him hear what His Father had done. Let us not be afraid to do that, too.

Thanksgiving came naturally to Jesus. It was His habit to give thanks before He ate and drank. Do you remember to thank God for the everyday things of life, as well as for the special blessings?

"Come, let us bow down in worship, let us kneel before the Lord our Maker" (Psalm 95:6).

QUESTION
Are these part of your prayer life? Worship, praise, gratitude, love, thankfulness, adoration.

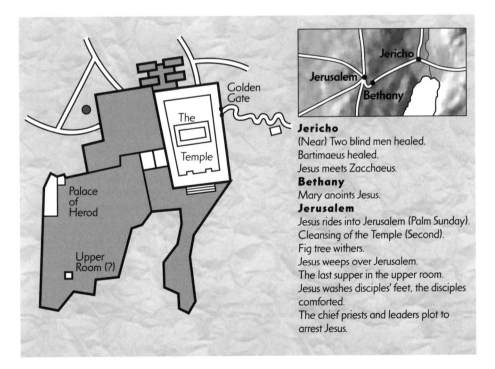

Jericho
(Near) Two blind men healed.
Bartimaeus healed.
Jesus meets Zacchaeus.
Bethany
Mary anoints Jesus.
Jerusalem
Jesus rides into Jerusalem (Palm Sunday).
Cleansing of the Temple (Second).
Fig tree withers.
Jesus weeps over Jerusalem.
The last supper in the upper room.
Jesus washes disciples' feet, the disciples comforted.
The chief priests and leaders plot to arrest Jesus.

DAY 260

Surrender
Matthew 6:10; 26:36–44; Luke 23:46

"Your will be done." We say it to our Father, but do we really mean it in our lives? Jesus was completely surrendered to His Father's will in all things. He did nothing except He saw the Father doing it (John 5:19). He wanted only to be obedient to His Father in all things, right to the bitter end.

"... not as I will, but as you will"

Jesus' prayer in the Garden of Gethsemane was wrung out of an anguish that we can't begin to understand. Taking the sins of the world on Himself meant total separation from His Father for a while. It was this, rather than the physical humiliation and pain, that Jesus' spirit shrank from. Yet He would not ask to be released from it if that were His Father's will.

We can only be totally sure of God's answer to our prayers when we are totally surrendered to His will. By His Holy Spirit He will reveal His will to us as we pray. Examine your own life to see if there are any areas which are not yet surrendered to Him.

"Do not offer the parts of your body to sin, as instruments of wickedness, but rather offer yourselves to God, as those who have been brought from death to life; and offer the parts of your body to him as instruments of righteousness" (Rom. 6:13).

◢ DEFINITION
Write out your definition of the word surrender.

PRAYER

Prayer is so simple;
It is like quietly opening a door
And slipping into the very
    presence of God,
There in the stillness
To listen to His voice;
Perhaps to petition,
Or only to listen;
It matters not.
Just to be there
In His presence
Is prayer.

DAY 261

Asking in faith
Matthew 6:11, 7:7–11, 9:38, 17:20; Luke 11–13

It seems too simple to most of us – ask and you will get it! If God knows what we need anyway, why should we ask for it? Surely it is selfish to ask for things for ourselves anyway? These and other questions have puzzled Christian people through the ages. The key to the answers is in the order of the pattern prayer in Matthew 6:9–13.

"Ask ... seek ... knock ..."

Firstly, we know God as our Heavenly Father who loves us, cares about us and knows our needs. Then we worship Him. As we worship, praise and exalt *Him*, we forget about ourselves – our selfish desires vanish. Then we submit ourselves completely to His will. Then we are ready to ask, as the Holy Spirit leads, for our own and other peoples' needs, practical and spiritual, in full assurance that we are praying according to God's will and that He will hear and answer.

Prayer is an exciting adventure. The Holy Spirit may lead you in ways that you have not thought of with your natural mind. Let Him lead you from today onwards in new dimensions.

"Until now you have not asked for anything in my name. Ask and you will receive, and your joy will be complete" (John 16:24).

■ **MEDITATION**
Philippians 4:6-7

Forgiveness

Matthew 6:12, 14–15; Mark 11:25; Luke 23:34

One of the most heart-rending prayers of Jesus is "Father forgive them ..." Even on the Cross, suffering excruciating pain for sins He hadn't committed. Jesus' thoughts were for those causing His pain. He forgave and He prayed for them.

"... when you stand praying ... forgive ..."

When I'm tempted with the sins of unforgiveness, resentment, anger or self-pity, I remember Jesus on the Cross. Nothing as bad as that has happened to me. If Jesus could forgive those who caused His agony, then so can I forgive the much lesser things that cause me hurt or annoyance. The Greek word *aphiemi* translated "forgive" in the New Testament literally means "to send away" or "let go".

When we forgive we push away the hurt done to us by another person, banish it out of existence, so that it can no longer damage the relationship between us. When we pray we must forgive, so that the Father will forgive us.

"Be kind and compassionate to one another, forgiving each other, just as in Christ God forgave you" (Eph. 4:32).

■ **STUDY**
Matthew 5:44; Luke 6:27–28

Salvation

Matthew 6:13; John 12:27–37

Jesus, Saviour of the world, did not ask His Father to save Him from the evil of death on the cross. He placed Himself at the mercy of evil men in order that *we* can pray, "deliver us from evil".

Salvation is a continual thing. At Calvary Jesus destroyed Satan's works and saved us from his power. If we trust in Jesus we are initially delivered from the kingdom of darkness and transferred to the kingdom of light. A continual abiding in Him safeguards us from the attacks and temptations of Satan and the world. We have a right, as sons and

"... sons of light ..."

daughters of God, to claim deliverance from, and protection against, the evil one. We can lift up the shield of faith to repel all the devil's fiery darts (Eph. 6:16).

We parents can pray for our families in this way, and for those in the Church we have responsibility for. Jesus has bought with His blood this full salvation for us. Pray continually, and expect to live in the freedom of that salvation.

"Oh, that salvation for Israel would come out of Zion! When the Lord restores the fortunes of his people, let Jacob rejoice and Israel be glad!" (Psalm 14:7).

■ **MY AFFIRMATION**
"I am trusting Thee, Lord Jesus, trusting only Thee; Trusting Thee for full salvation, great and free."

Intercession
John 17:1–26

Jesus prayed for you while He was here on earth! (v. 20) Doesn't that give you a sense of security in His love? This chapter has been called the greatest intercessory prayer ever prayed, for Jesus the Son interceded on our behalf to His Father.

"I pray for them..." Intercession means "standing in the gap," or "on behalf of". When we intercede for others we stand before the Father in the Name of Jesus and plead for those who cannot plead for themselves. It is a secret, hidden ministry, but a very important one in the Church. God is calling intercessors today to pray for the Church, the nation and the world. Consider your own responsibility in this area.

If God's children will not intercede, there is no-one else He can call on. Read again Jesus' requests for His (present and future) disciples. He prayed for protection (vv. 11,15), unity (vv. 11, 21, 23), joy (v. 13), sanctification (vv. 17, 19), fellowship with Him in heaven (v. 24) and love (v. 26). Jesus wants you to enjoy these gifts that He has asked for you to receive.

"Therefore he is able to save completely those who come to God through him, because he always lives to intercede for them" (Heb. 7:25)

◤ KEY THOUGHT
Christ Jesus – is at the right hand of God and is also interceding for us. Romans 8:34

Wedding invitation
Matthew 22:1–14

Each guest arriving at an Eastern wedding was given a wedding garment to wear. The feast was held at the bridegroom's house and all guests, no matter how poor and shabby or rich and expensively dressed when they arrived, would look alike and be treated the same way at the festivities.

"... many are invited, but few are chosen" This is a wonderful picture for us of the marriage feast of the Lamb, to which all are invited (Rev. 19:9).

When the Jews refused Jesus' invitation the offer was extended to the Gentiles. Good and bad alike came pouring in – and still come – accepting the pure white garment of righteousness bought with Jesus' blood at Calvary (Phil. 3:9). But we cannot enter the kingdom of God or sit down at His table, wearing our own clothes of sin or self-righteousness, for "all our rightcous acts are like filthy rags" (Isaiah 64:6).

There was no excuse for the man at the feast without a wedding garment, for one had been freely offered to him. Rejoice in God's provision today, and enjoy the privilege of being His guest. Put on the garment of righteousness and praise Him.

"Because of the increase of wickedness, the love of most will grow cold" (Matt. 24:12).

◤ REJOICE
Isaiah 61:10

Right: an ancient stepped road in Jerusalem with the Mount of Olives beyond

THE GREAT HIGH PRIESTLY PRAYER
John 17:1–26

Jesus offers a ninefold review of the past. He had:
given eternal life to all the elect (v. 2)
glorified the Father (v. 4)
completed His assignment (v. 4)
revealed the Person of God to man (vv. 6, 26)
declared the Word of God to man (vv. 8, 14)
kept the elect (v. 12; see also 18:9)
sent them into the world (v. 18)
sanctified (separated) Himself for them (v. 19)
shared with them His glory (v. 22)

He makes a ninefold request for the future. He asks the Father:
to glorify the Son (vv. 1, 5)
to keep the elect (v. 11)
to unify the elect (v. 11)
to fill them with joy (v. 13)
to protect them (v. 15)
to sanctify them (v. 17)
to guide them in the world (v. 23)
to gather them in the heavenlies (v. 24)
to fill them with love (v. 26)

In this prayer Jesus prays for Himself (17:1–5), for the disciples (17:6–19), and for the Church (17:20–26).

What a blessed "Father and Son" business meeting this prayer was! Now the Son is in His Father's house and the Holy Spirit is busily at work carrying out these great redemptive requests made by the Son on the eve of His crucifixion.

DAY 266

Insincerity exposed

**Matthew 22:15–22;
Mark 12:13–17; Luke 20:20–26**

A carefully laid trap was set for Jesus. He had previously placed the Pharisees in a position where either of two answers would be dangerous (Mark 11:31, 32), so now they attempted to snare Jesus in a similar way.

"... give ... to God what is God's"

The Herodians were a political party, irreligious and supporters of Rome. If Jesus said "Yes" to their question He would be denounced by the people as a traitor. If He said "No" He could be handed over the Romans.

The insincerity of the initial flattery did not deceive Jesus. He openly told the men that He saw through their trap. The contrast between the darkness of deceit and the light of truth is striking. Jesus then answered their question with profound wisdom, teaching us at the same time that we have a certain responsibility to human government.

We receive the benefit of law and order, amenities and education, so we should pay our dues. Our greater responsibility, however, is to God. Consider your own position on giving right honour and dues to God and to the nation's rulers.

"Show proper respect to everyone: Love the brotherhood of believers, fear God, honour the king" (1 Pet. 2:17).

**STUDY
Romans 13**

DAY 267

In step with God

**Matthew 22:23–33;
Mark 12:18–27; Luke 20:27–28**

It was the Sadducees' turn to be exposed. They did not believe in the resurrection so their question was a dishonest one. They adhered to Moses' law but refused to acknowledge the continual unfolding of spiritual revelation from God through the prophets until that present time. There are Christians like that today, living in the past and not seeing what new things God is doing in the Church today.

"... I am the God of Abraham ... Isaac, and ... Jacob"

Let us keep in step with God as He reveals His will today through the Scriptures and through prophets and teachers in the Church. The Sadducees were in error because they did not know the Scriptures or the power of God. A Christian is like a railway engine, which needs tracks to run on and the power to move. Without tracks it will career around all over the countryside, a danger to all. Without the power it will stay safely on the tracks and get nowhere.

The tracks are the written Word of God, the power is the Holy Spirit. Consider whether you have a balance of both in the walk with God.

"Jesus said to her, 'I am the resurrection and the life. He who believes in me will live, even though he dies' " (John 11:25).

THANKS
Lord, I thank You that I have received Your abundant resurrection life. There is no question in my mind that You are the risen Son of God. Praise Your name!

DAY 268

With all our heart
Matthew 22:34–40;
Mark 12:28–34; Luke 20:39–40

He was an honest Pharisee, judging by Mark's account of the incident. A genuine enquirer who was prepared, at least, to accept Jesus as a good teacher. We are not told whether he later entered the Kingdom and became part of the Early Church, but I like to think that he did.

"Love the Lord your God ..."

Jesus answered his question by combining Deuteronomy 6:4, 5 and Leviticus 19:18. Of the ten commandments given to Moses (Exodus 20:1–17) the first four govern our attitude towards God and the remaining six our actions towards our neighbours. If we love God, our whole lives will be geared to worshipping him and doing His will. If we genuinely love our neighbours we will be a positive living witness of the Gospel to them. Without the second the first is meaningless and without the first the second is impossible.

Read Mark 12:30 again and consider the "alls". Measure your own love for God by Jesus' standards. Then think of your "neighbours". Is there any way you could more actively love them?

"... all men will know that you are my disciples if you love one another" (John 13:35).

▌ FOR FURTHER READING
1 John 4:6–21

DAY 269

Fixed on Jesus
Matthew 22:41–46;
Mark 12:35–37; Luke 20:41–44

The Jewish leaders' extreme discomfort at Jesus' question shows their failure to understand the nature of the Messiah,

"What do you think about ... Christ?"

Jesus' quotation of Psalm 110:1 shows the Messiah as both God and man. As David's son He is man, but because David the king calls Him "Lord", He must be more exalted than David and, therefore, God. The Jews, looking for an earthly deliverer, could not conceive of a Heavenly One.

We, too, need to watch that we don't have our eyes so firmly fixed on worldly things that we fail to see the spiritual. We often strive and struggle to work through a difficult situation when God longs to step in and work it out His way. Let's remember He is God and can do all things.

Worship Him, turn to Him first and He will work things out either supernaturally or naturally, according to His will. The Jews' failure was the failure to recognise Jesus as God. Never forget His greatness, His majesty and glory.

"Simon Peter answered, 'You are the Christ, the Son of the living God' (Matt. 16:16).

▌ WORSHIP
"You are my God, and I exalt Thee You are my God and I will praise Thee."

Be real!
Matthew 23:1–31;
Mark 12:38–40; Luke 20:45–47

Beware of head knowledge! The scribes and the Pharisees knew Scripture. They could quote, argue and explain the law of Moses and the prophets, but they were spiritually blind and did not practise what they preached. What a sad denunciation in Matthew 23:3: "... do not do what they do." Compare this with the words of Paul (who was a converted Pharisee) in 1 Corinthians 11:1.

"Woe to you ..."

Unless my life and my actions measure up to my words and knowledge then I am equally as hypocritical as the Pharisees. One definition of hypocrisy is "pretending to be what one is not". Is your Christian life real? Are your innermost thoughts and attitudes in line with your manner and actions in public?

God desires truth in the inner parts, and the blood Jesus shed is able to cleanse deep sins as well as visible ones. Allow Him to make you transparent, real, true to Him through and through.

"Meanwhile, when a crowd of many thousands had gathered, so that they were trampling on one another, Jesus began to speak first to his disciples, saying, 'Be on your guard against the yeast of the Pharisees, which is hypocrisy' " (Luke 12:1).

QUESTION
What are the characteristics of hypocrisy?

Peril of rejection
Matthew 23:32–36

The Scribes and Pharisees had had their chance. They had met with Jesus, talked and argued with Him, experienced His power in the healings and miracles He performed. They had gazed at the purity of His life. The evidence was before them to accept or reject – and they continually rejected it. When people continually reject the Holy Spirit, the Spirit withdraws and there is no forgiveness. God's judgment inevitably falls on such people.

"... You brood of vipers!"

So great was the Jewish leaders' hatred and rejection of Jesus that they were determined to kill Him to prevent others from entering the kingdom that He promised. Yet still God hadn't finished with them. Still He would send them teachers and prophets after the outpouring of the Holy Spirit at Pentecost, to proclaim the Gospel of Christ crucified to them. Some of them, perhaps, were among the 3,000 who repented after Peter's first sermon (Acts 2:41).

God's judgment is just, righteous and inescapable for sinners who will not repent. But it is always tempered with mercy and patience.

"... if this is so, then the Lord knows how to rescue godly men from trials and to hold the unrighteous for the day of judgment, while continuing their punishment" (2 Peter 2:9).

PRAY
For those you know who have so far resisted the Gospel message.

DAY 272

Grief for a city
Matthew 23:37-39

Feel the heartache of Jesus as He grieved over Jerusalem. If you have ever been badly hurt by someone you love deeply, someone you have tried to help or your wife, husband or child, **"... you were** then you will understand **not willing"** something of the deep emotions Jesus experienced for the people of Jerusalem.

God had built His temple there, His dwelling place. He had spoken through His prophets there, revealing His plan and purpose for His beloved people. Think of Isaiah – he ministered in the temple in Jerusalem and received his commission from the Lord in a wonderful vision (Isa. 6:1-8). He spoke faithfully the words that God gave him to speak, foretelling the coming Messiah and of God's judgment on unfaithful Judah.

But the people didn't listen. God loved them and spoke to them over and over again, but they refused to hear. Now they refused the Son of God Himself. Ask God today for the kind of love and yearning over your town, city or village that Jesus had for Jerusalem

"He came to that which was his own, but his own did not receive him" (John 1:11).

✎ MEDITATION
Isaiah 6:5–8

DAY 273

Valuable to Him
Mark 12:41-44; Luke 21:1-4

"I can't do anything for you, Lord. I'm so small and insignificant and have nothing to give." I've felt like that, and I'm sure you have. It's true, too, in one way, that our offerings are noth- **"... she ... put in** ing in comparison to **everything ..."** God's greatness and wealth. Even giving ourselves completely and wholeheartedly to God is nothing compared to Jesus' sacrifice on the Cross for us. It is good to remember that, and to kneel before Him humbly, confessing our nothingness to Him.

The widow in today's passages knew that she was nothing. Widows in those days had no financial support and were often left to die. She realised that in giving her last farthing to God she could be

THE BEST THING TO GIVE ...

The best thing to give...
to your enemy is forgiveness;
to an opponent, tolerance;
to a friend, your heart;
to your child, a good example;
to a father, deference;
to your mother, conduct that
    will make her proud of you;
to yourself, respect;
to all men, charity;
to God, yourself.

condemning herself to death and no one would care. Yet she still gave – and God received her gift gladly.

The small insignificant amount of money from a nameless woman is still remembered today, 2,000 years later. It is written in God's book and in His heart.

It is not insignificant to Him. Whatever *you* give to Him, He will treasure and use.

"Give, and it will be given to you. A good measure, pressed down, shaken together and running over, will be poured into your lap. For with the measure you use, it will be measured to you" (Luke 6:38).

■ QUESTION
1 Cor. 1:20–31. What is Paul teaching here?

DAY 274

A new temple

Matthew 24:1–3; Mark 13:1–4; Luke 21:5–7

The new temple, still under construction in Jesus' time, was one of the architectural wonders of the Roman world. Herod was building it for the Jews, and it was being soundly constructed, in common with other building work going on in Judea at that time. There could have

"Tell us ... when will this happen"

been a note of pride in the disciples' wish to draw it to Jesus' attention. Jesus, however, knew that the usefulness of the earthly temple was soon to end. Our Lord had come to inaugurate a new temple, built with living stones, His

Church. There is a spiritual progression through the Scriptures which we need to understand. God is constantly the same – yet constantly doing new things. He never changes, yet He reveals new truths to the Church as we need them.

Let us be always open to hear and see what He is saying to us today. The disciples' question (Matt. 24:3) shows that they have grasped some, but not all, of the truth. As we wait on God we must seek to know His *whole* will. If we only grasp part of it there is a danger of going off at a tangent.

"Don't you know that you yourselves are God's temple and that God's Spirit lives in you?" (1 Cor. 3:16)

■ KEY THOUGHT
Lord, may my life be so lived that the temple of my body will be Your continual dwelling place.

DAY 275

End time signs

Matthew 24:4–31; Mark 13:5–10; Luke 21:8–11, 20–28

We will know when Jesus comes again – there will be no doubt about it whatsoever! Just as vultures instinctively gather around a carcass, so will God's people know, by spiritual awareness, of

"Watch out that no-one deceives you"

the second coming of the Lord.

The prophetic words of Jesus preceding these verses refer both to the times immediately following His death and, on a wider scale, to the times preceding His second coming.

The false Christs, wars, famines, persecution and desecration of the temple all happened during the 40 years between Christ's death and the final destruction of Jerusalem about AD 70. As we look around the world today we can see the prophecies being fulfilled in the wider sense.

We need carefully to note Matthew 24:12, 13. It is so easy today for Christians to succumb to the pull of the world. There must be no compromise. Let's encourage each other to stand firm in Jesus, the rock of our salvation, and not be deceived by worldly standards or by the enticing lies of the enemy.

"You also must be ready, because the Son of Man will come at an hour when you do not expect him" (Luke 12:40).

◤ **RESOLVE**
Philippians 2:15

DAY 276

Encouraging signs
Matthew 24:30–35;
Mark 13:28–31; Luke 21:29–33

The snowdrops are almost out and the daffodils pushing their way bravely through the frozen ground, as I write this, in February.

Even though snow is falling I know that spring is near, and I'm encouraged and uplifted. So it will be in the last days before Jesus comes again.

The world will get worse, times more difficult, Christians will suffer persecution. Yet, as we see and experience these things, we will know that the end is in sight – that Jesus is coming (Matt. 24:30). His coming will be sudden, but watch and you will be prepared. Matthew 24:34 can be interpreted in various ways, but verse 35 is quite unequivocal – the words of Jesus are sure, steadfast, absolutely reliable and eternal. Do you believe that, deep down in your heart?

"... my words will never pass away"

As wickedness and lawlessness begin to shake our society we, too, will be shaken unless our foundations are solid. Our foundation is Jesus. He will never be shaken, so have faith in Him.

"... but the word of the Lord stands for ever" (1 Peter 1:25).

◤ **DECLARATION**
Lord, my faith is in Your Word and Your ability to fulfil and bring to pass all You have promised in it.

Below: the Dung Gate in Jerusalem as it stands today

PROPHECIES CONCERNING THE END TIME

The Church	Mt. 16:13-19
The rapture	Jn. 14:2, 3
The second coming	Mt. 16:27 Mt. 25:31
The great white throne judgment	Mt. 7:21-23 Mt. 12:41,42 Rev. 20:11
The future resurrection	Jn. 5:28, 29
The last days	Lk. 17:26-30
Armageddon	Lk. 17:34-37
Future rewards	Mk. 10:28-31

DAY 277

Ready for His return
**Matthew 24:36–51;
Mark 13:32–37; Luke 21:34–36**

There are two opposite errors which we can fall into over the second coming of Jesus. One is to be so obsessed with the imminence of His return that we become impractical in our daily living. The other, totally opposite, attitude is to look around and think, "This and that hasn't happened yet, so His coming isn't imminent", and become lax and lethargic about our spiritual lives.

"Therefore keep watch ..."

That's why Jesus tells us to keep alert (Matt. 24:42) and keep working (vv. 45, 46). Our Lord, in fact, urged His disciples over and over again to "watch" – to study the Scriptures and the happenings in the world, to be spiritually aware of the signs of the times. He also reminded them to carry on their work faithfully in the Master's absence.

We should be spiritually ready if Jesus were to come today and practically prepared should His coming be delayed for years. One thing is certain – He will come! Rejoice in that glorious fact.

"Behold, I come like a thief! Blessed is he who stays awake and keeps his clothes with him, so that he may not go naked and be shamefully exposed" (Rev. 16:15).

◖ FOR FURTHER STUDY
Genesis 6:5–8, 2 Thessalonians 2:1–4; Revelation 1:5–7

No time for worry
Mark 13:11–13; Luke 21:12–19

"Do not worry." "Make up your mind not to worry beforehand ..." Mark and Luke add these comforting and encouraging words when looking to the end times. I have known Christians to tremble in fear at the thought of persecution. We read stories of violence and imprisonment of Christians in some parts of the world and wonder how we would cope with it ourselves.

"All men will hate you because of me ..."

Jesus told His disciples what to expect, but He also told them, and tells us, not to be anxious about it. He will give us, at the right time, words of wisdom that will confound our accusers. He will give us strength to overcome, and He will be with us constantly. He has prayed for our protection (John 17:11), given us the power of the Holy Spirit within us (Acts 1:8).

Take to heart Luke 21:19 and stand firm no matter what happens. Consider your commitment to Jesus in the light of the coming persecution. He died on the Cross for you – and He will be with you through whatever trials you encounter.

"Blessed are you when people insult you, persecute you and falsely say all kinds of evil against you because of me" (Matt. 5:11).

■ QUESTION
If you were accused in court of being a servant, follower and proclaimer of Jesus Christ, would there be enough evidence against you for conviction?

Totally secure
Luke 21:37–38

Despite the antagonism of the Jewish leaders and their threats and plots to kill Jesus, He was still teaching openly in the Temple.

"... all the people came ... to hear him ..."

Jesus lived what He preached. He told His disciples not to worry about persecution. He Himself had no fear of possible danger to His own life because He was secure in the knowledge that nothing could happen to Him until the appointed time and unless His Father allowed it.

We, too, need that sense of security, that same fearlessness that Jesus showed. He was not foolhardy. He didn't walk into unnecessary danger, but He calmly and determinedly obeyed His Father's will. These were the last days of Jesus' public ministry and He spent them teaching the people in His Father's house.

He spent the nights alone with His disciples on the hillside underneath the stars on the Mount of Olives. Let us learn from His dedication, sense of purpose and selflessness.

" 'David himself calls him 'Lord'. How then can he be his son?' The large crowd listened to him with delight." (Mark 12:37).

▟ MEMORISE
James 1:19

DAY 280
Filled and waiting
Matthew 25:1–13

The bride and her friend wait in her house for the bridegroom and his friends to come and escort them back to his home for the wedding feast.

The ten bridesmaids in this parable represent the church. They all have lamps, but only half carry spare oil. They all fall asleep, but half are ready instantly when the bridegroom comes. Will you be ready when our Bridegroom comes for "His own"?

It may be at midday, it may be at twilight,
It may be, perchance, that the blackness of midnight
Will burst into light at the blaze of His glory,
When Jesus receives His own.

Oil is a picture in the Bible of the Holy Spirit, who was poured out for us at Pentecost. Paul tells us to "be filled with the Spirit". The verb is in the continuous tense – go on being filled. We are not to rely only on our initial sealing with the Holy Spirit at conversion, or even on a baptism in the Spirit, but on the constant daily filling with the Spirit. To be constantly filled, we need to experience a continuous emptying of self to allow His full power to lighten the darkness around us. Then we will be ready for Jesus' coming.

"Therefore keep watch ..."

"You are all sons of the light and sons of the day. We do not belong to the night or to the darkness. So then, let us not be like others, who are asleep, but let us be alert and self-controlled" (1 Thess. 5:5–6).

A WEDDING IN PALESTINE

- The bride was dressed by her bridesmaids (Isaiah 61:10; Jeremiah 2:32 and Isaiah 49:18 and Revelation 21:2).
- The feast was prepared in the bridegroom's house.
- The bridesmaids were woken and trimmed their lamps.
- The whole procession, lit by the bridesmaids' lamps, walked through the streets to the house of the bridegroom.
- The bride waited with her bridesmaids.
- The bridegroom and groomsmen arrived at the bride's house.
- The wedding feast began.
- The door was barred and no one else could enter.

▌ PRAYER
Lord, give me a fresh infilling of the oil of Your Holy Spirit today, that I might be ready and burning brightly for You when You come.

DAY 281
Parable of the talents
Matthew 25:14–30

Some years ago a preacher gave out this word of knowledge in a meeting, "There is someone here who has a creative gift and isn't using it. It could be a gift of writing.". Then, pointing at me, "I think it's you?" He prayed and prophesied over me and I repented of my disobedience in not practising the ministry that I knew God was calling me to. One of the results of that word of knowledge is this book on the "Life of Christ". The preacher used his gift of the "word of knowledge" to encourage me to use the gift of writing. I am now using the gift that God has given me to encourage you

"Well done, good and faithful servant!" to use the gifts that He gives you. God gives both spiritual gifts and natural abilities. We need His wisdom and guidance to know how and when He wants us to use them. Note that (v. 25) it was fear that caused the man in the parable to hide his talent. Jesus has set you free from fear; step out in that freedom and be profitable for Him.

"Now it is required that those who have been given a trust must prove faithful" (1 Cor. 4:2).

EXAMINE
Examine your life to see if you are 'hiding' any gifts or abilities that you should be using for Jesus.

DAY 282

Serving each other
Matthew 25:31–46

How closely Jesus identified Himself with His disciples! (v. 45). Whatever we do for each other we are doing for Him. When we neglect one another, we neglect Jesus. We cannot say "I love Jesus" while failing to meet the needs of a brother or sister.

"Come, you who are blessed by my father ..." Some have been puzzled by the seeming "judgment by works" in this teaching, but the statement, "take your inheritance" (v. 34) puts it in context.

Inheritance belongs to sons and daughters – it is not merited. The works are a proof of the love shown by children of God to their Father and to each other.

Above: the ruins of a Second Century synagogue in Capernaum

The eternal fire is prepared for the devil and his angels – not for man. God has prepared eternal life for man through the death of His Son, and it is not His will for any to perish in the fire of hell. Knowing this, we should be zealous to tell people of the way of escape, so that on that judgment day our relations, friends and neighbours will also be at the King's right hand.

"You will be his witness to all men of what you have seen and heard" (Acts 22:15).

ACTION
Speak to someone today about the saving grace of Christ.

DAY 283

Arrest Him!

**Matthew 26:1–5; Mark 14:1–2;
Luke 22:1–2**

A definite decision had been made. Jesus must die, but He must be arrested secretly to avoid a riot among the people who looked to Him as their leader. Jesus, however, was not caught unprepared. He knew before the Jewish leaders did that the time had come for Him to be crucified. God's plan for the salvation of mankind was nearing its fulfilment.

"... they plotted to arrest Jesus ..."

This meeting of the leading members of the Sanhedrin was probably an informal one, at the palace of the reigning High Priest, Joseph Caiaphas, and took place on the Wednesday before Passover. The chief instigators of the plot to arrest Jesus were the Sadducees. They were all in agreement that Jesus must die, but did not know how to bring this about with as little fuss as possible. It is interesting that they were afraid of the crowds.

Jesus had escaped easily from the leaders several times before. Could it be that they were also afraid of His power, even though they professed not to believe who He was? Take courage in that fact that Jesus is always master of every situation.

"Jesus answered them, 'Destroy this temple, and I will raise it again in three days.' The Jews replied, 'It has taken forty-six years to build this temple, and you are going to raise it in three days?' But the temple he had spoken of was his body" (John 2:19–21).

◗ THOUGHT

A ready accuser is usually a self excuser.

DAY 284

Anointed – for burial

Matthew 26:6–13; Mark 14:3–9

The storm clouds were gathering round Jesus, but this little incident shines out like the sun through the clouds.

"... She has done a beautiful thing to me"

Our Lord was among His friends at Bethany, people who loved Him, when the woman came and poured the expensive perfume, not over His feet this time, but over His head. When, after Jesus' death, the women went to the tomb to anoint His body they were too late, because he had already risen from the dead.

Jesus received His anointing before His burial, while He was still alive. This shows us that we should take the opportunities as they are give us – if we delay we may be too late.

In anointing His head the woman was, consciously or unconsciously, proclaiming Jesus as King (Messiah means "Anointed One"), and her faith, love and humility must have rejoiced Jesus' heart. She poured out her love to Him extravagantly and unselfishly – and received His commendation for doing so. Take time today to pour out your love in worship to Jesus.

"And let us consider how we may spur one another on towards love and good deeds" (Heb. 10:24).

■ ACTION

What good works will you do today as an expression of your love for Jesus?

DAY 285

The traitor appears

**Matthew 26:14–16;
Mark 14:10–11; Luke 22:3–6**

The blood price for a servant – 30 shekels of silver! (see Exodus 21:32).

"he watched for an opportunity to hand him over"

Judas' love of money and his habit of helping himself from the common purse (John 12:6) led him further into sin. Satan knows our weakest points. If we give him an inch he will take a mile. Take care that you do not give the enemy any foothold in your life.

Judas may have been disappointed at the turn of events in Jerusalem. He had probably been expecting Jesus to be an earthly king, and it had now become obvious that Jesus had no such intention. So Judas turned traitor, and ingratiated himself with those who were plotting Jesus' death. Not a pleasant character!

It is hard to understand how he could have been so close to Jesus for three years and not come to love Him. There had to be a Judas, however, to fulfil the scriptural prophecies of Jesus' betrayal by a friend (Psa. 41:9). God brings good out of evil, but let us be careful not to be one who betrays Him or causes Him grief.

"Then he said to them, 'Watch out! Be on your guard against all kinds of greed; a man's life does not consist in the abundance of his possessions' " (Luke 12:15).

⬛ KEY THOUGHT
The love of money is the root of all evil.

DAY 286

A door for us all

John 12:20–36

Jesus' death on the Cross opened the door of the kingdom of heaven to *all* believers. It is significant that Jesus should again predict His death after the Greeks had diffidently sought an interview with Him, coming to Him through His Jewish disciples.

"... I ... will draw all men to myself"

We now have direct access to the Father through the Son, whatever race, colour or former creed we come from.

This is a passage of contrasts. Life and death, the troubled thoughts of Jesus' human heart and the glory of His Father's reassurance, the seeming insignificance of a death of one man on a Cross and the amazing eternal result (vv. 31 & 32), and the contrast between light and darkness. There is also the contrast between the crowd's dithering uncertainty, their unwillingness to accept a Messiah who tells them He is about to be crucified, and Jesus' firm awareness of who He is, why He has come and what the outcome will be.

We have a Saviour whose determination to do His Father's will never wavered. He was "lifted up" for you and me. Thank Him now and trust in Him fully.

"Just as Moses lifted up the snake in the desert, so the Son of Man must be lifted up, that everyone who believes in him may have eternal life" (John 3:14–15).

🚩 PRAYER
Please help me to be steadfast and unwavering in my walk with You, following Your example. Amen.

The praise that matters
John 12:37–43

One of the saddest statements in Scripture is, "... they loved praise from men more than praise from God." Praise from men can provide

"... they still would not believe in him" encouragement and make you feel good temporarily, but in eternity it counts for nothing. Praise from God lasts.

To understand the quotation from Isaiah 6:10 (v. 40) we need to remember that the Jews were given every opportunity to see and understand Jesus and to turn to Him but would not. *Therefore*

A last plea
John 12:44–50

Jesus was closing His public ministry. He cried out to the people He came to save, His own people, the Jews. His last words

"I have come into the world as a light ..." to them were a heartfelt plea to come out of their darkness and into His light.

It is not a word of judgment. There was no bitterness or anger in Jesus for the rejection He suffered, but a deep longing for the people to know His Father, to accept His word and receive eternal life.

Jesus summed up the purpose for which He came and the consequences of rejecting Him. Our Lord came to do His Father's will, to speak His message and

God blinded their eyes. God never prevents anyone who sincerely seeks Him from coming to Him. Only those who wilfully and continually refuse to believe will eventually find that their hearts are so hardened so that they cannot believe.

Many Jews were secret believers, afraid to come out in the open for fear of being excommunicated. They were not willing to take that final step of faith from the old to the new. Consider how you would help people who are fearful, for whatever reason, of committing themselves fully to Christ.

"Immediately the boy's father exclaimed, 'I do believe; help me overcome my unbelief!" (Mark 9:24).

■ QUESTION
What made the difference between John 12:42 and Acts 2:41?

LIGHT

Lamplighters in Victorian times carried a light on a long pole to light the gas lamps along the streets. The man could not be seen at the end of the pole, but he left a light in the darkness.

The Lord Jesus didn't say, "Let your light so twinkle" – but let it "shine"!

to show the world what the Father is like. On the final judgment day those who have rejected His words will be condemned.

"I *know* that his command leads to eternal life" (v. 50). We *know* that rejection of Him leads to eternal condemnation. Let us be zealous and positive in our conversations with non-Christians, that they may realise how important their choice is.

"In the same way, let your light shine before men, that they may see your good deeds and praise your Father in heaven" (Matt. 5:16).

COMPARE
John 1:9–12 with 12:46, 47, 50.

Simple trust

Matthew 26:17–19; Mark 14:12–16; Luke 22:7–13

Jesus exercised His supernatural gift of knowledge in directing His disciples to the chosen upper room. Peter and John went in simple trust that everything would happen just as He said it would. They had been with Jesus for three years and had learned that it wasn't necessary to question His word.

> "... the disciples did as Jesus had directed them ..."

The longer we walk with Jesus the more we trust Him, because He never lets us down. In the overcrowded city of Jerusalem at Passover time a special sign was needed to identify the man they had to follow. A man carrying a water jar was a rare sight – it was usually a woman's job.

We don't know who the owner of the house was, but we do know that he had exactly what Jesus needed at that time – a room – and that he willingly made it available for His use. It is encouraging for us to realise that we don't need to be spiritual giants to be of use to Jesus. It may be that you have a room in your house that could be offered to someone in need, or some other gift that is strategically important to Jesus at this time.

"Jesus replied, 'If anyone loves me, he will obey my teaching. My Father will love him, and we will come to him and make our home with him'" (John 14:23).

PRAYER
Lord Jesus, I offer my home and all that I possess, for your use when you need it. Amen.

Too well hidden

Matthew 26:20–25; Mark 14:17–21; John 13:21–30

Judas was not only a traitor (and, according to Matt. 26:25, a hypocrite) but he must have been a good actor, too. Apparently, none of the other disciples suspected him of treachery. How sad it is when people cover up their faults to such an extent that they even deceive their brothers and sisters in Christ and cannot, therefore, receive any help from them.

A fault or weakness confessed can be cleansed and removed. A fault hidden multiplies until it breaks out and provides a foothold for Satan and his demonic forces to enter that life. There is a sad, dramatic finality in John's closing words in this passage: "And it was night."

The custom of the host's offering of a special piece of food was usually reserved for the most honoured guest. Jesus' last act to Judas was one of love and honour. In accepting the bread, however, Judas rejected His Master's offering of love and confirmed his resolve to betray Him. Take care to root out sin of every form from your life. Then there will be no opportunity for the devil to use you in any way.

"Yes, it is you"

"Yet there are some of you who do not believe (John 6:64).

🔖 FURTHER READING
Ephesians 4:22–27

Tender preparation
John 13:31–35

The time was very near for Jesus' betrayal and death. He knew what was ahead of Him, yet His thoughts were for His disciples. Tenderly He called them once more for His departure. They had to understand that what was about to happen was planned beforehand and known already to Jesus. It was the Father's perfect, prepared plan of salvation that the Son would be glorified in His death.

"As I have loved you ... love one another"

The new commandment was that we should love one another as *Jesus loves us.*

Jesus' whole life was a life of service. He gave Himself completely to His disciples and to the ever-present crowds of needy people thronging round Him. Later He did not shrink from one of the most painful deaths devised by man so that we might live.

Jesus' attitude was one of humility, of a servant serving the people He came to save. Do you love your fellow Christians like that? Allow the Holy Spirit to search your heart, repent of any wrong attitudes or actions that He shows you and ask Jesus to fill your life afresh with His love.

"Dear friends, since God so loved us, we also ought to love another"
(1 John 4:11).

◀ EXHORTATION
1 John 4:7–8

The Lord's Supper
Matt. 26:26–29; Mark 14:22–25; Luke 22:14–23; 1 Cor. 11:23–26

Four cups of wine were drunk during the Passover meal, which was always eaten reclining rather than sitting. It is likely that Judas departed after the second cup of wine, and that the third cup was used by Jesus to institute the Holy Communion or Lord's Supper as we know it today.

The Passover meal commemorated the passing of the angel of death over the homes of the Israelites in Egypt when all the first-born born of the Egyptians were slain (Ex. 12:1–30). The blood of the lamb on their doorposts protected them. Jesus also reminded the disciples, by His use of the word "covenant," of the solemn agreement between God and man at Sinai (Ex. 24:8), also sealed by blood.

The new covenant between God and man at Calvary was sealed by Jesus' own blood and the red wine in the cup is a continual reminder to us of that eternal covenant made between God and man, the forgiveness of our sins. As Jesus broke the bread He gave a piece to each of His disciples, signifying that we are all part of His body. Take time today to meditate again on the wonderful significance of the new covenant.

"... gave thanks and broke it ..."

"Then Jesus declared, 'I am the bread of life. He who comes to me will never go hungry, and he who believes in me will never be thirsty!' " (John 6:35).

🏴 **MEDITATE**
Break thou the bread of life, dear Lord, to me,
As thou didst break the bread by Galilee:
Beyond the sacred page I see thee Lord;
My spirit pants for thee thou living Word.

Arguing!
Luke 22:24–30

Incredible, isn't it, that at such a solemn time the disciples started arguing? And what a subject to argue about, when Jesus was about to pour out His life for them. It shows that the disciples still had not understood what Jesus had been telling them about His death. They were still looking ahead to a glorious kingdom without taking into account the trials, the suffering, the serving that precedes the elevation to glory.

"... I am among you as one who serves"

Yet Jesus was very gentle with them. He does not, on this occasion, rebuke them, but patiently explains again the principles of greatness.

What encouraging words in verses 28 and 29! Even though the disciples were weak, foolish sometimes and argumentative, yet Jesus commended them for their faithfulness to Him. He commends you, too, for your love and faithfulness, your desire to know Him and to follow Him. You are His beloved son or daughter, and you will be with Him in glory one day. Praise Him!

GREETING A GUEST

Feet washing
A guest's feet would be hot and dusty from the road. His sandals were easily removed and his feet would be washed by a slave of the household.

Kiss of greeting
The kiss was on both sides of the face. A host always greeted his guests in this way when they entered his house (e.g. Genesis 29:11,13) and again when they left (Acts 20:37).

Anointing with oil
In the sultry Eastern climate both men and women used oil and perfumes for there was no soap to wash with. Oil was freshening and scented the body. A host always anointed the head of an arriving guest as a sign of happiness and joy.

"... but made himself nothing, taking the very nature of a servant, being made in human likeness" (Phil. 2:7).

📖 **THINK ABOUT IT**
"The one who rules should be like one who serves."

Be humble!

John 13:1–20

So important is the servant principle in the kingdom of God that Jesus gave a practical demonstration either during or after the Passover meal. He got up from His position of honour at the table and took on the role of a servant. He laid aside His clothes just as He was later to lay aside His life, put on a slaves' apron and washed the dirt of the day from His disciples' feet.

"... you know these things, you will be blessed if you do them."

Peter's protestations show his pride and lack of understanding. He was unwilling for his beloved Master to see his dirty, calloused feet and wash them for him. Jesus told His disciples to wash one another's feet (v. 14), meaning, symbolically, to serve each other humbly and to keep one another clean from the stains of the world.

We need to be humble enough to confess our faults and failings to one another to allow others to help us. Our initial acceptance of Jesus' sacrifice on the Cross is our first "bath". We are washed clean of all sin, but we still need a daily cleansing. Be humble enough both to wash another's feet – and have your own washed.

"Therefore, as we have opportunity, let us do good to all people, especially to those who belong to the family of believers" (Gal. 6:10).

■ CHALLENGE
Are you humble enough, if God asks you, to literally wash your brother's feet?

Peter's fall

Matthew 26:29–35; Mark 4:27–31 ; Luke 22:31–34; John13:36–38

Impulsive Peter was very often the disciples' spokesman. Matthew and Mark make it clear that all 11 men were emphatic that they would die with Jesus rather than deny Him. But Peter, as the leader, was singled out for a special word from Jesus.

"... I will never disown you"

In the book of Job we learn that Satan has to ask permission from God before attacking one of His children (Job 1:12). Jesus revealed to Peter that Satan desired to attack him, to "sift him as wheat", but the Lord had intervened on Peter's behalf. Jesus still has that ministry, sitting at His Father's right hand in heaven and interceding for us. Satan cannot do anything to us without the Father's permission and without Jesus knowing about it beforehand.

Because of Peter's pride he was allowed to fall – but not too far. He needed to learn humility but, having learned that lesson, he was lifted up again and became the leader of the Early Church. Humble yourself before God then you will not fall.

"Whoever acknowledges me before men, I will also acknowledge him before my Father in heaven. But whoever disowns me before men, I will disown him before my Father in heaven" (Matt. 10:32–33).

◤ MY PROMISE
Lord, I will confess You before men, as You confess me before my Father in heaven.

The one certainty
John 14:1-3

The disciples were still bewildered, uncertain, afraid of what was to come. One thing they knew – Jesus, their beloved Master, was leaving them. They didn't understand why or how, but they must have been conscious of this dark, threatening cloud hanging over them. Jesus comforted them as a Father would comfort little children. "Trust in God. I'm going to prepare a place for you, then I'm coming back to fetch you."

"Do not let your hearts be troubled ..."

Sometimes, when circumstances seem dark and difficult, the only thing we can hang on to is our trust in God. God never fails. He always has a plan for us and He knows the answer to every difficult situation even before it happens.

His ultimate and sure purpose for us is that we will be with Jesus where He is in heaven. Those two facts give us hope and banish all fearful and distressing thoughts from our minds no matter what we have to go through on this earth. Take Jesus' words (v. 3) into your heart today and meditate on them until they become part of you.

" 'I have told you these things, so that in me you may have peace. In this world you will have trouble. But take heart! I have overcome the world' " (John 16:33).

■ MEMORISE
Revelation 21:3, 4

The only way
John 14:4-14

"There are many different ways to God." "All religions are as good as one another." "It doesn't matter what you believe as long as you are sincere." Jesus' words in verse 6 contradict all these common statements. If we believe in Jesus at all we must believe that His words are true and that He is the only way to God the Father.

"... I am the way and the truth and the life"

We can be loving yet completely uncompromising when speaking with people from other religions, cults or sects: there is only one way – Jesus. If we know Jesus is the way, then we know the destination, for Jesus came to show us the Father.

Verse 12 is one of the most staggering statements in the Bible. Jesus was a great teacher. He healed the sick, performed miracles, cast out demons, raised three dead people to life and said that anyone who has faith in Him will do greater things. Because Jesus is now sitting at the right hand of His Father, anything that we ask will come to the immediate attention of the Father. Be bold in your asking.

"Then you will know the truth, and the truth will set you free" (John 8:32).

▲ PONDER
Think about the relationship between "will do what I have been doing" (v. 12) and "You may ask me for anything in my name, and I will do it" (v. 14).

The Holy Spirit promised
John 14:15–31

Jesus' return to the Father would release the Holy Spirit into the hearts of believers. Notice (v. 17) that the Spirit already lived *with* the disciples. After Pentecost He would live *in* them in a new way, empowering them to preach, to teach and to do the "greater things" that Jesus had already spoken of.

"... he will give you another Counsellor ..."

Jesus' love for His disciples shines through this passage of Scripture. He knows how they are feeling and He comforts them with the promise that they will not be left helpless or unloved. There is one proviso – that they obey His commandments and

His teaching. Obedience is the key to the Christian life. Just as Jesus was completely obedient to His Father's commands (v. 31) so should we be, and on this obedience hang our security (v. 20), love (v. 21) and peace (v. 27). You cannot say you love Jesus if you do not obey Him in your everyday life, living daily as He taught His disciples to live and obeying His specific commands to you as He gives them.

"And if the Spirit of him who raised Jesus from the dead is living in you, he who raised Christ from the dead will also give life to your mortal bodies through his Spirit, who lives in you" (Rom. 8:11).

QUOTE
"He who has the Holy Spirit in his heart and the Scripture in his hands, has all he needs."
Alexander McClaren

In the vine
John 15:1–17

The branch of a vine cannot be independent, self-centred or self-productive. We are totally dependent on Jesus for our life. Without Him we can do nothing. We are also inter-dependent with one another. Imagine the branches of a vine trying to draw away from one another, or fighting with one another!

"Remain in me ..."

As each of us remains in position, in Christ, respecting and loving one another, so we will grow, flourish and produce fruit to His glory. The vine is a wonder-

ful picture of the Church, rooted and grounded in Jesus, with His life flowing through us to produce beauty and usefulness.

There is, however, need for continual cleansing or pruning. The Greek word means both. We are already clean through the blood of Jesus, but we still need daily cleansing through His word, so that we go on producing good fruit. During the last hours that He had with His disciples, Jesus placed great emphasis on His command to love each other. How important it is that we obey that command.

"Whoever claims to live in him must walk as Jesus did" (1 John 2:6).

MEMORISE
1 John 3:6

PICTURES OF THE HOLY SPIRIT

A dove	John 1:32	Indicating purity and peace
Water	Isaiah 44:3	Indicating life and cleansing
Oil	Luke 4:18	Indicating healing and anointing for service
A seal	Ephesians 1:13	Indicating ownership, value, security and authority
Wind	John 3:8	Indicating power which is unseen, but felt and heard
Fire	Acts 2:3	Indicating purifying, cleansing and empowering

DAY 300

Nothing hidden

John 15:18–27, 16:1–4

When Jesus began His talk to His disciples He called them "my children" and comforted them as such (John 13:33). They needed to learn and grow quickly so that when Jesus left them they would know what to expect.

"... you also must testify ..." He called them friends (John 15:15) as He began to tell them about His suffering and death, hiding nothing from them.

They would not have understood then for, though Jesus was hated and the subject of plots by the Jewish leaders, He had not, up until then, suffered physical abuse. After the crucifixion, however, the 11 would recall and understand what Jesus had been telling them.

In parts of the world today Christians suffer intense persecution, imprisonment and torture. Let us remember them and faithfully and lovingly share their suffering in our prayers for them. Let us also be willing to stand up for Jesus here and now, no matter what it costs us. As the time grows nearer for Jesus' return, conditions in the world will get more hostile. Remember then Jesus' words: "You must also testify" (John 15:27).

"But you will receive power when the Holy Spirit comes on you; and you will be my witnesses in Jerusalem, and in all Judea and Samaria, and to the ends of the earth" (Acts 1:8).

■ ACTION
Who was the last person you witnessed to? Will you witness to someone today?

A Counsellor promised

John 16:5–15

The grief-stricken disciples were not able to take in all that Jesus wanted to tell them at that time. Their concern about their own personal loss at His leaving, instead of seeing beyond the Cross to the work that Jesus wanted them to do afterwards, must have saddened Him. Yet He understood their feelings.

"... I will send him to you"

The Counsellor, the Holy Spirit, would come to them and teach them the truth about Jesus' death, reveal to them God's glorious plan of salvation and guide them in their future work. The Holy Spirit, working through the Church, would also convict the world of sin, reveal Jesus' righteousness and, because Satan was defeated at Calvary, would be able to show the world the judgment to come.

God never overburdens us with more than we can take at one time. The Holy Spirit is always present now to teach and guide us day by day. Ask Him about anything you don't understand.

"When the Counsellor comes, whom I will send to you from the Father, the Spirit of truth who goes out from the Father, he will testify about me" (John 15:26).

QUESTION
Have you received the Holy Spirit since you believed? (Acts 19:2)

Birth pangs

John 16:16–28

If Jesus had said, "In about 18 hours' time you will lose sight of me for about 56 hours, then you will see me again," the disciples would still have been puzzled about what He meant.

"... I am going to the Father"

There are some things that we cannot understand until they happen, and some things that we don't understand even until years later.

Jesus likened His passion and death to a woman giving birth to a child. The pain is most intense just before the birth. The darkest time for the disciples would be between Jesus' death and resurrection. Then their grief would turn to joy and they would understand at last what Jesus had been telling them.

Jesus gently turned their attention again to the Father. He always glorified His Father rather than himself. He desired His beloved disciples to know and love their Father as He did, asking Him as children for anything they needed. Do you know your Father like that? Meditate today on Jesus' intimate relationship with His Father and seek to come closer to Him.

"For you did not receive a spirit that makes you a slave again to fear, but you received the Spirit of sonship. And by him we cry, 'Abba, Father' " (Rom. 8:15).

THANKS
I thank You, Lord, that I can stand in Your presence and say "Abba, Father" because You have made me a joint heir with Your Son, Jesus.

DAY 303

Faith's foundation

John 16:29–30

Faith is not an instant thing. The disciples' faith grew gradually
with each new revelation
they had of Jesus. They
had called Him Lord and
Master before, worshipped Him as God
and recognised Him as the Messiah, yet
their faith had been tried severely with
recent events in Jerusalem.

"... you came from God"

When Jesus began to speak of His
death, doubts flooded in about whether
He really was the expected Messiah after
all. A little thing, the fact that Jesus
knew what they were thinking about
(John 16:19) was enough for them to
declare their faith in Him again. It
wasn't, however, a very firm foundation
for faith, because soon they were to forsake Him.

James wrote, "... he who doubts is like
a wave of the sea, blown and tossed by
the wind" (James 1:6). It wasn't until
after Jesus' death and resurrection that
the disciples' faith became firm and
unshakeable. We need to be very sure
what our faith is based on.

**"In the beginning was the Word, and
the Word was with God, and the
Word was God" (John 1:1)**

■ **PRAISE AND PRAYER**
**Praise the Lord for the foundations He
has given you. Pray for Him to build
on them.**

RIPE FRUIT

An interpretation of Galatians 5:22–23.

"The fruit of the Spirit is an affectionate,
loveable disposition, a radiant spirit and
a cheerful temper, a tranquil mind and a
quiet manner, a forbearing patience in
provoking circumstances and with trying
people, a sympathetic insight and tactful
helpfulness, generous judgment, loyalty
and reliability under all circumstances,
humility that forgets self in the joy of others, in all things self-mastered and self-
controlled, which is the final mark of
perfecting."

DAY 304

Peace promised

John 16:31–33

A Christian man once became bankrupt.
He was about to lose his business, home,
possessions – everything. He knelt beside
his bed in tears.

"... in me you may have peace ..."

"Lord", he started,
"all I've got left is You."
Then a wonderful
sense of peace flooded
over him. Jesus is all we
need – He is everything.

There are times for all of us when we
feel utterly alone and friendless. Jesus
felt like that when all His friends deserted Him at the time of His trial, when He
most needed their support. Yet He knew
that He wasn't alone because His Father
was with Him (v. 32) and Jesus felt completely at peace in the situation.

God gives us one another in His family

so that we may love, encourage and support one another. Yet we are not dependent wholly on that support. Our peace and dependence is in God our Father and in Jesus His Son, who never leaves us, or forsakes us, never lets us down or falls short in any way. Consider who or what you are depending upon today.

Look to Jesus and receive His peace.

"And the peace of God, which transcends all understanding, will guard your hearts and minds in Christ Jesus" (Phil. 4:7).

MEDITATION
Hebrews 13:5b The Living Bible version.

DAY 305

The gulf bridged
Hebrews 9:11–28

Since Adam first sinned, God and man have been separated by that gulf of sin between them. God, however, loves and yearns over man so much that He longed to be "at one" with us again.

In the Old Testament atonement (making at one) was achieved by God's acceptance of the blood of sacrificial animals as a substitute for the death of sinners. "... without the shedding of blood there is no forgiveness" (Heb. 9:22). In the New Testament, although the word "atonement" is not used, the teaching of

"Christ ... offered himself unblemished ..."

Christ's atoning, sacrificial death on the Cross is all important (God Himself took the initiative of atonement because man was incapable of bridging the gulf between them).

Jesus shed His blood, once and for all, for the sin of the whole world. He is our High Priest and, at the same time, the unblemished sacrificial Lamb, perfectly acceptable to His holy Father, God. He has made it possible for all mankind to be at one with God. Meditate, at least for a few moments, on this aspect of Jesus' sacrifice for you.

"For there is one God and one mediator between God and men, the man Christ Jesus" (1 Tim 2:5).

CONSIDER
Exodus 30:10; John 1:29; 1 Peter 1:19; 2 Cor. 5:14, 15

DAY 306

Reconciled
Romans 5:1–21

There can be no reconciliation between two opposing parties unless the original cause of separation is removed and forgiven. Jesus' death on the Cross paid for the sin of the world and made forgiveness and cleansing of our individual sins possible.

"While we were still sinners, Christ died for us"

God has moved towards man in forgiveness and friendship, proclaiming peace. As we move towards Him, cleansed in the blood of Jesus and clothed in His righteousness, perfect reconciliation takes place. A wonderful picture of friends, separated for years by an unbridgeable gap, suddenly finding the way open for a close, loving relationship again.

In atonement the initiative is entirely God's. In reconciliation the first move was God's – in sending His Son to die for us – but we must then accept His offer of peace to experience personal reconciliation with Him. Are you truly reconciled to God, enjoying a close relationship with Him with no shadow of sin between you?

"Therefore, there is now no condemnation for those who are in Christ Jesus" (Rom. 8:1).

DAY 307

Resurrected!

1 Corinthians 15:1–58

"Where, O death, is your victory?"

Preachers and writers in the Early Church constantly emphasised the resurrection of Jesus from death. People had been brought back to life before – in Old Testament times as well as in the New. Jesus himself raised three people from the dead. But our Lord's own resurrection was different because the quality of His resurrection life was different.

He was able to move through closed doors, yet He was still able to eat. He was not always instantly recognisable and yet He was obviously the same Jesus that the disciples knew and loved. He ascended into heaven while they were watching Him. His resurrection life was not the same as the life He led before His death.

We, too, experience a complete change in our lives when we identify with Jesus in His death on the Cross, lay our sin on Him and accept His vicarious sacrifice. We are new creations in Him, not living any longer to indulge the flesh but by the Spirit. Death could not hold Jesus in its grip – and sin can no longer hold you.

"And if the Spirit of him who raised Jesus from the dead is living in you, he who raised Christ from the dead
will also give life in your mortal bodies through his Spirit, who lives in you" (Rom. 8:11).**

▲ **KEY TRUTH**
If Christ has not been raised, your faith is futile.

RESURRECTION APPEARANCES OF CHRIST

First, Mary Magdalene John 20:11–18

Second, On the road near Jerusalem Matt. 28:5–10

Third, Emmaus Road Luke 24:13–35

Fourth, Simon Peter Luke 24:34

Fifth, Upper Room Luke 24:36–43

Sixth, Upper Room (week later) John 20:24–29

Seventh, Sea of Tiberias John 21:1–25

Eighth, Mount Tabor Matt. 28:16–20

Ninth, The Upper Room Mark 16:14–18

Tenth, Mount of Olives Luke 24:50–53

DAY 308

Liberty!

Galatians 5:1–6; Romans 8:1–11

Jesus, by His death and resurrection, has liberated His people from sin, Satan, the law and death. A non-Christian cannot help sinning. A Christian is free to resist sin – and free to receive immediate cleansing if he does fall.

"... Christ has set us free ..."

Satan was defeated at Calvary and has no longer any statutory rights to a Christian's life. In Jesus' name we have authority over all the powers of darkness. The law, which was given by God to Moses, was impossible for sinful man to keep. Now we have the Holy Spirit dwelling in our hearts giving us both the guidance and the power to live according to God's will.

The penalty for sin is death – eternal separation from God. The gift of Christ is victory over death – eternal life with Him. Jesus has set us free from all bondage. Give to Him any fears, satanic bondages or besetting sins that are holding you back from enjoying the abundant life full of love, joy and peace that He has bought for you. Enjoy your freedom.

"Now the Lord is the Spirit, and where the Spirit of the Lord is, there is freedom" (2 Cor. 3:17).

◀ THOUGHT
Freedom is not the right to do what we want, but the power to do what we ought.

DAY 309

A servant heart

Philippians 2:1–11

Jesus Christ is Lord, the most high God, King of kings, glorious in majesty, might and power. Yet, He chose to humble Himself and become a man. The Son of God became a servant for us.
He gave His time on earth willingly to serve His disciples and the crowds who flocked unceasingly around Him.

"... he humbled himself and became obedient ..."

He gave us an example to follow when He washed His disciples' feet. He submitted Himself to unjustified arrest, beating and crucifixion in obedience to His Father's will. As a good servant always obeys his master, so Jesus always did His Father's will.

What an example to follow. Look at your own attitude to position in life, relationships with fellow Christians, family and employers. Are you willing to serve, as Jesus did? Only as we become like Jesus will the world see Jesus as He really is.

"Let us fix our eyes on Jesus, the author and perfecter of our faith, who for the joy set before him endured the cross, scorning its shame, and sat down at the right hand of the throne of God" (Heb. 12:2).

◀ REMEMBER
Your attitude should be the same as that of Christ Jesus.

Nobody like Him!
Colossians 1:1–20

Jesus Christ is worthy of all our worship, praise and adoration because He is

"... by him all things were created ..."

"before all things" (v. 17). There is nothing and nobody in this world or out of it more worthy of our worship.

You may find it helpful to take pen and paper and write down the attributes of Jesus mentioned in verses 15–20 and add to the list from other Scriptures as the Holy Spirit leads you. Some people have difficulty in finding words to express their worship of Jesus – such a list can be a helpful reminder.

There is no comparison between Jesus and any other person – He is just so great and wonderful and loving. Consider the Jesus who created the heavens and the earth and everything in them. Consider Him as the *only* perfect man, the *only* one who could take away the sins of the world. Consider His greatness and humility, love and justice, strength and meekness. Now worship Him with *all* your heart, soul and mind.

"In the beginning was the Word, and the Word was with God, and the Word was God" (John 1:1).

CHALLENGE
Worship the Lord in the beauty of holiness – today.

The eternal priest
Hebrews 7:1–3, 11–28, 8:1–2

The High Priest who meets our need (v. 26). That's Jesus. Earthly priests offered animal sacrifices to atone for the sins of the people, but they were not themselves holy and blameless. Jesus, our great High Priest, is pure and sinless.

"... he offered himself ..."

He offered Himself once and for all as a perfect sacrifice for all sin.

Earthly priests served for a lifetime only, but Jesus is eternal and is seated at the right hand of His Father, His work completed and effective for ever. There will never be a time when a sinner will look to Jesus to save him and fail to find Him alive and available.

Jesus' priesthood was made doubly certain because it was instituted by God and sealed with His oath (Heb. 11:21). It cannot fail, be superseded or changed. Take some time today to meditate on the absolute surety and finality of Jesus as our great High Priest. In this uncertain and changeable world, Jesus is our eternal steadfast rock who *never* changes.

"Therefore, since we have a great high priest who has gone through the heavens, Jesus the Son of God, let us hold firmly to the faith we profess" (Heb. 4:14).

STUDY
Take a Bible dictionary and look up the priesthood. See in what ways the Old Testament priests were foreshadows of Jesus.

CHRIST IN ALL THE SCRIPTURES

Genesis	The seed of the woman
Exodus	The Lamb
Leviticus	Our High Priest
Numbers	The Star of Jacob
Deuteronomy	The Great Rock
Joshua	Our Captain
Judges	The Messenger
Ruth	Our Kinsman-Redeemer
1 Samuel	The Great Judge
2 Samuel	The Princely King
1 Kings	As David's choice
2 Kings	The holiest of all
1 Chronicles	King by birth
2 Chronicles	King by judgment
Ezra	Lord of heaven and earth
Nehemiah	The Builder
Esther	Our Mordecai
Job	Our Risen, returning Redeemer
Psalms	The Good Shepherd
Proverbs	Our wisdom
Ecclesiastes	One above the sun
Song of Solomon	The Altogether Lovely
Isaiah	The suffering and glorified Servant
Jeremiah	The Lord our righteousness
Lamentations	The Man of sorrows
Ezekiel	The glorious God
Daniel	The Messiah
Hosea	Risen Son of God
Joel	Outpourer of the Spirit
Amos	The eternal Christ
Obadiah	The forgiving Christ
Jonah	The risen Prophet
Micah	The Bethlehemite

Nahum	The bringer of good tidings
Habakkuk	The Lord in His holy temple
Zephaniah	The merciful Christ
Haggai	The desire of all nations
Zechariah	The Branch
Malachi	Sun of righteousness
Matthew	King of the Jews
Mark	The Servant
Luke	Perfect Son of Man
John	Son of God
Acts	Ascended Lord
Romans	The Lord of righteousness
1 Corinthians	Our resurrection
2 Corinthians	Our comforter
Galatians	The end of the law
Ephesians	The head of the Church
Philippians	Supplier of every need
Colossians	Fullness of the Godhead
1 Thessalonians	He comes for His Church
2 Thessalonians	He comes with His Church
1 Timothy	The Mediator
2 Timothy	Bestower of crowns
Titus	Our great God and Saviour
Philemon	Payer of our debt
Hebrews	The fulfiller of types
James	The Lord drawing near
1 Peter	The vicarious sufferer
2 Peter	The Lord of glory
1 John	The Way
2 John	The Truth
3 John	The Life
Jude	Our security
Revelation	King of kings

Plain speaking
John 17:1–5

"Father, the time has come." Jesus speaks to His Father quite naturally, as any son would speak to his father. We, too, don't need flowery, theological words in our prayers.

"... completing the work ..."

Jesus is moving steadily towards the completion of His work on earth in an atmosphere of prayer. He wants, and needs, to be in close communication with His Father, and prays first of all for Himself. His request to be glorified does not stem from pride, but from His humble desire to glorify His Father.

Eternal life can only be available to sinners when the crucified Son is risen and restored to His former glory in heaven. It was for that purpose that Jesus came and He was determined that His Father's work should be completed. Meditate on verse 4. The Living Bible puts it: "I brought glory to you here on earth by doing everything you told me to." God has a work for *you* to do here on earth, too. Seek to glorify Him in your obedience.

"My food," said Jesus, "is to do the will of him who sent me and to finish his work" (John 4:34).

PRAYER
Lord God, please make clear to me what particular work you want me to do here, and enable me to do it. Amen.

Praying for His disciples
John 17:6–9

Jesus' great love for His disciples comes over so clearly in this prayer. It is the prayer of our great High Priest interceding for the disciples and also the prayer of a man for His beloved friends.

"Sanctify them by the truth ..."

Jesus had been in their company for three years and had faithfully given them the teaching that His Father had shown Him to give (v. 8). He had protected them and kept them safe (v. 12) and sent them out into the world (v. 18).

Any parent who has had the experience of a child leaving home will know how Jesus felt. He hands them over to His Father in His prayer, asking Him to protect them, keep them united (v. 11) and sanctify them by the truth of the Word of God (v. 17). He also desires that they will have a full measure of joy (v. 13). Jesus had confidence in His Father that He would do as He asked. We, too, must have that confidence that God will answer our prayers for those we commit to His care.

"... being confident of this, that he who began a good work in you will carry it on to completion until the day of Christ Jesus" (Phil. 1:6).

QUESTION
What does it mean to be sanctified?

DAY 314

Key to unity
John 17:20–26

This is Jesus' prayer for you! He has given us His glory so that we might be one with each other in the same way that Jesus and the Father are one. That's something to really think about! Jesus' will was always to do His Father's will. They moved together, worked together, communicated with each other constantly, having the same love and the same goal.

"... that all of them may be one ..."

That is how the fellowship of believers should be – and how Jesus longed and prayed for it to be. The key is in verses 21 and 26: that "they also be in us". We can only be one with one another in as far as we are one with God and His love is in us.

The purpose is made clear in verse 23: that the world may know. One of the main criticisms of the Church is that we are so divided. Make sure that you have no lack of love for your fellow Christians, so that Jesus' prayer may be fulfilled in you.

"How good and pleasant it is when brothers live together in unity!" (Psalm 133:1).

STUDY
1 John 4:7–12, 19–21

DAY 315

No easy way through
Matthew 26:30, 36–46; Mark 14:26, 32–42; Luke 22:39–46; John 18:1

Gethsemane. Jesus had often been there before with His disciples. He withdrew to that familiar, friendly place to experience the greatest agony, anguish and loneliness anyone has ever known. He was feeling the weight of the sin of the world and wrestling with Satan's temptation not to go through with it. Jesus longed for the prayer support of His friends – but they fell asleep.

"My soul is overwhelmed with sorrow ..."

We can, perhaps, excuse them by saying that they didn't understand what Jesus was going through. Nevertheless, they had been asked to keep watch with Him – and they failed. Think about your own faithfulness in prayer and support for friends experiencing particular difficulties.

Jesus' one desire was to do His Father's will, but He didn't find it easy. It was a tremendous struggle, and we need to remember that when we are tempted to take an easy way out of a situation. There is to be no compromise in the Christian life, only obedience to our Father's will.

"I tell you the truth, unless a grain of wheat falls to the ground and dies, it remains only a single seed. But if it dies, it produces many seeds" (John 12:24).

REQUEST
**"Lest I forget Gethsemane,
Lest I forget Thine agony,
Lest I forget Thy love for me,
Lead me to Calvary."**

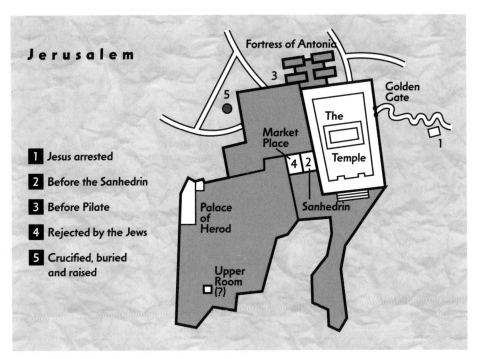

Jerusalem

Fortress of Antonia

3

5

Golden
Gate

The

Market
Place

4 2 Temple

1

1 Jesus arrested

2 Before the Sanhedrin

3 Before Pilate

4 Rejected by the Jews

5 Crucified, buried
and raised

Palace
of
Herod

Sanhedrin

Upper
Room
(?)

Betrayed and arrested

**Matthew 26:47–55;
Mark 14:43–49; Luke 22:47–53;
John 18:2–11**

The temple guards had been thwarted once before when they attempted to arrest Jesus in the temple. This time they meant to make sure they got Him. They came with a large crowd, armed, at dead of night when only the 11 disciples were with Him, and with the treacherous Judas to identify Him. Yet they could not have taken the Son of God had He not willingly given Himself up to them. His calm demeanour produced terror and awe in the watching crowd (John 18:6).

"... seizing him, they led him away ..."

Jesus stepped forward and identified Himself, protecting His disciples (John 18:8). This small act was symbolic of all that Jesus was about to take for us – the beating for our healing, the mocking and ridicule, the exposure, suffering and, finally, death.

Jesus accepted what was coming to Him in obedience to His Father's will. The time had come, and Jesus gave Himself up. Consider your own willingness to accept hardship and suffering for Jesus' sake.

"Greater love has no-one than this, that one lay down his life for his friends" (John 15:13).

THANKS
Lord Jesus, thank you that you were willing to be obedient, even to the death of the Cross.

DAY 317

Deserted!
Matthew 26:56; Mark 14:50-52

The disciples failed Him in His need for prayer support, then deserted Him completely. The two things often go together. Those people **"... everyone deserted him ..."** whom we faithfully support in prayer are the people we will give practical help to when they need it. When we neglect to pray, not only do we become insensitive to people's needs, but less likely to stand by them in their trials.

Think about whether any brothers or sisters are suffering because of your withdrawal of prayer or practical support from them. Jesus had to go to the Cross alone. He alone was worthy to suffer and die for us, but the complete desertion of His friends at the time must have added to His anguish and sense of loneliness.

Let's learn to encourage, support and stand by one another as the world grows darker and persecution increases.

"Let us not give up meeting together, as some are in the habit of doing, but let us encourage one another – and all the more as you see the Day approaching" (Heb. 10:25).

▌ COMMITMENT
**Tho' all forsake thee yet will I follow,
Tho' all forsake thee yet will I follow,
Tho' all forsake thee yet will I follow,
No turning back, no turning back.**

DAY 318

Son of God on trial
John 18:12-14, 19, 23

An informal inquiry into Jesus' case was conducted at night by Annas, probably at his house. Annas had been deposed as High Priest in AD 15 by the Romans, but as the Jews regarded **"... why did you strike me?"** the office as a lifetime one he was still held in high honour by them. Jesus, unnecessarily bound, refused to plead for Himself or to offer explanations for His teaching and behaviour. The truth does not need defending, and Jesus knew that He had to die whatever the result of the trial. A lamb about to be slaughtered does not kick and struggle. Here the Lamb of God meekly accepts the beginning of His humiliation and hurt.

Jesus had set His face towards the Cross. Not once did He draw back from it or seek to alleviate His own suffering. Consider how much of Jesus' lamb-like nature can be seen in you.

"... but with the precious blood of Christ, a lamb without blemish or defect" (1 Peter 1:19).

◆ STUDY
John 1:29; 1 Cor. 5:7; Rev. 7:9, 15:3

Facing the Sanhedrin

Matthew 26:57, 59–66;
Mark 14:53, 55–64; Luke 22:54;
John 18:24

Many of the witnesses against Jesus were, no doubt, bought with the same money handed over to Judas. It is much more difficult, however, to lie consistently than to tell the truth and the Sanhedrin had problems. They had to produce concrete evidence against Jesus, sufficient to warrant a sentence of death, but they had no success with their false witnesses.

"... Jesus remained silent"

Finally Caiaphas put Jesus on His oath and compelled an answer (Matt. 26:63).

By using those words he was assured of a truthful answer and Jesus gave it, adding a warning of His position in glory and of His coming again in judgment. Caiaphas wasn't listening – he had heard the words he was waiting for: "I am".

So Jesus was condemned by His own people for blasphemy. They didn't stop to think of the enormity of their sin, whether Jesus was right and they were wrong. Pray for people today who dismiss the claims of Jesus without properly considering them.

"He was oppressed and afflicted, yet he did not open his mouth; he was led like a lamb to the slaughter, and as a sheep before her shearers is silent, so he did not open his mouth" (Isa. 53:7).

STUDY
Exodus 3:14; John 8:58; Rev. 1:8; Heb 1:1-4

A TRAVESTY OF JUSTICE

The Sanhedrin was both the religious and legal Jewish Supreme Court. Its sessions would be attended by the 70–72 members, comprising:

a. The high priest (president).
b. The heads of the 24 priestly service divisions.
c. The scribes and lawyers.
d. The elders (the representatives of the laity).

Here Christ stood during His third illegal trial (Matt. 26:65, 66; 27:1,2). Here also He was blindfolded, spat upon and beaten.

His trial before the Sanhedrin was a travesty of justice.

a. The Sanhedrin acted as both prosecution and judges.
b. No defence witnesses were called and the prosecution's testimonies did not agree.
c. The Sanhedrin normally met in a semicircle with the prisoner. This was not done: Jesus was blindfolded.
d. Two clerks were appointed, one to record the votes for acquittal, the other for conviction. In Christ's case this was not done.
e. If the vote was for acquittal, the prisoner was set free there and then. If the vote was for conviction, condemnation could not be pronounced until the following day. Jesus' sentence was immediate.

Mocked all night

Matthew 26:67–68; Mark 14:65; Luke 22:63–65

Jesus, condemned, bound and blindfolded, spent the rest of the night in the hands of the guards. Only His Father was with Him. Even at that stage Jesus could have used His position as Son of God to escape, but He chose to stay and suffer the insults and mockery of the ignorant guards.

"... mocking and beating him ..."

There can be few things more unpleasant than being spat on in the face. Jesus was allowed no sleep and, presumably, offered no refreshment during that long night. He was continually hit with fists and open palms, beaten with rods and mocked, yet He offered no resistance, self-defence or retaliation for the ill-treatment He suffered.

We see in all this the absolute perfection and maturity of Jesus. He had no pride, hatred, self-pity or thought for Himself. Think about how you react to personal insults and injustice. Christ dwells in you – allow His perfection to shine out through your life in *all* circumstances.

"He was despised and rejected by men, a man of sorrows, and familiar with suffering. Like one from whom men hide their faces he was despised, and we esteemed him not" (Is. 53:3).

**FOR MEDITATION
Isaiah 50:6–7; 1 Peter 2:23**

A marked man

Matt. 26:58, 69–75; Mark 14:54, 66–72; Luke 22:54–62; John 18:15–18, 25–27

Peter was recognised. He was a marked man because he had been with Jesus. However hard he tried to deny it, people knew that he was one of the disciples. Do people recognise you as one of Jesus' followers? There should be something about a Christian that marks him as different from the world.

"... he went outside and wept bitterly ..."

We can imagine the conflict that was going on in Peter's mind that traumatic night. He had been rebuked by Jesus, first for falling asleep and then for using his sword to defend Him. Now Jesus was condemned and being mocked and spat upon. Peter's world was falling apart. It's easy to feel critical of him for denying knowledge of Jesus, but I wonder how you and I would have stood up to that test?

Peter, brash and outspoken, had to learn that he was weak, helpless and fallible. When we see ourselves in that light and repent, as Peter did, then Jesus can lift us up, fill us with His Holy Spirit and use us in His kingdom.

"The Lord is close to the broken-hearted and saves those who are crushed in spirit" (Psa. 34:18).

**PONDER
On Acts 1:15, 2:14, 4:13; 1 Peter 5:6**

DAY 322

Eyes on the future
Matthew 27:1–2; Mark 15:1; Luke 22:66–71

At dawn the full council of Jewish leaders, chief priests and lawyers met to formally try to sentence **"They ... led him away ..."** Jesus. According to rabbinical law, trials had to take place during daylight hours, so the previous night session was either illegal or a mere fact-finding commission.

This session at daybreak appears to have been a mere formality – the Jewish leaders had already decided on Jesus' crime and punishment.

Jesus, however, was not concerned with the intrigues, the illegality of the trial, the humiliation of it all. He was looking to the future (Luke 22:69). He saw the glory of the finished work of the Son of Man on the Cross. He saw Himself, not as a victim of man's injustice, but in His rightful place, seated at God's right hand in glory.

As you are in Him and He in you, consider how you see yourself. A child of God, under His protection and love, assured of your future? Is this foremost in your thoughts, as it was in Jesus', when you go through trials and tribulations?

"By oppression and judgment, he was taken away. And who can speak of his descendants? For he was cut off from the land of the living; for the transgression of my people he was stricken" (Isa. 53:8).

◼ DECLARATION
Jesus, I am in You and You in me. I know I am safe no matter what I may have to go through.

DAY 323

Failed to repent
Matthew 27:3–10; Acts 1:18–19

Remorse is not the same as repentance. The Greek word used in Matthew 27, verse 3 to describe Judas' reaction to his betrayal of Jesus is not the usual one used in the New Testament to denote true repentance.

Compare Judas with Peter. Judas was concerned about what he had done, **"I have sinned ..."** angry with himself and, seeking a human solution, he tried to obliterate his sin by taking his own life.

Peter, after his threefold denial of Jesus, wept bitterly in true repentance. Jesus forgave him, lifted him up, filled him with the Holy Spirit and set him at the head of the Church in Jerusalem. What a difference!

The discrepancies in the two accounts of Judas' last hours are not so great as would appear. By Jewish law a purchase made with money returned to the temple was made in the name of the man to whom the money once belonged. Therefore, legally, Judas "bought the field". The accident described in Acts could have happened while Judas was attempting to hang himself. A sad end to a sad man. If he had truly repented he could have been forgiven.

"My guilt has overwhelmed me like a burden too heavy to bear" (Psa. 38:4).

◼ FOR MEDITATION
1 John 1:9

DAY 324

Pilate's hypocrisy

Matthew 27:11–14; Mark 15:2–5;
Luke 23:1–5; John 18:28–38

It was a series of trumped-up charges mixed with lies and hypocrisy. Jesus was not a political revolutionary threatening Roman government. He had never said that paying taxes to Caesar was illegal and had never claimed a worldly kingdom. Yet, because the Jewish council could not, under Roman law, impose the death sentence, these were the charges they brought against Jesus before Pilate. How preposterous that they should then refuse to defile themselves by entering the Roman palace.

"... it is as you say ..."

Those seeking the death of the spotless Lamb of God whose blood would cleanse from every inward sin were more concerned about outward cleanliness and the ritual sacrifice of the Passover lamb. They were so spiritually blind that they could not see the true fulfilment of the feast of the Passover in front of them.

Pilate was equally hypocritical. He could find no fault in Jesus, yet he sought to appease the Jews. Search your heart for hypocrisy today.

"With his mouth the godless destroys his neighbour, but through knowledge the righteous escape" (Prov. 11:9).

◢ PRAYER
Father, grant me truth in my innermost being, and a hatred for lies and hypocrisy. Amen.

DAY 325

Herod thwarted

Luke 23:6–11

Pilate passed the buck. He was unwilling to handle Jesus' trial and sent Him to his enemy, Herod Antipas. It was usual for there to be a large army presence in Jerusalem at feast times and Pilate and Herod would both have been there to attempt to keep law and order.

"... Jesus gave him no answer"

Herod had heard a lot about Jesus in Galilee with a certain amount of apprehension (Mark 6:14–16). He wanted to

PILATE AND HEROD

Pontius Pilate was Roman procurator of Judea, AD 26–37. He was in charge of the army of occupation, which was usually stationed at Caesarea with a small detachment in Jerusalem. He had power to reverse or ratify capital sentences passed by the Sanhedrin and was also in charge of temple funds and the appointment of high priests. He appears to have been a rather weak man, more concerned with pleasing Emperor Tiberius by quelling unrest in Judea than in executing justice in the province.

Herod Antipas inherited the kingdoms of Galilee and Perea from his father, Herod the Great. He had already antagonised the Jewish people by marrying the wife of his half-brother and then imprisoning and beheading John the Baptist. Jesus described him as "that fox" (Luke 13:31), and was later mocked and ridiculed by him during His trial. The father of Herod's first (divorced) wife, king Arctas of Nabatea, fought and defeated Herod's forces in AD 36. This was regarded by many as God's judgment for the killing of John the Baptist.

see Jesus now only in the hope of seeing a miracle performed, and, when none was forthcoming, he turned spiteful, angrily mocking and ridiculing the Son of God. Not a very nice character!

Jesus remained silent, answering neither Herod's questions nor the accusations of the priests and lawyers. It is good to know when to keep silent. Most of us need to learn how to control our tongues in awkward situations, speaking wisely and lovingly when prompted by the Spirit, guarding against words which we would later regret.

"A man of knowledge uses words with restraint, and a man of understanding is even-tempered" (Prov. 17:27).

■ PONDER
On Ecclesiastes 3:7; James 3:5–6

Patience and dignity
Luke 23:11–16

Mocked and ridiculed by Herod's soldiers, Jesus was shuttled back to Pilate again. Can you imagine how He was feeling? He had had no sleep for He had been arrested during the night after His prayer in the garden.

"... I have ... found no basis for your charges ...

Since that time Jesus had been tried by Annas, then the Sanhedrin and again by the full council of Jerusalem, by Pilate twice and Herod once.

Our Lord had been beaten and mocked by the temple guards and by Herod's soldiers. He had been ridiculed and vehemently accused, having had no opportunity of sleep, food or drink, a wash, or possibly even the chance to sit down. Yet Jesus bore it all patiently, with dignity, love and forgiveness in His heart. He knew the end from the beginning. He knew, too, that the suffering was inevitable and part of His Father's plan for full salvation for believers.

It helps, when we go through times of suffering, to remember that Jesus suffered so much and understands what we go through. He is with us and has a perfect plan through suffering to peace.

"For just as the sufferings of Christ flow over into our lives, so also through Christ our comfort overflows" (2 Cor. 1:5).

■ DECLARATION
Lord, I will seek to live in such a way that others will not find fault in me.

Crowd stirred up
Matthew 27:15–26;
Mark 15:6–15; Luke 23:13–25;
John 18:39–40, 19:1

This must have been one of the original rent-a-crowds! "... the chief priests and elders persuaded the crowd ... they shouted all the louder ... an uproar was starting" (Matt. 27:20, 23, 24). How many of those people, I wonder, had acclaimed Jesus as King when He rode into Jerusalem? How many had followed Him and been amazed at His miracles? Yet, now, stirred up by the envy of their Jewish leaders, they demanded His crucifixion. Think about the awful seriousness of their words in Matthew 27:25 (compare with 2 Cor. 3:14–16).

Consider Pilate's position, too. He knew Jesus was innocent. He saw through the accusations of the Jewish leaders and his unease was confirmed by his wife's dream – yet he was too weak to see that justice was done.

"Crucify him!" You and I can only guard against being carried along by the crowd, or giving way to our own weakness by putting roots deep down in Jesus, being filled and empowered by the Holy Spirit and relying on His strength, not our own.

"It is impossible for those who have once been enlightened, who have tasted the heavenly gift, who have shared in the Holy Spirit, who have tasted the goodness of the word of God and the powers of the coming age, if they fall away, to be brought back to repentance, because to their loss they are crucifying the Son of God all over again and subjecting him to public disgrace" (Heb. 6:4–6).

▆ **READ, MARK, LEARN**
Ephesians 6:10–13

Suffered to conquer
Matthew 27:27–31; Mark 15:16–19; John 19:2–3

Safe in their own armour, the Roman soldiers mocked and ill-treated an innocent and defenceless prisoner. It is a miracle that Jesus remained **"... king of the Jews!"** conscious after being flogged with the barbed Roman scourges and persistently struck on the head with staves.

The scarlet robe was the cloak worn by Roman officers, fastened with a buckle on the right shoulder. Such a cloak was also a mark of royalty. In the mockery of obeisance to the "King of the Jews" the soldiers were as much ridiculing the Jewish nation as Jesus Himself.

Jesus suffered so much for us, not only on the Cross but during the hours of trial before His final condemnation. Because He suffered, and conquered, He has won eternal victory for us. Compare Jesus' defenceless position in the hands of the Roman soldiers with our position in the armour of God – secure against all attacks of the enemy! Thank Him now for what He went through for you, and put on the whole armour of God.

"... but made himself nothing, taking the very nature of a servant, being made in human likeness" (Phil. 2:7).

▆ **STUDY**
Ephesians 6:14–17

In Father's care
John 19:4–12

The Jews slipped up by reverting to their original charge of blasphemy, subject to the death sentence according to Jewish, but not Roman law. Pilate became even more apprehensive about the case and asked Jesus a very pertinent question: "Where do you come from?" Unless we are sure about where Jesus came from our faith is based on shaky foundations.

Jesus didn't answer that question, but reaffirmed His certainty that He was in His Father's care rather than at the mercy of Pilate, and offered the comfort that Judas' betrayal was a greater sin than Pilate's condemnation.

"Here is the man!" "From then on" Pilate tried to set Jesus free. Previously he had realised Jesus' innocence and made some effort to get Him released. Now that Jesus had shown him a personal kindness, Pilate warmed towards Him and redoubled his efforts to free Him.

Knowing about Jesus is good. Experiencing His love personally changes our lives – and our attitudes.

"The next day John saw Jesus coming towards him and said, 'Look, the Lamb of God, who takes away the sin of the world!' " (John 1:29).

■ **ACTION**
Declare to someone today, "Behold the man Christ Jesus, the Saviour of the World."

DAY 330

Death sentence
John 19:13–16

The Jews, having gone back to their political accusations against Jesus, kept up a continual barrage of shouting before Pilate. At 6 a.m. Pilate gave way and sat down on the judges' seat (John reckoned time from midnight to noon and noon to midnight).

After one last appeal to the Jews, "Shall I crucify your king?" he finally pronounced the death sentence and handed Jesus over to be crucified.

The Jewish statement, "We have no king but Caesar," was so hypocritical.

'Here is your king ..." They who hated their Roman masters, despised the Roman religion and kicked against the foreign laws imposed upon them, had to descend to owning allegiance to Caesar to get their Messiah sentenced to death.

Ponder on the Father's grief over His chosen people at that moment. He had sent His Son to redeem them, yet out of their religious hypocrisy, their envy and disbelief they rejected Him, treating Him with cruelty and contempt, even pretend-

ing allegiance to Rome in order to secure His death. Pray for Israel today.

"... God, the blessed and only Ruler, the King of kings and Lord of lords" (1 Tim. 6:15).

▮ **THOUGHT**
Caesar after Caesar tyrannised and massacred the Jewish nation. Yet the King they crucified still loves them.

FLOGGING

Flogging was the usual preliminary to capital punishments. The condemned criminal was publicly stripped and tied, bent forward, to a pillar. He was then beaten on the back with a Roman scourge, a stick with long leather thongs barbed with lumps of lead or jagged pieces of bone. Sometimes the blows fell on the head and face, causing terrible disfigurement. Often the victim fainted and sometimes even died under the punishment.

The walk to Golgotha

**Matthew 27:32–34;
Mark 15:20–23; Luke 23:26–32;
John 19:17**

Jesus' last prophetic words before His death were to the weeping women of Jerusalem. In the words of Hosea's prophecy (Hosea 10:8), He told them that a time of far worse suf-

"... Golgotha ..."

fering was to come in their lifetime. If, in the days of comparative peace, an innocent man could be treated so cruelly, what would it be like when evil became rampant? We, too, need to pray for ourselves and our children for the time of persecution that is coming.

Simon from North Africa was probably part of the Jewish community there. His sons were evidently well-known disciples in the Early Church (Rom. 16:13) and he himself may have been the Simeon mentioned in Acts 13:1. Staggering under the weight of the already blood-soaked cross bar, no doubt helped along by Roman curses and kicks, Simon must have been thinking, "Why me? Oh, why did they have to pick on me?"

Later, he would have realised the privilege he'd been entrusted with. Let us trust God in every trying situation, realising that His love and His purpose for us never fails.

"Carry each other's burdens, and in this way you will fulfil the law of Christ" (Gal. 6:2).

◤ PRAYER
Lord, I trust You with my life. Please be my strength in every situation. Amen.

Crucified

**Matthew 27:35–44;
Mark 15:24–32; Luke 23:33–43;
John 19:18–22**

How do you feel when you are insulted, mocked or unfairly accused? Very few of us are so mature that we feel no temptation to answer back and defend ourselves. Yet Jesus, in tremendous

"... they crucified him ..."

agony on the Cross, displayed no anger, touchiness or resentment towards those who hurled insults at Him. At the height of His pain He forgave, and asked His Father to forgive His tormentors.

As we look at Jesus on the Cross we see spiritual perfection and maturity.

Examine your own life to see if there are areas of touchiness likely to cause you to sin. Ask Jesus to heal and release you those areas.

Before He was nailed to the Cross, Jesus was offered analgesic wine to dull the pain. He refused. He took the full measure of suffering for us. The repentant thief, suffering as Jesus was, had a clearer insight than any at that time of who Jesus was when he said, "... when you come into your kingdom ..." It is often those who suffer who see God most clearly.

"For we do not have a high priest who is unable to sympathise with our weaknesses, but we have one who has been tempted in every way, just as we are – yet was without sin" (Heb. 4:15).

◢ MEDITATION
Romans 8:17-18

Nothing stops God!

John 19:23-27

"... here is your son ..."

Jesus' seamless garment, common in Galilee, was reminiscent of the garment of the high priest, woven "entirely of blue cloth, with an opening for the head" (Ex. 28:31-32). It was made so that it would not tear. The callous soldiers, in fulfilling the prophetic words in Psalm 22:18, show so clearly how God has His hand even on those who do not believe in Him. God's Word will be fulfilled no matter what man attempts to do. That is an absolute certainty.

There was no self-pity in Jesus. In the midst of His suffering His thought was for others. His love and care for His mother shines out from the Cross, not only as the love of a Son for His mother, but as part of the atoning work of the High Priest.

Jesus started the work there of creating a fellowship of believers. Because of their common loyalty to Jesus, Mary and John were united as part of His family, overriding the bond between Mary and her other sons. Jesus prayed for unity (John 17:21) and He showed the practical application of it on the Cross. Consider your own commitment to fellow Christians. There should be no lonely people in the Church if we all follow Jesus' example.

"This is how we know what love is: Jesus Christ laid down his life for us. And we ought to lay down our lives for our brothers" (1 John 3:16).

STUDY
James 1:27, 2:14; Acts 4:32

Darkest darkness

Matthew 27:45-49; Mark 15:33-36; Luke 23:44-45; John 19:28-29

"... Jesus cried out in a loud voice ..."

I remember an afternoon in the early 1950s when thick darkness fell over London. I felt a momentary anxiety and I prayed – it was so unnatural. Headlines in papers the next day proclaimed that people had feared the end of the world. Imagine the fear in Judea when darkness fell over the whole land at 12 mid-day (Matthew, Mark and Luke reckon time from 6 a.m. to 6 p.m. and 6 p.m. to 6 a.m.). There was no smog then to explain the phenomenon.

The sun stopped shining, because the close bond between Father and Son had, for a time, been broken. Jesus had the sin of the world on His shoulders, and the holy Father could not look on sin. Jesus was alone for that short space of time in eternity, and He cried out for His Father as a small child might in the dark. The physical suffering was nothing compared with the infinitely greater spiritual suffering of being separated from His Father God.

He thirsted, not only for water, but for God, but accepted the small comfort of the soldiers' sour wine. Spend time today meditating and thanking Him for what He went through – for you personally.

"The light shines in the darkness, but the darkness has not understood it" (John 1:5).

THANKSGIVING
Thank You, Lord, that You were willing to become sin for me.

Mission completed

Matthew 27:50; Mark 15:37; Luke 23:46; John 19:30

Jesus knew that His work was finished. What a glorious satisfaction that knowledge gave to one who had toiled, struggled and suffered to complete the task that His Father had given Him to do. Yet even greater than that sense of completion and satisfaction was His desire to be once again in the presence of His Father. His thirst was not only intense physical need, but intense longing for fellowship with His Father (Psalm 42:1-2; 63:1).

".... into your hands ..."

The kind gesture of the sponge soaked with sour wine enabled Jesus to make one final loud cry, heard by all the crowd, "It is finished." The work was accomplished, the perfect sacrifice accepted, the way opened for all men to be reconciled to God.

Jesus had revealed the Father and His last earthly act was to bow His head in submission to Him, voluntarily giving His Spirit into His Father's care. As you bow before Him today, perhaps you would like to re-dedicate your life to Jesus.

"No-one takes it from me, but I lay it down of my own accord. I have authority to lay it down and authority to take it up again. This command I received from my Father" (John 10:18).

◆ PRAYER
Lord Jesus, as You gave Yourself for me completely, so I give myself to You afresh, totally and unreservedly, holding nothing back. Amen.

AGONY ON THE CROSS

The details of Christ's crucifixion are not gone into by the writers of the Gospels. The agony of the crucified victim was brought about, firstly, by the painful, but not fatal, wounds inflicted by the nailing of the hands and feet to the cross. It was the abnormal position of the body which caused great suffering – the slightest movement bringing additional torture. A third factor was fever induced by hanging for such a long time. Death came through the blood sinking into the lower extremities of the body and causing heart failure.

Poured out for us

John 19:31–37

The soldiers in charge of the crucifixion were experienced – they knew their job. They found Jesus already dead after only six hours on the Cross yet, to make doubly sure, one of them thrust a spear upwards under the left rib cage, piercing the stomach, lung and heart.

John testifies, as an eye witness, that his statement is true, refuting the rumour that Jesus went into a coma on the Cross and later revived in the tomb. Roman soldiers would not have made that mistake.

The blood and water that flowed from Jesus' side is an accurate medical description of the nature of His death.

Yet it has far greater spiritual significance. Jesus' blood was poured out for us for salvation and redemption – the blood of the sacrificial Lamb, sacrificed on our behalf. The water flowed for our sanctification and cleansing.

"... so that the scripture would be fulfilled ..."

It also reflects Jesus' words in John 7:37 and 38 – the water of life, invigorating all who drink from Him. Receive from Jesus today all that He has for you.

"A righteous man may have many troubles, but the Lord delivers him from them all; he protects all his bones, not one of them will be broken" (Psa. 34:19, 20).

▪ FOR STUDY
Eph. 1:7; Rom. 5:9; 1 Pet. 1:18–19; 1 John 5:6–8; Rev. 22:17

Tragedy and triumph

Matthew 27:51–56; Mark 15:38–41; Luke 23:47–49

The death of Jesus was both a tragedy and a triumph. A tragedy for the Jews and for Pilate who put the Son of God to death. A seeming tragedy for His disciples and the weeping women at the Cross. But a glorious triumph for God and righteousness.

"Surely he was the Son of God!"

The temple veil was rent from top to bottom so that any man could enter into God's presence in the Holy of holies, the innermost sanctum of the temple. No longer was atonement the annual job of the reigning high priest. Jesus, our eternal High Priest, had made atonement once and for all between man and God. The earth was shaken and many dead came out of their tombs – death could no longer hold them.

Perhaps the greatest miracle of all, however, was the recognition of the Son of God by a Gentile centurion, a hardened, worldly, Roman soldier. Jesus had opened the door, not only for Jewish believers but for Gentiles. God is still a God of miracles today – look for them and you will see them.

"If anyone acknowledges that Jesus is the Son of God, God lives in him and he in God" (1 John 4:15).

▼ THOUGHT
He who has nothing to say about Jesus Christ has nothing to say.

Garden of life

Matthew 27:57–61; Mark 15:42–47; Luke 23:50–56; John 19:38–42

It was the Friday before the Sabbath of Passover week. Jesus had died at 3 p.m. and it was important that He should be buried before sunset, the start of the Sabbath.

There wasn't time for the usual embalming, but Joseph and Nicodemus wrapped Jesus' body hastily in linen cloths with spices and placed it in Joseph's own tomb.

Both these men were members of the Sanhedrin and it was probably this that prompted Pilate to grant their request to take Jesus' body. Prominent men, secret followers of Jesus, prepared and placed by God for a specific purpose. Pray for such men today. There was further evidence of Jesus' death in the testimony of

"... there came a rich man ..." the centurion to Pilate.

The garden where Jesus was buried was "at the place where He was crucified" (John 19:41). It was in a garden that Adam sinned and brought about the downfall of all mankind. In a garden Jesus paid the price for that sin and redeemed mankind. God's purposes are so completely worked out and fulfilled in every detail.

"He was assigned a grave with the wicked, and with the rich in his death, though he had done no violence, nor was any deceit in his mouth" (Isa. 53:9).

■ **THANKSGIVING**
Lord, thank You that You bring Your Word to pass and that Your prophetic Word is true and sure.

....

Nothing could hold Him
Matthew 27:62–66

The Jewish leaders weren't taking any chances! Neither was Pilate, who must have been anxious to have the whole affair over and done **"... 'After three days I will rise again' "** with by then. Presumably they checked to make sure the body was still in the tomb before sealing it and posting the guard. They were only afraid of the disciples stealing the body, but how incongruous to think that the Son of God could be confined to a tomb by a seal and a guard!

Jesus had predicted that He would rise again after three days. He was buried on Friday, before the Sabbath started at sunset on Friday evening, and He rose again early Sunday morning. So according to Jewish reckoning He was in the tomb Friday, Saturday and Sunday – three days.

The feelings of the disciples and the women during that time can be imagined – complete desolation and bewilderment. They grieved and mourned for Jesus without understanding. But we who know the end of the story know that we can trust God implicitly – even when we don't understand.

"Where, O death, is your victory? Where O death, is your sting?" (1 Cor. 15:55).

◆ **FOR STUDY**
Ephesians 4:9; 1 Peter 3:18–19

....

He's alive!
Matthew 28:1–4; Mark 16:1–4; Luke 24:1–2; John 20:1

As soon as they could after the Sabbath rest the three devoted women went to anoint and wrap Jesus' body.

It would have been a very unpleasant task for them, considering the awful wounds and disfigurement that Jesus had suffered. Yet they went because they loved Him and because it was their duty to see that their Master's body was anointed for burial in proper, customary manner after the hasty burial three days previously.

The women were sincere in their service, yet they were looking for a dead Christ instead of a living one. They had their minds fixed on the past rather than the future.

While we remember always, with thankfulness, the death of Jesus on the

Cross for us, let us never fall into the trap of worshipping only a crucified

"... on the first day of the week ..." Saviour. Neither the Cross not the tomb could hold Him. The stone is rolled away – Jesus is risen! We worship a living, reigning, eternal Saviour.

"But Christ has indeed been raised from the dead, the firstfruits of those who have fallen asleep" (1 Cor. 15:20).

■ **MEDITATE**
on Acts 2:2

A wonderful dawn

Matthew 28:5-8; Mark 16:5-8; Luke 24:3-8

"Remember how he told you ..." In their grief neither the women nor the disciples had remembered what Jesus had told them. Even when they remembered, after the angel's prompting, the women were still trembling and bewildered. And yet Matthew tells us they are also "filled with joy". What a mixture of emotions!

"Do not be afraid ..." Grief-stricken, puzzled, alarmed by the angels, bewildered by the message, burdened by the responsibility of conveying it and yet with a dawning, joyful hope that something wonderful must have happened.

The angels invited them into the tomb so that they were sure and could testify that the body had gone. This is a graphic picture of the dawning realisation of a sinner that his past life holds nothing for him – there must be a better way forward. When we seek to lead people to Christ let's be careful not to rush them into a decision too quickly. A Christian who is certain that his past is dead and has no hankering after worldly pleasures is one who will stand strong in resurrection life.

"So do not fear, for I am with you; do not be dismayed, for I am your God. I will strengthen you and help you; I will uphold you with my righteous right hand" (Isa. 41:10).

◆ **THOUGHT**
In resurrection stillness there is resurrection power

Seeing and believing

Luke 24:9-12; John 20:2-10

Even though the women's words seemed to be making no sense, impetuous Peter got up and started running. He wanted so much to believe – he needed a second chance with Jesus.

John, probably the younger of the two, outran Peter but was fearful of entering the tomb. Peter had no such inhibitions, even though, to be a good Jew, contact with a dead body would have meant ceremonial uncleanness.

Peter saw the position of the linen clothes and wondered. John saw and believed. In a very honest declaration John tells us (20:9) that they still did not understand from the Scriptures that Jesus would rise again, but in the darkness of the empty tomb he had a sudden revelation from God – and he believed.

Later, John understood the prophecies in the Old Testament, linked them with Jesus' words and with his personal experience, and all three agreed. Direct revelation is always in agreement with God's

"Peter ... got up and ran ..."

word. Check always that your experience and revelation tie up with Scripture.

"When the perishable has been clothed with the imperishable, and the mortal with immortality, then the saying that is written will come true:

'Death has been swallowed up in victory' " (1 Cor. 15:54).

■ **REJOICE!**
Up from the grave he arose
With a mighty triumph o'er his foes.
He arose a victor from the dark domain
And he lives forever with his saints to reign,
He arose, He arose, Hallelujah, Christ arose!

DAY 343

Doubt flees
Mark 16:9–11; John 20:11–18

Mary was still weeping for the body of Jesus – while the risen Jesus was standing behind her. Consider whether you sometimes get so engrossed in misery, problems, difficulties or the past that

"... he appeared ..."

you can't see Jesus waiting to show you His answer to your need.

There was something different about Jesus after His resurrection. He was not instantly recognised even by those who had been close to Him. As

soon as Mary heard her name spoken, however, she knew her Master.

There was no more doubt, no further need for angels, for hearsay, or for the evidence of the tomb and the grave-clothes. Mary had met and spoken with Jesus and she was convinced. Straight away she was entrusted with the mission of telling the disciples. Good news is meant to be shared. Whatever you know of Jesus share it.

"He was delivered over to death for our sins and was raised to life for our justification" (Rom. 4:25).

■ **DECLARATION**
Jesus, what you reveal to me of yourself I will declare to others.

DAY 344

"Tell my brothers"
Matthew 28:9–10

"Suddenly Jesus met them." Although Jesus met first with Mary Magdalene alone, He did not forget

"Do not be afraid ..."

the other faithful and loving women who had gone to the tomb to look for Him. Like Mary, they wanted to clasp Him. So Jesus had to gently explain that He would not be staying with them. He

had to return to His Father.

The women worshipped Him, bowing before Him and holding on to His feet, recognising who He was. Often we find that women in the Church today are quicker to receive spiritual revelation than the men, freer in worship, more ready to express their love for God. But notice, that Jesus said to them, as He said to Mary, "Go and tell my brothers."

The women needed the men as leaders. It was the men who led the Early Church, who wrote the Gospels, who searched the Scriptures and explained them. We need one another, men and women, in the Church.

"For what I received I passed on to you as of first importance: that Christ died for our sins according to the Scriptures, that he was buried, that he was raised on the third day according to the Scriptures" (1 Cor. 15:3, 4).

▌ THOUGHT
Our Lord has written the testimony of resurrection not in his Word alone, but in every leaf of springtime.

Can't be hushed up
Matthew 28:11–15

A dilemma for the poor guards! Whether they told the truth or concocted a lie they would still have got into trouble.

So the soldiers took the money ..." They told the truth to the chief priests – at whose request the guard had been set – and the priests immediately set about concealing the whole ignominious episode.

A large amount of "hush money" was required. The story was believed quite widely, was written about by Justin in AD 150, and is still propagated in some circles today. Careful examination of all the evidence, however, will convince any honest seeker after truth that Jesus did, indeed, rise from the dead. He was seen and heard by numerous people who were willing to testify even at the risk of their own lives.

The greatest evidence, though, was the changed lives of the disciples. From terrified men hiding behind locked doors, they became bold fearless preachers of the Word of life. That's the power and the truth of the resurrection.

"For the love of money is a root of all kinds of evil. Some people, eager for money, have wandered from the faith and pierced themselves with many griefs" (1 Tim. 6:10).

◢ RECOMMENDED READING
The Evidence for the Resurrection by Sir Norman Anderson (IVP) and Who Moved the Stone by Frank Morrison (Faber).

One glimpse enough
Mark 16:12–13; Luke 24:13–32

"He was a prophet," said Cleopas, "powerful ... before God ... we had hoped ..." Hope is good, but hope can be disappointed. Faith had not yet been given to Cleopas and his companion. They could not believe the reported message of the angels and were still upset and puzzled over all the events in Jerusalem over the previous three days. Like Mary, they were so concerned with their own grief that they failed to recognise Jesus as He walked and talked with them.

Mark makes it clear, though, that Jesus was different from the man they had known intimately before. Even as He rebuked them for their slowness to understand and explained all the Old Testament prophecies about Himself,

"How foolish you are, and how slow of heart ..." they still didn't recognise Him. Only in the familiar gesture of breaking the bread did light finally dawn, and they "saw" Him.

Then He was gone – but that glimpse was enough. Pray that you will recognise Jesus in ordinary everyday happenings and know His presence just as much at work or in the kitchen as at church or in the prayer meeting.

"Immediately Jesus reached out his hand and caught him. 'You of little faith,' he said, 'why did you doubt?'" (Matt. 14:31).

■ **FOR MEDITATION**
Hebrews 11:1

It's true!
Luke 24:33–35

Rumours are annoying, elusive things. They tend to grow, get distorted, denied, whispered, gossiped, categorically denied, reborn.

"The Lord has risen ..." Sometimes the truth never emerges. Rumours were rife in Jerusalem that first day of the week.

Everyone knew about the death of Jesus. That was undisputed. But there were stories flying around about an empty tomb, guards frightened away by strange manifestations, women who said they had seen angels, and even Jesus Himself. Then suddenly, *"It's true!"* The evidence was too strong to be denied. Simon Peter had seen Him, the women had seen Him, Cleopas and his companion had seen Him. Jesus was alive!

Cleopas would have been able to explain from the Scriptures more clearly now, how everything that had happened to Jesus had been prophesied. As they shared together things would become plainer. Sharing and listening is an important part of fellowship.

"With great power the apostles continued to testify to the resurrection of the Lord Jesus, and much grace was upon them all" (Acts 4:33).

■ **ACTION**
Witness to someone today about the resurrection of the Lord Jesus.

Unbelief rebuked
Mark 16:14; Luke 24:36–43; John 20:19–23; 1 Corinthians 15:5

Unbelief has always been a sin most severely rebuked by God. Only Peter, among the disciples, had so far seen the risen Jesus. The others refused to believe reports of His resurrection and were hiding behind locked doors, still thinking that

"... Jesus ... stood among them ..." their lives, too, were in danger. Then Jesus appeared and rebuked their unbelief.

Even in their joy and amazement they still refused to believe at first that it was really Him. Our emotions, fear, sorrow, joy can deceive us often if we allow them to. Faith does not depend on emotion, but on personal knowledge of God and the Word of God plus a willingness to depend on Him completely even in the face of what we feel or see with our natural eyes. Faith is an act of will, a conscious decision to believe God.

The conflicting emotions of the ten disciples were calmed only when Jesus showed them His wounds and ate with them. He was then able to give them His peace and breathe on to them the Holy Spirit. Take time to look at Jesus when you are troubled or confused – and receive His peace.

"After that, he appeared to more than five hundred of the brothers at the same time, most of whom are still living, although some have fallen asleep" (1 Cor. 15:6).

■ STUDY
Acts 9:1-22

Facing doubts honestly
John 20:26–29

Thomas has come down through history as "Doubting Thomas". I sometimes wonder what label history would attach to me if it had a chance – I certainly would not want that particular one.

"My Lord and my God!"

But labels are unfair. Jesus met Thomas at his point of honest and confessed unbelief and reassured him.

Thomas repented (changed his attitude completely) and worshipped Jesus as Lord. The episode was over as far as Jesus and Thomas were concerned – forgiven and forgotten.

Faith cannot be pretended or worked up. If you have honest doubts, confess them. Seek the Lord, spend time with Him, touching His throne and asking for further revelation. Search the Scriptures to see what the Word says about your particular area of doubt. Having done all that, there comes a point where you have to step out, acting as though you believe what God says. That's faith.

"Immediately the boy's father exclaimed, 'I do believe; help me overcome my unbelief!'" (Mark 9:24).

■ COMPARE
Matt. 17:20, 21:21; Luke 18:8; Rom. 1:17, 10:17; 2 Cor. 5:7; Gal. 3:23–25; 2 Thess. 1:3–4; Heb. 11:1

THOMAS ■■■ ■■■■■■■■ ■■■■■■■■■

1. A twin: the word *didymus* (used in referring to him) means this (see Jn. 11:16).

2. Pessimistic in outlook: hearing Jesus' decision to attend Lazarus' funeral, he responded "Let us also go, that we may die with him" (Jn. 11:16).

3. At the Last Supper it was Thomas who asked "Lord, we don't know where you are going, so how can we know the way?" (Jn. 14:5).

4. Absent on the first Easter Sunday when Christ appeared to the apostles in the upper room (Jn. 20:24).

5. Doubtful: because of his absence, he could not believe the other disciples' report that Jesus had risen (Jn. 20:25).

6. The Lord appeared to him a week later and Thomas fell at His feet, crying, "My Lord and my God!" (Jn. 20:28).

7. Present with six other disciples when Jesus cooked breakfast on the shore by Lake Galilee (Jn. 21:2).

8. Tradition says he laboured in Parthia, Persia and India and suffered martyrdom near Madras, India.

DAY 350

Don't jump too soon!

John 21:1–4

Obedient to Jesus' instructions, the disciples had returned to Galilee – but for what? They had forsaken their jobs and were without a leader or sense of direction.

"... Jesus stood on the shore ..."

Peter was, as usual, the first to make a move. They might as well do something as nothing. But their efforts humanly conceived and carried out in their own strength, produced nothing.

They were tired and hungry and fed up before Jesus appeared and told them exactly what to do. How often we move off too early in some project, without waiting for specific instructions from the Lord, trusting our own judgment instead of His. Let us learn to wait for His direction and His timing and to leave the outcome to Him, too.

Jesus already had fish cooking on the fire (v. 9) and He gave a practical lesson to the disciples to teach them the conditions for successful "fishing for men". Simple obedience is all that is required.

" 'Come, follow me,' Jesus said, 'and I will make you fishers of men' " (Matt. 4:19).

▮ ACTION

Two Biblical pictures Christ gives are a shepherd and a fisherman. We are to reach people by hook or by crook today.

DAY 351

Restored

John 21:15–23

Peter had been so eager to meet Jesus again that he had swum and waded 100 yards through the water to be the first to greet his Master. His denial

"... do you truly love me?"

of Jesus must have still weighed heavily on his mind, but he had to wait until they had all finished breakfast before Jesus spoke directly to him.

What tremendous love, forgiveness, compassion and understanding Jesus then showed towards His disciple. He knew that Peter needed an opportunity to expunge completely from his memory his feeling of guilt and failure. Jesus gave him three opportunities to declare his love for Him and three corresponding reassurances of His trust shown by the responsibilities He was placing upon Peter.

Loving Jesus can never be in word only. Loving involves service. Peter was allowed to express his love in words but had to understand that his whole life after that should be spent in single-mindedly being a shepherd to Jesus' sheep. "Follow me," Jesus said. Peter looked round at John and was rebuked. Keep your eyes always on Jesus, not on other people.

"We love because he first loved us" (1 Jn. 4:19).

◆ QUESTION

Do you love me more than these?

DAY 352

Worldwide commission
Matthew 28:16–20; Mark 16:15–18; 1 Corinthians 15:6

Until the disciples had met the risen Jesus and been fully convinced of His resurrection from death they had no good news to preach. Now that they knew and understood, at least in part, Jesus could commission them to go out to "all nations". Jesus' own ministry had been almost entirely to the Jews, but since His death and the rending of the temple veil, the Gospel was available to all mankind without distinction.

"Go ... and preach the good news ..."

Baptism is expected to follow belief in Jesus, but baptism is not mentioned in the second part of Mark 16:16. It is unbelief that leads to condemnation, not the failure to observe a ritual baptism.

Consider your own obedience and commitment to Jesus' commission. We, too, are His disciples. The command was not just for those called to be evangelists, but for all His followers. He did not say, "Sit in your churches and wait for people to come to you," but, "Go".

"Again Jesus said, 'Peace be with you! As the Father has sent me, I am sending you' " (John 20:21).

THOUGHT
We will never move people until we ourselves are moved.

DAY 353

Jesus met him
1 Corinthians 15:7

James, brother of Jesus, was not one of the twelve. Both Mark and John make it clear that, during Jesus' lifetime, His own family did not understand who He was (John 7:5, Mark 3:21).

It is often those closest to us who fail to see God's hand in our lives. They know us too well, see all our faults and failings and find it hard to believe that we can change. Make sure that you recognise the ministries of your own family. See Jesus in them, encourage, support and pray for them, being quick to praise and slow to rebuke.

"... he appeared ..."

We do not know where James was at the time of the crucifixion. Perhaps he did not recognise the Son of God until Jesus made a special post-resurrection appearance to him. James became the leader of the Jewish church at Jerusalem. This should encourage us to pray, and go on praying, for those relatives, friends, work colleagues, national and international leaders who seem to be so hardened, indifferent and antagonistic to the claims of Christ. God can, and does, reach down and transform lives for His use and glory.

" 'Who are you, Lord' Saul asked. 'I am Jesus, whom you are persecuting,' he replied" (Acts 9:5).

FOR STUDY
Acts 12:1–17, 15:13, 21:17–19; Galatians 1:19; James 1:1

DAY 354

Fully equipped

Luke 24:44–49; Acts 1:3–8

Jesus had said "Go to all nations." Now He says, "Wait until ..." Once more we see how important is God's timing. We need to know, not only "what" but "when" from God before we obey His commands.

"... stay in the city ..."

Patience is perhaps one of the hardest lessons to learn in our Christian walk, but so essential to successful Christian service. God does not send His servants out unprepared. He teaches us the basics of what we need to know and equips us with the necessary tools. Then He works alongside us, teaching us more and more as we go on.

Read Luke 24:45 again. Do you sometimes find that as you read the Bible nothing seems to go in? Ask the Lord to open your mind and give you understanding. He has the key to your mind. The Holy Spirit who gives power for witness will also interpret and bring life to the Scriptures. The power of the Holy Spirit is for you – and all believers.

"On one occasion while he was eating with them, he gave them this command: 'Do not leave Jerusalem, but wait for the gift my Father promised, which you have heard me speak about' " (Acts 1:4).

◼ CONSIDER
What takes first place in your mind. Write down, honestly, the first five things that take priority in your thoughts. Then bring them to the Lord and ask Him to put them in His order of priority.

DAY 355

Joy in Jerusalem

Mark 16:19–20; Luke 24:50–53; Acts 1:9–12

Confidence had replaced doubt in the disciples' minds. Their fear, sorrow, confusion and puzzlement had changed to love, joy, peace and understanding. Even though they stood and gazed up into heaven after Jesus had disappeared from sight, we know from Mark that they understood what had happened.

"... he was taken up into heaven ..."

Luke tells us that they returned to Jerusalem with great joy. They had the promise of the Holy Spirit and the promise that Jesus Himself would return

one day. They had learned to believe Jesus' promises and to trust Him absolutely. We catch in these Scriptures the excitement of a new chapter about to unfold.

Jesus finished His work on earth and sat down at the right hand of His Father in heaven. There He is the radiance of God's glory, glorious in majesty, power and honour. Bow before Him and worship in thankfulness and adoration today.

"Therefore, since we have a great high priest who has gone through the heavens, Jesus the Son of God, let us hold firmly to the faith we profess" (Heb. 4:14).

◆ MEDITATE
On Colossians 3:1–4

Life-changing words
John 20:30–31, 21:25

"That *you* may believe ... and have life" – that was John's purpose in recording the life of Jesus. Not just to interest or provide facts about a much disputed person. Not just to excite and thrill, but to produce an active faith in his readers that would result in eternal life for them.

"... that you may believe ..."

Believing in Jesus as Son of God, crucified, risen and ascended requires a response from us. Either Jesus is who He said He is and the Gospel message is all true, or He was a deluded blasphemer. The evidence in the Gospels and the changed lives of the disciples point to the truth of His life, death and resurrection. Belief must lead to a total life commitment to Jesus.

The "name" of God in Scripture means far more than the name by which we call Him. It means all that He is, His whole nature. To have life "in His name" means life lived by the power and according to the nature of God. That is the reason John wrote his Gospel.

"As long as it is day, we must do the work of him who sent me. Night is coming, when no-one can work" (John 9:4).

■ CONFESSION
Lord, today I will believe my beliefs and doubt my doubts.

The Spirit comes
Acts 2:1–14, 22–24, 33–41

Jesus' redeeming work for all mankind would have been in vain had there not been some way of proclaiming it. Just before He left the earth Jesus commanded, "Go and tell," and repeated His promise of sending the Holy Spirit.

"All of them were filled ith the Holy Spirit ..."

The disciples waited in Jerusalem as they had been told and, at Pentecost, the promised Holy Spirit came.

They were empowered to witness fearlessly to the reality of the good news of Jesus. Peter spoke with boldness and clarity. The Holy Spirit worked through this uneducated fisherman and also in the hearts of the Jewish hearers, convincing and convicting of sin. About three thousand men that day believed in Jesus, repented and were forgiven.

The rivers of living water that Jesus had promised (John 7:38–39) had started flowing. Will you let that same Spirit, the same waters of life, flow through you to those around you by proclaiming Jesus as Lord and Saviour?

"Then Peter and John placed their hands on them, and they received the Holy Spirit" (Acts 8:17).

▨ STUDY
Write, from Peter's sermon, the essential points of the Gospel message.

DAY 358

Reigning supreme

**Colossians 1:15–23;
Hebrews 1:1–4, 8–12**

Jesus came to show us the Father. The once invisible God became visible in Jesus and man was able to appreciate for the first time the nature and glory of God.

"... by him all things were created ..."

Jesus has always existed and is responsible for all creation. Not only did he create the universe initially, but He holds it together now.

Jesus is head of the Church, holding a unique place in our worship and directing the life of His body of believers. Jesus was the only One who could recon-cile God and man by shedding His blood on the Cross. He is now seated in the place of highest honour in heaven, at God's right hand, where He reigns in glory and majesty. His throne is eternal. We worship Jesus because His name is high above every other name in heaven or earth.

Let's seek to appreciate more and more the absolute supremacy and authority of Jesus. There is nothing and no one more worth knowing, more worth loving, more worth serving, than Him.

"In the beginning was the Word, and the Word was with God, and the Word was God" (John 1:1).

🌿 THANKS
Thank You, Lord, that You are the centre of the universe and by Your power You hold all things together.

DAY 359

He's coming back

1 Thessalonians 4:13–18

Jesus is coming back! We can look forward to His second coming in glory as our King with great anticipation and excitement.

"... the Lord himself will come down ..."

Very few people were aware of His arrival in Bethlehem, but everyone will know of His second coming. At His command and with a loud trumpet call from heaven, those believers who have died will rise up to meet Him, followed by those of us still alive on earth at that time. What a meeting that will be!

Jesus told His disciples that He would return (Matt. 24:30–31), and He warned us to be ready when He comes (Matt. 24:42). We don't know exactly when, but as we study the Scriptures and look around at world events we can only conclude that it could be soon. Think about your readiness to meet Him. Will you be watching, waiting, serving Him faithfully when He comes?

"... so Christ was sacrificed once to take away the sins of many people; and he will appear a second time, not to bear sin, but to bring salvation to those who are waiting for him" (Heb. 9:28).

🚩 QUESTIONS
How would your life be if Jesus were to return today? Are you ready and expectant?

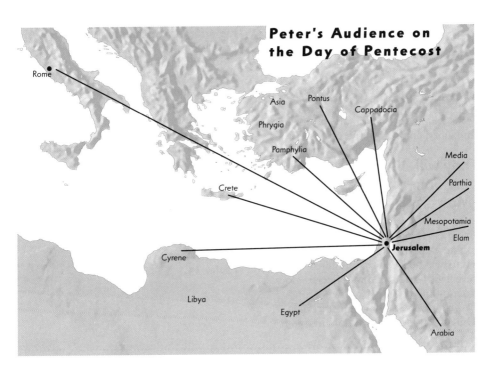

Peter's Audience on the Day of Pentecost

Rome · Asia · Pontus · Cappadocia · Phrygia · Pamphylia · Media · Parthia · Crete · Mesopotamia · Elam · Jerusalem · Cyrene · Egypt · Arabia · Libya

DAY 360

Mighty return
Acts 1:11; Zechariah 14:4–7

Jesus' departure from the world was a foretaste of how He will come back. The angels explained to the disciples that they were not to expect Jesus to come back as a man in any conventional way, but that His second arrival would be in a dramatic way from heaven.

"... Jesus ... will come back in the same way ..."

The assurance that He would come back was a great encouragement and comfort to the disciples then – and should be to us. No matter how dark and terrible this world may become in the last days we know that Jesus is coming and that He will turn the darkness into light (Zech. 14:7).

When He returns to stand again on the Mount of Olives He will bring the holy ones with Him. It is clear that Jesus' feet will actually touch the earth again, shaking the very mountain. It will be a fearful time for those who have rejected Him, but a time of joy and wonder for us who love Him.

"At that time they will see the Son of Man coming in a cloud with power and great glory" (Luke 21:27).

▼ MEDITATION AND PRAISE
Zechariah 14:9

DAY 361

Joy awaited

Matthew 24:30; 1 Peter 1:7; 4:13

Jesus will be revealed in all His power and glory, coming on the clouds in the sky. It will be a time of mourning and terror for the nations, for those who have gone their own way and sought their own pleasure without regard to the living God. It will, on the other hand, be a time when the suffering, persecuted saints will be lifted up and filled with joy, revealed to the world in reflected glory, honour and praise.

"... They will see the Son of Man ..."

It isn't easy to rejoice in suffering. Only the hope of a triumphant end to the sufferings can sustain us. Jesus gives us that hope.

Suffering refines us as fire refines gold and, when Jesus comes, He will find us purified and ready to meet Him. We will have a genuine faith and be overjoyed, not because our suffering has ended, but because His glory is revealed. Fix your eyes on Jesus and live your life to His praise and glory now.

"Look, he is coming with clouds, and every eye will see him, even those who pierced him; and all the peoples of the earth will mourn because of him. So shall it be! Amen" (Rev. 1:7).

■ **STUDY**
Psalm 24.

DAY 362

Judging the nations

**Matthew 25:32; John 5:22;
Jude 14–15; Revelation 20:11–15**

Every nation and person will be called before the Son of God for judgment. Those who have rejected Him will be condemned. Those who, by faith, have trusted in the finished work of Christ will be acquitted, free to continue in the eternal life that they have already received in Christ.

"All the nations will be gathered before him ..."

We have a just and righteous judge, one who knows what man is like because He was a man. Jesus knows all the temptations, weaknesses and difficulties of the human race, yet He is also the holy incorruptible God, perfect in all His ways. We know with absolute certainty that we can trust His judgment. It will be fair and impartial. That gives us confidence for judgment day.

The Bible also speaks of judgment of Christians according to our stewardship of the gifts and opportunities that God has given us, and according to how our lives have been lived. It will be a fatherly judgment (1 Peter 1:17), not jeopardising our place in His family and His love but, nevertheless, a future certainly to be borne in mind.

"This will take place on the day when God will judge men's secrets through Jesus Christ, as my gospel declares" (Rom. 2:16).

■ **STUDY**
**John 3:36; 1 Cor. 3:12–15;
2 Cor. 5:10**

Worthy of honour

Matthew 25:31;
Revelation 19:4–5

A throne is a seat of honour for a person of supreme importance. It implies dignity, authority and the right to rule and judge. Jesus, Son of God, Son of Man, perfect Lamb seated on the throne in heaven for ever, is worthy of all our worship, praise and adoration.

"... his throne in heavenly glory ..."

In heaven the angels are continually praising Him. How much more should we, whom He has redeemed, thank and praise Him all our waking hours.

Consider, though, whether you really acknowledge His right to rule in *your* life. It is easy to give Him honour with words, but not so easy to submit to His rule and authority in everyday life. We can sing, "Jesus, we enthrone you, we proclaim you our King ..." But is it real? Is Jesus king in your life, reigning in your heart? Has He your complete allegiance and obedience in all aspects great and small? Take stock now, and bow before Him.

"At once I was in the Spirit, and there before me was a throne in heaven with someone sitting on it" (Rev. 4:2).

■ **PRAYER**
Jesus, Lord and King, take my heart and make it Your throne. Rule over me in every aspect of my life.

A glorious kingdom

Daniel 7:13–14, 18, 27

The kingdom of God is unlike any earthly kingdom, because it will never end. All through history kingdoms and empires have risen and fallen, but God's kingdom can never fall because there is no greater power than He. It is also a universal kingdom – all people, all nations, all races will worship at His throne.

His dominion is an everlasting dominion ..."

God's kingdom is established now in the hearts of all believers, but it will be established in a wider sense as a visible and triumphant reign of glory and peace after the second coming of Christ. Satan and all his hosts will be condemned to eternal torment (Rev. 20:10), and there will be no more evil, darkness or death.

We who have bowed before His throne will reign with Him. We will receive the kingdom from Him as a trust and rule under His direction. Prepare now to be trustworthy in that future kingdom.

"... your kingdom come, your will be done on earth as it is in heaven" (Matt. 6:10).

▮ **STUDY**
Look up, in a concordance, the New Testament references of the kingdom.

SIGNPOSTS TO THE SAVIOUR

The Bible is a Christ-centred book. Jesus Himself said the Old Testament spoke of Him (John 5:39). One way it does this is through events in the lives of Old Testament men and women which point to and remind us of the Saviour's ministry.

O.T. character	Event	Old Testament	New Testament
Adam	Headship over a new creation	Gen. 1:28	Rom. 5:17-19; 1 Cor. 15:22, 45, 47; Heb. 2:7-9
Moses	Prophetic ministry	Deut. 18:15-18	Heb. 3:5, 6
Melchizedek	Priestly ministry	Gen. 14:18-20; Ps. 110:4	Heb. 5-8
David	Kingly ministry	2 Sam.. 7:1-17	Mk.11:10; Rev. 5:5, 22:16
Jeremiah	Sorrows	Jer. 3:20; 5:1-5; 8:20-22; 9:1; 10:19; 11:19	Lk. 13:34; 22:44; 23:34
Joseph	Sufferings		
	Hated without a cause	Gen. 37:4, 8	Jn. 15:25
	Ridiculed	Gen. 37:19	Lk. 22:63
	Plotted against	Gen. 37:20	Matt. 26:3, 4
	Stripped of his robe	Gen. 37:23	Jn. 19:23, 24
	Sold for silver	Gen. 37:28	Mt. 26:14-16
	Lied about	Gen. 39:14	Mt. 26:61
	Placed in captivity with two guilty men	Gen. 40:1-3	Lk. 23:32, 33
	Unrecognised by his own	Gen. 42:8 Jn. 1:11	
Isaac	Death	Gen. 22:2, 8, 10	Mt. 26:36, 42, 43
Jonah	Resurrection	Jon. 1:17	Mt. 12:40; 16:4; Lk. 11:29
Joshua	Victorious life	Josh. 1:3, 5, 6, 8, 9	Jn. 10:17, 18, 19:30
Noah	His saving life	Gen. 6:13, 14, 17, 18	1 Pet. 3:18-22
Abraham	His father	Gen. 22:7, 8	Mt. 26:36, 42, 43
Daniel	Acceptance by the Father	Dan. 9:23; 10:11,19	Mt. 3:17; 17:15
Elijah	His forerunner	Isa. 40:3, 4	Mt. 17:11, 12
Elisha	Miracles	2 Ki. 2:9	Jn 3:2
Ezekiel	Parables	Ezek. 17:2; 20:49	Mt. 13:3
Ruth	His Church	Ruth 2-4	2 Cor. 11:2
Boaz	His love for the Church	Ruth 2-4	Eph. 5:25-27
Ezra	Zeal for the Scriptures	Neh. 8	Mt. 21:42; 22:29; Mk. 12:10, 24; Lk. 4:21; 24:27; Jn. 10:35
Nehemiah	Zeal for the Holy City	Neh. 1-2	Mt. 23:37-39; Lk. 19:41
Absalom	Opposition		
	1. Absalom was a betrayer and member of David's inner circle, as was Judas of Jesus' inner circle	2 Sam. 15	Mt. 26:14
	2. Absalom plotted against the Davidic throne, as will the antichrist	2 Sam. 15	Rev. 13
Solomon	Wisdom	1 Ki. 3:11-13	Lk. 4:22; Jn. 7:46
Lot	His backslidden followers	Gen. 19	2 Pet. 2:7

The unchanging Christ

Hebrews 13:8;
Philippians 3:7–11, 14

The Jesus we have read about and whose life we have studied over the past year is the same Jesus today. He is the same in His humility and glory, in His death and resurrection life. His teaching still holds true. His promises still stand and His prophecies will be fulfilled.

"I want to know Christ ..."

You cannot look at Jesus and remain the same if you honestly consider His claim on your life. He has bought you with His own blood – you are His. He desires to live His life in you, not changing your personality or individuality, but showing His love, power, glory and authority to the world through you.

We cannot be like Jesus through striving. Only as we allow His wonderful work of grace in our lives day by day through surrendering completely to His will, will we become like Him. The word "Christian" means "little Christ". Are you willing, like Paul, to count everything else as loss to become like Him?

"... and through him to reconcile to himself all things, whether things on earth or things in heaven, by making peace through his blood, shed on the Cross" (Col. 1:20).

■ ACTION
Pray a fresh prayer of dedication today.

■■■■■■■■■ A PRAYER OF DEDICATION ■■■■■■■■■

Jesus, Saviour and Lord, thank You for Your willingness to come to this earth for me. Thank You for Your example of a perfect life lived in complete submission to Your Father's will. Thank You for suffering and dying on the Cross, for shedding Your blood to atone for my sins, for reconciling me to God. Lord Jesus, I bow in wonder at the evidence and the power of Your resurrection, the glory of Your ascension and reign in heaven, and I look forward to when You come again and establish Your kingdom for ever. Lord Jesus, I want to re-commit my life totally to You, holding nothing back. I want to be obedient to You in every aspect of my life. Please take me as I am and change me into what You want me to be, so that Your love and power may be channelled through me to the world. Lord, I ask You to show me day by day what particular tasks You have for me here on earth – and equip me to do them. I worship, praise, honour and adore You, my Lord and King. Amen.

ALSO AVAILABLE FROM CWR

Character by Character
Selwyn Hughes & Trevor J Partridge

Tracing the amazing interplay of divine providence with human personalities, this one year reading plan provides profiles of 58 of the Bible's most fascinating and instructive characters.

A specific lesson is drawn from the lives of each character, which along with daily thoughts, helps personal application and spiritual growth.

1 85345 120 7   224 pages   hardback   Available from 5.9.97

Through the Bible
Selwyn Hughes & Trevor J Partridge

A popular daily reading plan, used by over 80,000 people, to help you discover the whole Bible in one year. Arranged in the order events took place, it shows God's purposes unfolding over the centuries and how all of God's Word fits together.

1 85345 010 3   188 pages   hardback

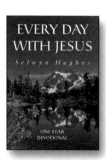

Every Day with Jesus
One Year Devotional
Selwyn Hughes

A new one year daily devotional containing six popular past editions of Every Day with Jesus with topical index for easy reference.

- 365 undated daily readings
- Prayers and further study questions
- Topical index for easy reference
- Ribbon marker

1 85345 119 3   376 pages   hardback   Available from 20.6.97